The BEST Book of
BASKETBALL
FACTS
& STATS

A FIREFLY BOOK

Published by Firefly Books Ltd., 2003

First Printing   *638208*

Publisher Cataloging-in-Publication Data (U.S.)
(Library of Congress Standards)

Strasen, Marty.
The best book of basketball facts & stats / Marty Strasen. –1st ed.
          [304] p. : cm.
Summary: A reference guide to all NBA teams, important players,
coaches, games, and statistics
ISBN 1-55297-782-X (pbk.)
1. Basketball – Records.   2. Basketball players.
3. National Basketball Association.   I. Title.
796.323/64/03 21   GV885.55 .M446 2003

National Library of Canada Cataloguing in Publication Data

Strasen, Marty   ·
The best book of basketball facts & stats / Marty Strasen.
"STATS Inc."
ISBN 1-55297-782-X
1. Basketball—United States—Miscellanea. 2. National Basketball Association—
Miscellanea.I. Sports Team Analysis and Tracking Systems, Inc II. Title.
GV885.515.N37S77 2003   796.323'64'0973   C2003-903359-7

First published in the United States in 2003 by
Firefly Books (U.S.) Inc.
P.O. Box 1338, Ellicott Station
Buffalo, New York 14205

First published in Canada in 2003 by
Firefly Books Ltd.
3680 Victoria Park Avenue
Toronto, Ontario M2H 3K1

Commissioning Editor: Martin Corteel
Project Editor: Luke Friend
Production: Lisa French

Printed and bound in Great Britain

The BEST Book of
BASKETBALL
FACTS
& STATS

Marty Strasen

STATS INC

FIREFLY BOOKS

CONTENTS

CONTENTS

CONTENTS

CONTENTS

D r. James Naismith never could have imagined when he first hoisted a peach basket at a YMCA in Springfield, Massachusetts what a global phenomenon he had tipped off. Some 55 years after that 1891 day, the Basketball Association of America—a forerunner of the National Basketball Association—was formed. The average salary was $4,500 per year and the average player stood a shade under 6 feet, 4 inches.

If Dr. Naismith would have been stunned by the growth of his game in its first half century of existence, imagine his reaction if he sat courtside today watching the 7'5" Yao Ming of the Houston Rockets battle the 340-pound Shaquille O'Neal of the Los Angeles Lakers.

Yes, basketball has grown in a myriad ways since Naismith first threw a ball into a peach basket and needed a ladder to retrieve it. At its basic level, however, it remains among the purest athletic tests of all —a sport that has captivated a world-wide audience in recent years while remaining a mainstay in American towns large and small.

This book takes you inside the game at its highest level. The Franchise Histories chapter relives the glory years of the Boston Celtics, tracks the movement of the Lakers from the cold of Minneapolis to the glitz of L.A., charts the absorption of ABA clubs into the NBA and documents highlights of every team.

Selecting the best of the best for the players section was not unlike trying to win a game on a tightly-guarded 3-point shot. So many legends have graced the hardwood, from early stars like Joe Fulks to incomparable centers Wilt Chamberlain and Bill Russell to more recent greats Julius Erving, Larry Bird, Magic Johnson and Michael Jordan. We have settled on 80, with apologies to those who weren't far behind.

Basketball coaches are among the most visible in all of sports, and

INTRODUCTION

the NBA has had its share of greats. We will introduce you the most innovative and successful, though most of their names you probably know already. Red Auerbach, Jack Ramsay, Chuck Daly, Lenny Wilkens need little introduction.

Of course, we remember these teams, players and coaches mainly for what they do once the game clock starts ticking. Games can be memorable for a variety of reasons. Some, like Chamberlain's 100-point outing, are important for a statistical feats never before reached. Others, like the many Jordan capped with buzzer-beating heroics, become etched in our memories for the drama that unfolds before our eyes.

We've selected some of the most significant and memorable outings in NBA history to help mark the league's progress from the early days to the 2002–03 season.

The book concludes with a comprehensive Facts & Stats chapter that lists career statistical leaders, single-game and single-season leaders for both the regular season and playoffs. This chapter also features complete standings and NBA Finals results for every season and a complete list of Hall of Famers, MVPs and other award winners.

Marty Strasen
June 2003

EASTERN CONFERENCE

ATLANTIC

Boston Celtics
Miami Heat
New Jersey Nets
New York Knicks
Orlando Magic
Philadelphia 76ers
Washington Wizards

BOSTON CELTICS

One of the legendary teams in all of sports, the Boston Celtics quickly became synonymous with championship basketball, not unlike baseball's New York Yankees or hockey's Montreal Canadiens.

Their reputation comes well-earned. In fact, no team in professional sports can match the Celtics' run of 11 championships in 13 seasons from 1957–69. In all, the boys in green have earned 16 NBA titles, losing in the Finals just three times. The team's all-time greats could open their own wing in the Hall of Fame. Red Auerbach, Bill Russell, Bob Cousy, John Havlicek, Dave Cowens, Sam Jones, Robert Parish, Larry Bird and Kevin McHale are just a handful of the names that made Celtic green the winningest color in NBA history. Even their floor—the old parquet of the Boston Garden—and their announcer, the incomparable Johnny Most, were the stuff of legend. While the team's dynasty years came in the late 1950s and throughout the 1960s under the coaching genius of Auerbach, Boston was that rare team with the ability to sustain its success. The Celts won two more titles in the 1970s and rode the Bird-McHale-Parish trio to three more championships in the 1980s. The Celtics of the new FleetCenter have not recreated the magic of the Garden, but fans of the great green machine cling to hope that a long line of glory is not yet complete.

FRANCHISE RECORD			
	W	**L**	**Pct.**
Regular Season	2656	1773	.600
Postseason	285	202	.585
NBA Finals	**19** (1957, 1958, 1959, 1960, 1961, 1962, 1963, 1964, 1965, 1966, 1968, 1969, 1974, 1976, 1981, 1984, 1985, 1986, 1987)		
NBA Championships	**16** (1957, 1959, 1960, 1961, 1962, 1963, 1964, 1965, 1966, 1968, 1969, 1974, 1976, 1981, 1984, 1986)		

BOSTON CELTICS

1946–47   The Celtics finish 22–38 in the Basketball Association of America.

1950–51   Boston acquires Ed Macauley and Bob Cousy. The former is awarded to the team in an NBA reorganization. Cousy's name is drawn out of a hat in a dispersal draft.

1955–56   Coach Red Auerbach pioneers the "sixth man" role, bringing Frank Ramsey off the bench.

1956–57   With Tom Heinsohn Rookie of the Year, Cousy MVP and Bill Russell making his NBA debut, Boston wins its first championship.

1958–59   After giving up their title for one year, the Celtics regain the crown with the first of eight straight championships.

1962–63   Cousy's last season concludes with another ring.

1965–66   Auerbach steps down as coach after winning his eighth title in a row.

1967–68   Russell wins the first of his back-to-back championships as player-coach.

1973–74   With stars like Dave Cowens, John Havlicek and Jo Jo White, Boston wins the first of two 1970s titles.

1979–80   Larry Bird enters the NBA and helps Bill Fitch's Celtics make a 32-victory leap.

1980–81   By trading for Robert Parish and drafting Kevin McHale, the Celts build perhaps the greatest frontcourt ever. Bird, Parish and McHale win the first of three titles in the 1980s.

1983–84   K.C. Jones guides the Celtics to the championship in his first season and wins another in 1986.

1986   No. 2 overall draft choice Len Bias dies after a cocaine overdose.

1992–93   Another sorrowful season. Bird retires before it starts, and promising 27-year-old Reggie Lewis collapses on the court in the playoffs. He dies after a similar collapse in the off-season leaves him in cardiac arrest.

1995   The Celtics move to the FleetCenter and stock up on young talent while looking toward the future.

MIAMI HEAT

Theirs was the most futile start in NBA history. The Miami Heat, who entered the NBA with the Charlotte Hornets in 1988–89 as the first two teams in a four-club expansion, lost their first 17 games—a league record for failure at the beginning of a season.

It did not take long, however, for some shrewd drafting and wise player moves to pay dividends. Behind Glen Rice, Rony Seikaly, rookie Steve Smith and coach Kevin Loughery in 1991–92, the Heat became the first of the four expansion clubs to reach the playoffs. The team took on a rugged, defensive style with new coach Pat Riley and center Alonzo Mourning leading the charge beginning in the late 1990s. Twice, Michael Jordan and the champion Chicago Bulls were the one obstacle keeping the Heat—a perennial playoff qualifier—from a possible berth in the NBA Finals.

FRANCHISE RECORD			
	W	**L**	**Pct.**
Regular Season	559	639	.467
Postseason	20	31	.392

MIAMI HEAT

1988   The Miami Heat and Charlotte Hornets enter the NBA, one year before the Minnesota Timberwolves and Orlando Magic round out a four-team expansion. Rory Sparrow scores the first points in Heat history.

1988   After a record 17 straight losses to start the season, Miami edges the Clippers 89–88 for its first franchise win.

1989–90   Rony Seikaly wins the NBA's Most Improved Player Award after averaging 16.6 PPG (up 10.9 from the previous season) and 10.4 RPG (a 7.0 improvement).

1991–92   With Kevin Loughery taking the coaching helm from Ron Rothstein, Miami makes the playoffs for the first time.

1992–93   Brian Shaw sets an NBA record by making 10 treys in a game against Milwaukee.

1994–95   Glen Rice sets a franchise record by scoring 56 points in a nationally-televised game against state rival Orlando.

1995–96   Former Lakers and Knicks coach Pat Riley takes over the Heat. On the eve of the season, he pulls off a trade with Charlotte that lands Alonzo Mourning.

1996–97   Miami is the NBA's most improved team with a 61–21 mark, winning the Atlantic Division title. Along the way, the Heat win 14 consecutive road games. They fall to the Bulls in the playoffs for the second straight year.

1998–99   Mourning wins the first of his two consecutive NBA Defensive Player of the Year Awards and finishes second in the MVP balloting.

1999–00   American Airlines Arena becomes the Heat's new waterfront home, but some things remain constant. Miami and New York meet in the playoffs for the fourth consecutive year.

NEW JERSEY NETS

Consider the Nets' periods of success a pair of bookends: One back in the days when Julius Erving ruled the ABA, the other in the 21st century, when New Jersey finally reached the NBA Finals.

In between, the team struggled through more than its fair share of adversity. The ABA wanted to start its league with a team in New York City. But after a long search, team owner Arthur Brown could not find a suitable site in Manhattan. As a result, the New Jersey Americans opened the 1967–68 season in a Teaneck, N.J., armory. It was the first of the club's six arenas in the New York City area. "Dr. J" rescued the franchise in 1973, gracefully leading the Nets to championships in two of the ABA's last three seasons. The NBA, though, was not as kind to New Jersey, especially after Erving was sold to Philadelphia. Strings of five and seven straight losing campaigns haunted the Nets. However, all the losing made the team's dramatic turnaround sweeter. New Jersey improved by a staggering 26 wins in 2001–02, reaching the Finals for the first time as an NBA club and serving notice to Eastern Conference rivals that the Nets are no longer a team that can be taken lightly.

FRANCHISE RECORD			
Formerly: New York Nets			
	W	**L**	**Pct.**
Regular Season	903	1279	.414
Postseason	34	45	.430
NBA Finals	**2** (2002, 2003)		

NEW JERSEY NETS

1967–68 The New Jersey Americans open ABA play in Teaneck, N.J., with average home crowds of less than 1,000. Their court is booked for a circus and a back-up arena's floor is deemed unplayable for a one-game playoff with Kentucky, costing the Americans a forfeit.

1971–72 With Rick Barry starring and Lou Carnesecca coaching, the New York Nets reach the ABA Finals, falling to the Pacers.

1973–74 The Nets obtain Julius Erving from Virginia to the delight of fans and New York-area media. Dr. J wins MVP honors and leads the team to its first title.

1975–76 The Nets are champs in the ABA's final season before a merger puts them in the NBA, where they sell Dr. J to Philadelphia and suffer five straight losing seasons.

1981–82 Playing in East Rutherford, N.J., under Larry Brown, the Nets make a 20-game leap from the previous season to reach the playoffs.

1983–84 Coach Stan Albeck promises fans the Nets will win their first playoff series. Otis Birdsong, Darryl Dawkins and the Nets respond with a five-game win over Philadelphia.

1991–92 New Jersey posts its seventh straight losing season, but the emergence of rookie Kenny Anderson—a New York prep legend—sparks a return to the playoffs.

1992–93 One month after the playoffs, 28-year-old Drazen Petrovic is killed in an auto accident in Germany.

1997–98 For the first time since 1993–94, the Nets finish with a winning record.

2001–02 A trade for All-Star guard Jason Kidd triggers the Nets' best NBA season. They win a club record 52 games and go to the NBA Finals for the first time.

NEW YORK KNICKS

Only two charter members of the NBA remain in the cities they started in—the Boston Celtics and New York Knickerbockers.

The Knicks won the first game ever played in the Basketball Association of America in 1946. Madison Square Garden was largely booked for hockey and college basketball in those days, so the Knicks played many of their home games at the 69th Street Regiment Armory. Over the last 55 years, however, their famed Garden has been home to more pro basketball memories than any gym in the world. The Knicks of Dick McGuire, Carl Braun and Harry Gallatin reached the Finals three straight times in the early 1950s, but the glory years came two decades later. Willis Reed and Walt Frazier drove New York to the 1970 NBA title with scoring averages of 20-plus points, and were key cogs on a second championship team three years later. Those 1972–73 champs also featured Bill Bradley, Dave DeBusschere and Earl "The Pearl" Monroe. The 1980s and '90s brought Knicks fans another dominant center in Patrick Ewing and two more Finals appearances—in 1994 and '99—but a three-decade championship drought has New Yorkers feeling long overdue.

FRANCHISE RECORD			
	W	**L**	**Pct.**
Regular Season	2271	2154	.513
Postseason	179	172	.510
NBA Finals	**8** (1951, 1952, 1953, 1970, 1972, 1973, 1994, 1999)		
NBA Championships	**2** (1970, 1973)		

NEW YORK KNICKS

1946   The Knicks win the first game in Basketball Association of America history, a 68–66 road victory over Toronto.

1950–51   New York reaches its first NBA Finals, losing to Rochester. Nathaniel "Sweetwater" Clifton is among the first African-American players in the league.

1952–53   Dick McGuire and the Knicks fall to the Lakers in the Finals for the second straight year.

1960–61   New York wins a franchise-low 21 games.

1964–65   Willis Reed is drafted by the Knicks and wins Rookie of the Year honors.

1969–70   Under coach William "Red" Holzman, New York wins 18 straight games and 60 on the season. MVP Reed, after sitting out Game 6 of the Finals with a leg injury, scores the Knicks' first two buckets in Game 7 as the Knicks beat the Lakers.

1972–73   With Reed, Jerry Lucas, Earl Monroe, Walt Frazier, Bill Bradley and Dave DeBusschere leading the way, New York overpowers the Lakers for its second NBA title.

1977–78   Holzman, who was replaced by Reed the year before, is brought back as coach as the Knicks begin to falter.

1984–85   Bernard King becomes the first Knick to lead the NBA in scoring, averaging 32.9 PPG.

1985   The Knicks win the first draft lottery and use the top pick on 7-footer Patrick Ewing.

1991–92   Pat Riley, winner of four rings with the Lakers, takes over as head coach.

1993–94   One year after winning 60 games, the Knicks return to the Finals, falling to Houston in seven.

1998–99   New York becomes the first No. 8 playoff seed to reach the Finals, but San Antonio claims the championship.

ORLANDO MAGIC

The Magic have crammed a stunning amount of history into their relatively short existence.

It took them only six years to reach the NBA Finals, thanks largely—and we mean largely—to the 1992 drafting of Shaquille O'Neal. The powerful 7-footer led the Magic to the best record in the Eastern Conference in 1994–95 and a runner-up finish to the Houston Rockets in the Finals that year. It was no fluke, as Orlando proved with 60 victories the following year. While certainly the biggest in size and stature, Shaq was not the only star to put his imprint on the team that entered the NBA along with the Minnesota Timberwolves in 1989–90. Scott Skiles, Dennis Scott, Nick Anderson, Penny Hardaway, Horace Grant, Grant Hill and Tracy McGrady are among the headliners who helped the Magic compile 10 consecutive seasons without finishing under .500, a remarkable feat for such a young franchise.

FRANCHISE RECORD			
	W	**L**	**Pct.**
Regular Season	567	549	.508
Postseason	26	34	.433
NBA Finals	**1** (1995)		

ORLANDO MAGIC

1986   A group led by Jim Hewitt heads Orlando's bid for a franchise. Former 76ers GM Pat Williams is enlisted. One year later, the NBA grants their wish.

1989–90 Under coach Matt Guokas, the Magic open at Orlando Arena. Their first victory comes against the Knicks two nights later.

1990–91 Scott Skiles is the NBA's Most Improved Player and Dennis Scott makes 125 treys, most by a rookie in league history.

1992–93 Orlando wins the first pick in the NBA Draft and takes Shaquille O'Neal. Shaq becomes the first rookie All-Star starter since Michael Jordan in 1985 and wins Rookie of the Year honors.

1993–94 A draft-day trade for top pick Chris Webber brings Anfernee Hardaway to Orlando as a perimeter complement to O'Neal. The team wins 50 games.

1994–95 Remarkably, the Magic reach the NBA Finals in just their sixth season. Houston wins in four straight.

1995–96 A lineup of O'Neal, Hardaway, Scott, Nick Anderson and Horace Grant wins 60 games, but the 72-win Bulls overpower the Magic in the playoffs.

1997–98 Two legends—Chuck Daly (coach) and Julius Erving (executive V.P.)—join an organization that lost Shaq to free agency in 1996 and several players to injury.

1999–00 Glenn "Doc" Rivers becomes the fifth rookie named Coach of the Year and the first non-playoff qualifier to win the award.

2000–01 Free agents Grant Hill and Tracy McGrady join the Magic. While Hill encounters injury troubles, T-Mac develops into one of the NBA's top superstars.

PHILADELPHIA 76ERS

Though the 76ers boast a decorated NBA history, it did not begin in Philadelphia or with the name "76ers."

It started in the college town of Syracuse in the National Basketball League in 1937. Then called the Nationals, the team played with some distinction before joining the NBA in 1949–50 and falling to Minneapolis in the Finals. One could say it was a sign of things to come, as the franchise would become accustomed to achieving regular-season success before falling tantalizingly short of the ultimate goal. That was not always the case. The Nats bested Fort Wayne in a thrilling 1955 Finals. Following in the footsteps of Hall of Fame career of Dolph Schayes, a better one—Wilt Chamberlain—made a huge impact after the team made a 1963 move to Philadelphia and became the 76ers. The next year, the Sixers traded for Chamberlain, a move that ultimately produced another championship in 1967. Before their next title, though, 76ers fans endured a 9–73 mark in 1972–73—a record for futility. The purchase of Julius Erving from the ABA in 1976 signaled a desire to build a winner, and it paid off with another championship after center Moses Malone joined him in 1982–83. Twenty years later, the 76ers await their next close call. Allen Iverson led the team to the Finals in 2001, but the Lakers put the next Philly celebration on hold, at least for the time being.

FRANCHISE RECORD		
Formerly: Syracuse Nationals		
W	**L**	**Pct.**
Regular Season 2312	1942	.543
Postseason 204	183	.527
NBA Finals	**9** (1950, 1954, 1955, 1967, 1977, 1980, 1982, 1983, 2001)	
NBA Championships	**3** (1955, 1967, 1983)	

PHILADELPHIA 76ERS

1937   The Syracuse Nationals begin play in the National Basketball League.

1949–50   The Dolph Schayes-led Nats race into the NBA, compiling a 51–13 mark. They win 31 of 32 home games but fall to Minneapolis in the Finals.

1954–55   Syracuse wins its only championship, thanks to a 92–91 Game 7 win over Fort Wayne.

1963–64   After the Warriors' move to San Francisco left Philadelphia without pro basketball the previous season, the Nationals bring it back, leaving Syracuse to become the 76ers.

1964–65   Midway through the season, the 76ers trade three players and cash to the Warriors for Wilt Chamberlain.

1966–67   Philly wins 45 of its first 49 games en route to a 68–13 record and NBA title. Chet Walker and Billy Cunningham are perfect complements to Chamberlain on one of the all-time great teams.

1972–73   Just four years removed from a 62–20 mark, the 76ers stumble to 73 losses—ineptitude that has not been matched.

1976–77   The rebuilding process begins in earnest when the 76ers pay $6 million to acquire Julius Erving from the ABA. Erving and George McGinnis combine for 40-plus PPG.

1982–83   After continually falling short, the 76ers break through with a title. The addition of Moses Malone makes Philly the most complete team in the NBA.

1986–87   After the season, Erving retires with 30,026 ABA/NBA points. Charles Barkley becomes the team's dominant player.

1996–97   Allen Iverson arrives and the 76ers begin making progress after several lean years. It takes him just three years to win a scoring title.

2000–01   Iverson leads the 76ers to the Finals for the first time since 1983. They fall to the Lakers in five games.

WASHINGTON WIZARDS

From Walt Bellamy to Wes Unseld to Michael Jordan, this franchise has treated its fans to star power.

That has not translated into a slew of championships—only one, in fact, in 1978—but it has made for some interesting storylines along the way. Few teams in the NBA have undergone as many transformations as this one. The Wizards entered the league in 1961 as the Chicago Packers, changed their name to the Zephyrs and moved to Baltimore as the Bullets. One more move, to the Washington.D.C. area, and yet another name change put the franchise where it is today. The team's winningest stretch came in the 1970s, when four trips to the Finals and one title were achieved by standouts like Unseld and Elvin Hayes. Hard times followed, but fans again flocked to the team in recent seasons when Jordan decided to play his final years in a Wizards uniform.

FRANCHISE RECORD			
Formerly: Chicago Packers, Chicago Zephyrs, Baltimore Bullets, Capital Bullets, Washington Bullets			
	W	**L**	**Pct.**
Regular Season	1560	1841	.459
Postseason	69	97	.416
NBA Finals	**4** (1971, 1975, 1978, 1979)		
NBA Championships	**1** (1978)		

WASHINGTON WIZARDS

1961–62   The NBA's first expansion ushers in the Chicago Packers. Walt Bellamy averages 31.6 PPG and 19 RPG, franchise records that stand for decades.

1962–63   The Packers change their name to the Zephyrs, then move to Baltimore in March 1963 as the Bullets.

1968   One year after drafting Earl Monroe, a second straight No. 2 overall choice nets Wes Unseld as the Bullets start to build a winner.

1968–69   Unseld joins Wilt Chamberlain as the only men in history named Rookie of the Year and MVP in the same season. Gene Shue wins Coach of the Year.

1970–71   The Bullets reach the Finals for the first of four times in the 1970s. Their loss to Milwaukee is the first of their three runner-up finishes that decade.

1977–78   In Dick Motta's second year as coach, the Bullets—in Washington since 1974—win their lone NBA title. Unseld, Elvin Hayes and Bob Dandridge help erase a 3–2 deficit against Seattle in the Finals.

1985–86   Washington makes one of the most intriguing draft choices in history, selecting 7-foot-7 Manute Bol in the second round. Two years later they add 5-foot-3 Muggsy Bogues.

1996–97   After an eight-year drought, Chris Webber and Juwan Howard help the Bullets return to the playoffs. After the season, the team drops "Bullets" for "Wizards" in an anti-violence statement.

2001–02   Michael Jordan leaves the front office and returns to the NBA, leading the Wizards in scoring, assists and steals. Washington tops the NBA in regular-season attendance.

2002–03   Jordan represents the Wizards in his 14th and final All-Star Game.

EASTERN CONFERENCE
CENTRAL

Atlanta Hawks
Chicago Bulls
Cleveland Cavaliers
Detroit Pistons
Indiana Pacers
Milwalkee Bucks
New Orleans Hornets
Toronto Raptors

ATLANTA HAWKS

Few teams have packed and unpacked as frequently as the Hawks, who debuted as the Tri-Cities Blackhawks in 1946 in Moline and Rock Island, Ill., and Davenport, Iowa, and later played in Milwaukee and St. Louis before finding a home in the south.

Some of the top players in the game served for the Hawks in those early years. Bob Pettit, Cliff Hagan and Ed Macauley starred on the 1957–58 team that won the franchise's only championship, with Charlie Share helping hold off the Celtics in the Finals despite a broken jaw. The team's move to Atlanta in 1968–69 did not bring the peach state the same winning product, but fans' patience paid off when Dominique Wilkins' arrival in 1982 gave them a "Human Highlight Film" and a path to better success. The team won a division title under coach Mike Fratello in 1986–87 and set a club record with 57 victories under Lenny Wilkens in 1993–94, but its emergence coincided with a dynasty in Chicago that helped prevent Atlanta from ever rediscovering its 1958 championship status.

FRANCHISE RECORD			
Formerly: Tri-Cities Blackhawks, Milwaukee Hawks, St. Louis Hawks			
	W	**L**	**Pct.**
Regular Season	2142	2114	.503
Postseason	119	153	.438
NBA Finals	**4** (1957, 1958, 1960, 1961)		
NBA Championships	**1** (1958)		

ATLANTA HAWKS

1946–47   The Tri-Cities Blackhawks join the National Basketball League.

1949–50   In the first NBA campaign, the Blackhawks fire coach Roger Potter and replace him with Red Auerbach. Auerbach bolts for Boston after the season ends.

1951–52   Before the season starts, the team relocates to Milwaukee as the Hawks.

1955–56   With MVP Bob Pettit leading the NBA in scoring and rebounding, the Hawks move to St. Louis and make the Western Division finals.

1957–58   In an NBA Finals rematch, St. Louis has the talent and depth to oust Boston for the title. Pettit sets a playoff record with 50 points in the decisive Game 6.

1965   Pettit retires with two MVP Awards and four All-Star MVP honors. Lou Hudson is drafted the following year and becomes the team's star player.

1968–69   The Hawks fly south to Atlanta under new ownership.

1972   A new home, the Omni, and new coach, Cotton Fitzsimmons, signal change for the Pete Maravich-led Hawks. Richie Guerin steps down with 327 wins.

1982–83   A trade for rookie Dominique Wilkins sets the tone for the next decade. Dominique's acrobatic jams become the team's signature.

1986–87   Atlanta wins 57 games with Wilkins and Glenn "Doc" Rivers leading the way.

1993–94   Coach Lenny Wilkens comes aboard and guides the team to its first division title since 1987. The next year, Wilkens becomes the NBA's winningest head coach.

1996–97   The addition of 7–2 center Dikembe Mutombo helps the Hawks become one of the NBA's top defensive clubs.

1999–00   The Hawks move into Philips Arena and delve into a rebuilding project that remains in place.

CHICAGO BULLS

To most, the Chicago Bulls are forever defined by one incomparable player—Michael Jordan—and for good reason.

There has never been a competitor quite like No. 23, who brought long-suffering Bulls fans six championships in the 1990s and starred in enough highlight videos to fill Lake Michigan. Chicago's NBA history, however, did not begin when the Bulls chose M.J. with the third pick in the 1984 draft. It started in 1966, when the Bulls joined the league as an expansion team. The early '70s brought their first taste of success, as standouts like Bob Love, Chet Walker, Norm Van Lier and Jerry Sloan made their names known. Chicago reached the Western Conference finals in 1974 and '75. Hard times followed over the next dozen years, but Jordan lifted the Bulls to heights they had never before seen—first with his youthful array of basket-attacking moves and later with a competitive fire that drove the franchise to dynasty status. With sidekick Scottie Pippen and a reliable group of role players fulfilling the schemes of coach Phil Jackson and offensive guru Tex Winter, Jordan's Bulls twice won three straight titles (1991–93 and 1996–98). Not even a brief retirement by Jordan and his ill-advised minor-league baseball career between the two "three-peats" could keep the Bulls from their status as the NBA's "team of the '90s."

FRANCHISE RECORD			
	W	**L**	**Pct.**
Regular Season	1543	1458	.514
Postseason	147	106	.581
NBA Finals	**6** (1991, 1992, 1993, 1996, 1997, 1998)		
NBA Championships	**6** (1991, 1992, 1993, 1996, 1997, 1998)		

CHICAGO BULLS

1966–67   The Bulls join the NBA. They win their first three games en route to a playoff berth and 33–48 record, tops for a first-year franchise.

1968–69   In the midst of four straight losing seasons, the Bulls acquire Bob Love.

1971–72   Chicago adds Norm Van Lier and enjoys a 57–25 campaign.

1973–74   The Bulls make the first of two straight trips to the Western Conference finals.

1974–75   After building a 3–2 lead over the Warriors in the Western finals, the Bulls drop the final two games.

1976–77   Artis Gilmore joins Chicago in the ABA dispersal draft and averages 22 PPG.

1980–81   The Bulls post their last winning record of the pre-Michael Jordan era.

1984   Fate smiles on the Bulls when Houston drafts Akeem Olajuwon and Portland uses the second pick on center Sam Bowie, leaving Jordan to the Bulls.

1990–91   Chicago's 25th season produces its first title. With Phil Jackson at the helm and Scottie Pippen providing a No. 2 scoring threat, the Bulls whip the Lakers in five.

1991–92   A championship repeat requires a seven-game win over the Knicks in the East.

1992–93   Jordan wins his seventh straight scoring title and third consecutive ring as Chicago downs Phoenix. One month later, Jordan's father is murdered in a carjacking.

1994–95   After a two-year "retirement," Jordan returns wearing No. 45.

1995–96   With No. 23 again on his jersey, Jordan powers the Bulls to the first of three more championships. The team gains rebounding strength in Dennis Rodman.

1997–98   Jordan caps his Bulls career by hitting the game-winning jumper against Utah to clinch a sixth title.

1999–00   Elton Brand shares Rookie of the Year honors as the Bulls begin rebuilding.

CLEVELAND CAVALIERS

Bill Fitch uttered a fitting phrase when describing the coaching job he took on with the expansion Cleveland Cavaliers in 1970.

"Remember," he said. "The name is Fitch. Not Houdini." There was no magic for the first 15 games of the team's existence, all losses, before the Cavs outscored another expansion team—the Portland Trail Blazers—for their first win. After five straight losing seasons, Cleveland finally posted a winning mark in 1975–76 and each of the two subsequent years. However, a stretch of nine more losing campaigns followed, including a wretched 15–67 mark in 1981–82 that "featured" four head coaches and 23 players. It wasn't until coaches George Karl and Lenny Wilkens put their respective stamps on the team in the mid- and late-1980s that prolonged winning took root. With Ron Harper, Hot Rod Williams, Brad Daugherty and Mark Price forming the nucleus, Cleveland started to blossom in 1988–89. Despite two 57–25 seasons in the span of four years, the Cavs could not figure out a way to beat the Michael Jordan-led Chicago Bulls in the playoffs. Still looking for their first trip to the Finals, Cleveland began the 21st century hoping its youngsters will grow into contenders.

FRANCHISE RECORD			
	W	L	Pct.
Regular Season	1172	1502	.438
Postseason	28	49	.364

CLEVELAND CAVALIERS

1970   The Cavaliers enter the NBA with the Portland Trail Blazers and Buffalo Braves.

1970–71   After 15 losses in a row, a 105–103 win in Portland lets coach Bill Fitch's team taste victory for the first time.

1974–75   The Cavs leave Cleveland Arena for the Coliseum in Richfield, but it can't save them from a fifth straight losing campaign.

1975–76   Jim Chones is one of seven Cavs to average double-figures as the team wins the Central Division and makes the playoffs for the first time.

1978–79   The Fitch era ends when he resigns to coach the Celtics.

1981–82   With four coaches calling the shots at times, Cleveland wins 15 games against 67 losses, one of the worst marks in NBA history.

1984–85   A young George Karl takes over as coach and returns the Cavs to the playoffs.

1986–87   The team's biggest leap takes place before this season, when Wayne Embry becomes V.P./General Manager, Lenny Wilkens is hired as coach and Brad Daugherty, Mark Price and Ron Harper arrive via the draft.

1987–88   Michael Jordan averages 45.2 PPG against Cleveland in the playoffs as the Bulls start a tradition of eliminating the Cavs. The next year, M.J.'s famous turnaround jumper over Craig Ehlo does it again.

1991–92   Larry Nance becomes the NBA's career blocked shots leader and Price and Daugherty make the All-Star Game. Cleveland wins 57 games for the second time in four years.

1997–98   Shawn Kemp becomes the Cavs' first All-Star starter.

2002–03   Cleveland stumbles to one of its worst seasons ever, then wins the draft lottery and selects homestate phenom LeBron James.

DETROIT PISTONS

Detroit's "Bad Boys" didn't start out so rough at all. The Pistons' roots date back to the 1941 National Basketball League, when they were established in Fort Wayne, Ind., and they became a charter member NBA club in 1949.

Hall of Famer George Yardley was their main man, leading the team to the NBA Finals in 1955 and 1956 where they lost to Syracuse and Philadelphia, respectively. A move to Detroit in 1957 did not give the Motor City a winner for more than a decade, thanks to 13 consecutive losing seasons. Finally, Dave Bing and Bob Lanier began to change that, but it wasn't until Chuck Daly became head coach in the mid-1980s that the Pistons grew into a championship club. Fiery point guard Isiah Thomas was the sparkplug, and his defensive-minded supporting cast featured Joe Dumars, Bill Laimbeer and Dennis Rodman. Known as the "Bad Boys" for their take-no-prisoners approach, the Pistons made it back to the Finals in 1988. Then, ending a 41-year championship drought that ranked among the longest in pro sports, the Pistons won back-to-back titles the next two seasons before turning over NBA dominance to rival Chicago. By the 21st century, Detroit had returned to 50-victory status, confident that another four-decade title drought was not in the cards.

FRANCHISE RECORD			
Formerly: Fort Wayne Pistons			
	W	**L**	**Pct.**
Regular Season	2077	2241	.481
Postseason	127	132	.490
NBA Finals	**5** (1955, 1956, 1988, 1989, 1990)		
NBA Championships	**2** (1989, 1990)		

DETROIT PISTONS

1941   Auto magnate Fred Zollner starts a National Basketball League team bearing his name—the Zollner Pistons—in Fort Wayne.

1949–50   Fort Wayne makes the playoffs in its first NBA season.

1954–55   Twelve seconds separate Fort Wayne from a title, when George King's free throw and steal lead Syracuse to a 92–91 Game 7 Finals win against George Yardley's Pistons. It's the first of two straight runner-up finishes.

1957–58   The Pistons suffer through the first of 13 consecutive losing seasons in their new town, Detroit.

1961–62   Cobo Arena becomes the team's home and Bailey Howell continues to provide scoring and rebounding. After the season, Detroit drafts Dave DeBusschere, who later becomes player-coach at age 24.

1966–67   Dave Bing earns Rookie of the Year honors on his way to seven All-Star appearances.

1970–71   Detroit adds an inside presence to Bing's perimeter excellence by drafting center Bob Lanier.

1973–74   Under Coach of the Year Ray Scott, the Pistons win 52 games.

1981–82   Isiah Thomas and Kelly Tripucka are first-round draftees. Bill Laimbeer arrives in a 1982 trade.

1987–88   With Chuck Daly in charge and Joe Dumars igniting the defense, Detroit reaches the Finals for the first time in 32 years.

1988–89   Detroit ushers in The Palace of Auburn Hills with a 63-win season and its first NBA title, sweeping the Lakers.

1989–90   The Pistons survive Chicago in a seven-game Eastern Conference final en route to their second straight crown.

1994–95   The versatile Grant Hill enters the NBA as a triple-double machine.

2001–02   Defensive Player of the Year Ben Wallace leads resurgence.

INDIANA PACERS

If their ABA rivals thought of the Pacers in the same vein as the Boston Celtics, it was with ample reason.

Indiana won three league titles and reached the Finals two other times between the 1968–69 and 1974–75 seasons. The Pacers missed the championship game in just four of the ABA's nine campaigns. Roger Brown, Mel Daniels and George McGinnis were among the cornerstones. The team's 1976 jump to the NBA did not bring the same level of success. In fact, the Pacers finished with winning NBA records just twice through 1992–93. High-scoring Clark Kellog ultimately gave way to All-Stars like Reggie Miller and Chuck Person as the team began to build some chemistry in the 1990s. Miller has become the franchise's most identifiable player. His 3-point shooting and leadership were largely responsible for Indiana's first berth in the NBA Finals in 1999–2000. In the last of Larry Bird's three seasons as head coach, the Pacers fell in six games to the Los Angeles Lakers.

FRANCHISE RECORD			
	W	**L**	**Pct.**
Regular Season	1054	1128	.483
Postseason	63	63	.500
NBA Finals	**1** (2000)		

INDIANA PACERS

1967   Eight businessmen pitch in a few thousand dollars apiece to launch the Pacers under coach Larry Staverman.

1968–69   The Pacers reach the ABA Finals for the first time, falling in five games to Oakland.

1969–70   Indiana wins its first ABA title. Its Finals victory against the Los Angeles Stars features a 53-point game by Roger Brown.

1971–72   George McGinnis leads the Pacers to a second title—their first of two straight.

1976–77   The ABA folds and the Pacers join the NBA, a move that costs the franchise several million dollars.

1977   Elmer Snow, the GM of a local TV station, holds a telethon to help the Pacers reach the 8,000-plus season-ticket sales they need to keep the team in Indiana.

1979   Ann Meyers, 24, becomes the first woman invited to an NBA tryout camp.

1980–81   Jack McKinney wins Coach of the Year honors as the Pacers finish with a winning NBA record for the first time.

1982–83   Rookie Clark Kellogg leads the team with 20.1 PPG and 10.6 RPG.

1985–86   Chuck Person wins the NBA Rookie of the Year Award.

1987   The Pacers draft Reggie Miller as the 11th overall pick. He will become their all-time scoring king.

1993–94   Larry Brown takes over as coach and begins steering the Pacers toward the top of the standings.

1998–99   Indiana reaches the conference finals for the second straight year.

1999–00   Larry Bird coaches the Pacers to the NBA Finals, where the Lakers prevail in six games.

2000–01   After Bird's resignation, another Indiana legend—Isiah Thomas—becomes head coach.

MILWAUKEE BUCKS

Tails, the Bucks win. The fate of Milwaukee's pro basketball team literally turned on a coin flip in 1969.

Phoenix owner Dick Bloch called heads, and the half-dollar landed on tails. The Bucks won the right to draft Lew Alcindor after their first season in the NBA and, well, the rest is history. The towering center who later changed his name to Kareem Abdul-Jabbar went on to become the No. 1 scorer in NBA history. He and Hall of Fame guard Oscar Robertson helped Milwaukee become the fastest team in major professional sports history to win a league championship, doing it in just its third year of existence. The Bucks' success did not stop there. Amazingly, the club made the playoffs in all but four of its first 23 seasons through the early 1990s, and it earned a trip to the conference finals as recently as 2000–01 after posting the East's best record during the regular season.

FRANCHISE RECORD			
	W	**L**	**Pct.**
Regular Season	1545	1293	.544
Postseason	99	102	.493
NBA Finals	**2** (1971, 1974)		
NBA Championships	**1** (1971)		

MILWAUKEE BUCKS

1968–69 After the Bucks' inaugural season, they win a coin toss against Phoenix for the right to draft first in 1969. They select center Lew Alcindor.

1970–71 Milwaukee trades for veteran guard Oscar Robertson. The Bucks win 66 games in the regular season and lose just twice in the playoffs en route to the championship.

1972–73 The Bucks become the first team to win 60-plus games three years in a row.

1975–76 Kareem Abdul-Jabbar is dealt to the Lakers. In six seaons in Milwaukee, the center formerly known as Lew has won three MVP awards.

1976–77 Don Nelson replaces Larry Costello as coach and loads up in the next two drafts with Quinn Buckner, Alex English, Marques Johnson, Kent Benson and Ernie Grunfeld.

1979–80 Center Bob Lanier arrives from Detroit. The Bucks win 60 games in 1980–81, Lanier's first full season in Milwaukee.

1982 On March 6, the Bucks and Spurs set a single-game scoring record in a 171–166, triple-OT win for San Antonio.

1986–87 Nelson takes a job with Golden State after the season. His Bucks won seven straight division titles but tasted much playoff disappointment.

1990–91 Coached by Del Harris and led by All-Stars Alvin Robertson and Paul Pierce, the Bucks record their 12th straight winning season.

1998–99 A string of seven straight playoff-less seasons ends under new coach George Karl, with Glenn Robinson and Ray Allen providing the offense.

2000–01 The Bucks win their first division crown since 1986 and fall one game short of the NBA Finals, losing the Eastern crown to the 76ers.

NEW ORLEANS HORNETS

It made all the sense in the world, putting an NBA team near Tobacco Road, home to the most rabid college basketball fans anywhere.

The idea was first proposed in earnest by George Shinn in a 1985 meeting with NBA commissioner David Stern, and a little more than three years later the Charlotte Hornets took the Charlotte Coliseum floor for the first time in easily recognizable teal and white jerseys. Attendance was strong in the early years despite woeful play by the expansion team, which took its first giant steps when it drafted Larry Johnson in 1991 and Alonzo Mourning the following year. The Hornets made the playoffs in 1992–93 and won their first series over Boston. They won 50 games for the first time in 1994–95 and topped that total in two of the next three years. However, 10 straight seasons without a losing record in Charlotte could not keep the Hornets from buzzing to a new hive. Some thought Shinn was using New Orleans as leverage to secure a sweeter deal in Carolina when he first mentioned relocating the team there. The surprising move became a reality, though, when the Hornets hit the Big Easy in 2002–03.

FRANCHISE RECORD			
Formerly: Charlotte Hornets			
	W	**L**	**Pct.**
Regular Season	589	609	.492
Postseason	21	31	.404

NEW ORLEANS HORNETS

1986   While its bid to become an expansion team is considered, Charlotte sells nearly 8,500 season tickets, topping their goal by 1,000.

1987   Ticket sales swell to 13,000-plus. The NBA announces that Charlotte and Miami will join the league in 1988–89.

1988–89   With Dell Curry the team's top pick in the expansion draft and Rex Chapman its first choice in the college draft, Charlotte debuts with a 20–62 record.

1990–91   After just 19 victories the year before, rookie Kendall Gill helps the Hornets win 26 games. Larry Johnson arrives in the 1991 draft.

1992–93   In Alonzo Mourning's rookie campaign, Charlotte becomes one of the fastest expansion teams in pro sports to win a playoff series. The Hornets upset the Celtics in the first round on Mourning's buzzer-beating 18-foot jumper.

1994–95   Charlotte achieves 50 victories, a feat it will top twice in the next three years. After the season, Mourning is traded to Miami in a deal that nets Glen Rice.

1996–97   Rice earns MVP honors in his second All-Star Game after setting records for points in a quarter (20) and a half (24).

2000–01   The Hornets lose their chance to reach the Eastern Conference finals when they squander a double-digit lead at home against Milwaukee in Game 6, then drop Game 7 on the road.

2001–02   Attendance declines despite emerging standouts like Baron Davis and Jamal Mashburn. By season's end, the Hornets announce they will move to New Orleans.

2002–03   The NBA returns to New Orleans for the first time since the Jazz left for Utah in 1979.

TORONTO RAPTORS

Basketball in Canada was not a new concept when Toronto was lobbying for an NBA team.

After all, the game was invented by a Canadian named James Naismith. And the first game ever played in the Basketball Association of America saw the Toronto Huskies host the New York Knicks on Nov. 1, 1946. Still, it was a national milestone for Canada and an international one for the NBA when the Raptors took the court in 1995, with former Pistons great Isiah Thomas serving as general manager. Diminutive guard Damon Stoudamire was the team's first star and Marcus Camby joined him in the team's second season. Though 1998–99 was a short campaign, it featured two important debuts for the Raptors—the arrival of Rookie of the Year Vince Carter and the opening of Air Canada Centre. Toronto reached the playoffs for the first time the following season and hopes to build on its recent successes in the years to come.

FRANCHISE RECORD			
	W	**L**	**Pct.**
Regular Season	248	376	.397
Postseason	8	12	.400

TORONTO RAPTORS

1995   After many obstacles, Toronto officially becomes an NBA franchise on May 16, putting top-level pro basketball back on the Canadian map for the first time in 50 years.

1995–96   First-round draft choice Damon Stoudamire leads the team in scoring and assists, finishing fifth in the NBA in the latter category. The Raptors win 21 just games, but three come against the teams with the best records in the NBA—Chicago, Seattle and Orlando.

1997–98   Isiah Thomas, considered by many to be the heart and soul of the franchise, severs his front-office ties with the Raptors and accepts a job as an NBC Sports analyst.

1998–99   Toronto christens its Air Canada Centre with a victory over Canadian rival Vancouver. Dee Brown leads the NBA in treys made and attempted and the high-flying Vince Carter wins Rookie of the Year honors.

1999–00   Carter captures the NBA Slam Dunk Competition on All-Star Weekend and leads the Raptors to their first playoff appearance.

2000–01   Toronto wins its first postseason series with a Game 5 triumph over New York at Madison Square Garden, then pushes league MVP Allen Iverson and the 76ers to seven games in the Eastern Conference semifinals.

2001–02   With Carter injured and out of the lineup, the Raptors rally by winning 12 of their final 14 games to make the playoffs.

2002–03   The Raptors slip in the standings, but a reorganization of the team's ownership group gives the club hope that a winning direction is on the horizon.

WESTERN CONFERENCE

MIDWEST

Dallas Mavericks
Denver Nuggets
Houston Rockets
Memphis Grizzlies
Minnesota Timberwolves
San Antonio Spurs
Utah Jazz

DALLAS MAVERICKS

The Dallas Mavericks greeted the NBA with a game plan.

Despite the availability of veterans Rick Barry, Earl Monroe, Spencer Haywood and Pete Maravich in the 1980 NBA expansion draft, the team instead opted for youth in an effort to grow into a contender for owner Donald J. Carter and founding president Norm Sonju. For a while, the plan seemed to be working. The Mavs posted a winning record in just their fourth season and stayed above .500 for five straight years, including a 55–27 mark in 1986–87. The following year, with Mark Aguirre and Rolando Blackman filling the nets, Dallas came within one game of reaching the NBA Finals. But the 1990s saw the Mavs take a nosedive, with forgettable 11- and 13-win seasons among their 10 consecutive losing campaigns. However, an infusion of talent and teamwork under veteran coach Don Nelson now has Dallas among the most feared teams in basketball.

FRANCHISE RECORD			
	W	L	Pct.
Regular Season	814	1040	.439
Postseason	39	47	.453

DALLAS MAVERICKS

1980   Donald J. Carter's dream comes to fruition when Dallas is awarded an NBA franchise. Norm Sonju serves as president/GM and Dick Motta is the first head coach.

1980–81 The Mavericks debut. The season highlight is the mid-year signing of guard Brad Davis.

1981–82 The 1981 NBA Draft sets the stage for success. Mark Aguirre (the top pick), Rolando Blackman (ninth) and Jay Vincent (24th) come aboard.

1983–84 Aguirre becomes the first Dallas All-Star and leads the team to its first playoff appearance. The Mavs beat Seattle in the first round.

1985–86 One year after getting Sam Perkins in the 1994 NBA Draft, the Mavs add more frontcourt talent by drafting Detlef Schrempf and trading for 7-foot-2 James Donaldson.

1986–87 Motta wins his 800th game and coaches the Mavericks to a 55–27 record. He resigns after a first-round playoff exit.

1987–88 Dallas, coached by John MacLeod, tops 50 wins for the second straight year and makes an inspired playoff run, ousting Houston and Denver before falling to the Lakers in Game 7 of the Western Conference finals.

1991–92 In October 1991, Roy Tarpley is banned from the NBA for his third violation of the substance-abuse policy.

1992–93 The Mavericks barely avoid the all-time record for futility (9–73) with 11 wins.

1997–98 A.C. Green sets an NBA record by appearing in his 907th consecutive game.

2001–02 Dirk Nowitzki and Steve Nash make the All-Star Game. Coach Don Nelson's rejuvenated Mavs reach the second round.

2002–03 A 14–0 start is just one shy of the best in NBA history.

DENVER NUGGETS

Some NBA teams, especially those that have been around for a while, suffer from something of an identity crisis.

As new players and coaches come along, new styles and systems are adopted. That's the rule rather than the exception. Then there are the Denver Nuggets. For most of this team's 36-year existence as an ABA and NBA franchise, it has been a high-scoring, freewheeling outfit that keeps fans on the edges of their seats. Win or lose, the Nuggets have—by and large—found a way to entertain for most of their history. They were a successful ABA franchise and won their first eight NBA games after a merger of the rival leagues in 1976. In fact, 10 of their first 14 NBA seasons produced winning records and All-Star players like Alex English, David Thompson, Dan Issel and Kiki Vandeweghe. Although hard times have plagued the franchise since 1990, history tells us the Nuggets are never far away from their next scoring spree.

FRANCHISE RECORD			
	W	**L**	**Pct.**
Regular Season	981	1201	.450
Postseason	39	59	.398

DENVER NUGGETS

1967–68   Pro basketball returns to Denver after 18 years in the form of the ABA Denver Rockets.

1969–70   The Rockets sign rookie Spencer Haywood, who grabs 31 rebounds in a game before leaving for Seattle of the NBA.

1975–76   Dan Issel and Rookie of the Year David Thompson lead Denver to the ABA Finals and a runner-up finish to Dr. J and the Nets.

1976–77   The Nuggets race into the NBA by winning their first eight games—50 total.

1977–78   On the last day of the season, Thompson makes a bid for the NBA scoring title with 73 points against Detroit. Later that day, the Spurs' George Gervin nets 63 to nip Thompson by .07 points.

1980–81   In Alex English's first full season with the team, the Nuggets start a string of five consecutive years averaging 120-plus PPG.

1983   On Dec. 13, Denver drops a 186–184, triple-OT decision to the Pistons—the highest-scoring game in NBA history. Kiki Vandeweghe scores 51 points.

1987–88   Doug Moe guides Denver to a 54–28 mark to win Coach of the Year honors.

1990–91   Denver breaks its own NBA record for points allowed, yielding an average of 130.8 and winning only 20 games.

1992–93   Mahmoud Abdul-Rauf, formerly Chris Jackson, wins the Most Improved Player Award.

1993–94   Denver shocks Seattle, becoming the first No. 8 seed in playoff history to eliminate a No. 1 seed.

1999–00   The Nuggets hope a new home brings a new direction as they move from McNichols Arena to the Pepsi Center.

HOUSTON ROCKETS

They grow 'em big in Texas, so the saying goes. Or in the case of the Houston Rockets, they find 'em big elsewhere and use them to win basketball games.

The Rockets are the NBA's "team of the big man," from big forward Elvin Hayes in their San Diego days 30 years ago to centers Moses Malone, Ralph Sampson, Hakeem Olajuwon and Yao Ming. No team in the league has employed as many big-name pivot men as the Rockets, who moved from Southern California to Houston after just four years. They spent far longer than that chasing an elusive championship. Malone's MVP heroics could not produce one, nor could the "Twin Towers" era in which the team used Sampson and Olajuwon in the same lineup to pose unprecedented match-up problems. Finally, in 1994 and 1995, the Rockets turned size into substance with back-to-back championships behind Olajuwon's unstoppable turnaround jumper and dominant play in the paint. Houston's newest giant, the 7-foot-5 Yao Ming, could turn out to have the same-sized impact. Rockets fans hope he, too, can take the "team of the big man" to the biggest prize of all.

FRANCHISE RECORD		
Formerly: San Diego Rockets		
	W	**L**	**Pct.**
Regular Season	1447	1473	.496
Postseason	100	99	.503
NBA Finals	**4** (1981, 1986, 1994, 1995)	
NBA Championships	**2** (1994, 1995)	

HOUSTON ROCKETS

1967–68   The expansion San Diego Rockets lose an NBA record 67 games.

1968–69   Elvin Hayes wins the NBA scoring title as a rookie.

1971   Recalling the 50,000 Astrodome fans who once saw Hayes battle UCLA, a group from Houston purchases and relocates the team. NBA crowds fall short of expectations.

1974–75   Rudy Tomjanovich and Calvin Murphy lead the team to its first playoff berth since moving to Houston.

1977   On December 9, a fight breaks out. As Tomjanovich runs to the scene, the Lakers' Kermit Washington lands a punch that causes massive jaw, eye and cheek injuries.

1978–79   Moses Malone wins the first of his three MVP Awards.

1980–81   Despite a 40–42 record, the Rockets reach the Finals. Murphy breaks an NBA record by sinking 78 consecutive free throws.

1984   In a draft that also produces Michael Jordan, the Rockets use the top pick on Akeem (later Hakeem) Olajuwon. He joins fellow 7-footer Ralph Sampson to form the "Twin Towers."

1985–86   As they did five years earlier, the Rockets fall in six games to Boston in the Finals.

1993–94   A Game 7 win over the Knicks gives Houston its first title. Olajuwon wins MVP and Defensive Player of the Year. Tomjanovich, in his second full season, is the winning coach.

1994–95   The Rockets acquire Clyde Drexler down the stretch and become the fifth team in NBA history to repeat as champions.

1998–99   Three potential Hall of Famers—Olajuwon, Charles Barkley and Scottie Pippen—join forces.

2002–03   Yao Ming, the 7-foot-5 rookie from China, makes a worldwide impact, leading All-Star vote-getters.

MEMPHIS GRIZZLIES

The Memphis Grizzlies' original tracks are in Canada. The addition of Toronto and Vancouver in 1995–96 brought top-tier pro basketball north of the border for the first time in 50 years.

But poor play and lagging support seemed to go hand-in-hand for the Griz. As a result, their stay in Vancouver lasted only six years. During that time, forward Sharif Abdur-Rahim and center Bryant Reeves provided most of the entertainment, and the club did manage to avoid the Midwest Division cellar once—when Denver managed only 11 victories in 1997–98. Before playing their first game in Memphis in 2001–02, the Griz traded Abdur-Rahim for the draft rights to Pau Gasol, a magnificently talented Spaniard who won NBA Rookie of the Year honors. Before 2002–03, Memphis added the winning experience of Jerry West to the front office and Hubie Brown as head coach and began what is hoped will be a steady climb.

FRANCHISE RECORD			
Formerly: Vancouver Grizzlies			
	W	**L**	**Pct.**
Regular Season	152	472	.244
Postseason	0	0	–

MEMPHIS GRIZZLIES

1994 With local sports magnate Arthur Griffiths having made a strong pitch, the Vancouver Grizzlies get the official NBA go-ahead as the league's 29th franchise, joining Toronto in a two-team expansion into Canada.

1995 Vancouver selects Knicks guard Greg Anthony as its top pick in the expansion draft and Oklahoma State 7-footer Bryant "Big Country" Reeves in the first round of the college draft.

1995–96 The Grizzlies defy expansion logic by winning their first two games, but the remainder of their first season includes a stretch of 23 straight losses. They finish with a 15–67 mark.

1996–97 Team president Stu Jackson takes over for the team's first coach, Brian Winters, in mid-season, but not even star rookie Shareef Abdur-Rahim can keep Vancouver from a franchise-worst 14–68 season.

1998 Vancouver finds a backcourt complement to the play of Reeves and Abdur-Rahim in the paint when it takes Mike Bibby with the second overall pick in the NBA Draft.

2000–01 In the midst of another last-place finish and declining support in Vancouver, Grizzlies executives visit Memphis. Owner Michael Heisley aks for permission to move his team there, and the NBA grants it.

2001–02 Memphis welcomes the Grizzlies. Pau Gasol, acquired in a preseason trade for Abdur-Rahim, wins NBA Rookie of the Year honors.

2002–03 Hall of Famer Jerry West joins the club as director of basketball operations and Hubie Brown, with a coaching resume that includes five NBA playoff appearances and an ABA title, becomes the sixth head coach in franchise history.

MINNESOTA TIMBERWOLVES

In almost three decades after the Lakers' 1960 departure for Los Angeles, Minnesota enjoyed only two brief run-ins with pro basketball—the Muskies and the Pipers for one season apiece in the 1960s.

So you can forgive the state's basketball fans if some were a little skeptical when the Minnesota Timberwolves arrived in 1989–90 as part of a two-year, four-team NBA expansion. More than a decade later, the team has become a playoff regular behind the exciting skills of six-time All-Star Kevin Garnett. Minnesota's rise from the despair of four consecutive 60-loss seasons is far from complete, however. If fans in the Twin Cities have become accustomed to playoff games since the mid-1990s, they have also become somewhat disenchanted with the first-round exits their team has suffered regularly. It will take better than that to warm up the winters in an area where hockey—professional and otherwise—is king.

FRANCHISE RECORD			
	W	L	Pct.
Regular Season	460	656	.412
Postseason	7	22	.241

MINNESOTA TIMBERWOLVES

1987   Businessmen Harvey Ratner and Marv Wolfenson see the fruits of their efforts materialize when the NBA announces the Timberwolves will join Charlotte, Miami and Orlando as expansion teams.

1989–90   Bill Musselman coaches the Wolves to a 22–60 record, best among the four new teams. An NBA record 1,072,572 spin the Metrodome turnstiles.

1991–92   Luc Longley becomes the first Australian to play in the NBA.

1992–93   Jack McCloskey, architect of two championship teams in Detroit, becomes GM and the wheeling and dealing begins. Chuck Person, Micheal Williams and rookie Christian Laettner are among the newcomers.

1993–94   Rookie Isaiah Rider makes an early impact. Also, the NBA Board of Governors vetoes the sale of the team to a group that wanted to move it to New Orleans.

1995–96   Kevin McHale, replacing McCloskey, starts to rebuild a team that has lost 60 or more games in a record four straight seasons. High schooler Kevin Garnett is the fifth overall draft choice in 1995.

1996–97   The Wolves make their playoff debut, as Garnett and the versatile Tom Gugliotta become the team's first All-Stars.

1997–98   Stephon Marbury and Garnett drive Minnesota to its first winning mark (45–37).

1999–00   Garnett makes the All-NBA First Team and the All-Defensive First Team. Shortly after the season, Malik Sealy is killed in an auto accident.

2001–02   The Timberwolves' sixth straight trip to the playoffs ends in their sixth straight first-round setback. Wally Szczerbiak joins Garnett in the All-Star Game.

2002–03   Garnett wins the All-Star Game MVP Award with 37 points.

SAN ANTONIO SPURS

What started as a ragtag ABA franchise in Dallas, that featured six head coaches in six years and one single-game attendance total of less than 200, has evolved into one of the sturdiest outfits in the NBA.

It took a while to get things turned around. The team's move to San Antonio in 1973 kept it afloat, and the presence of four-time NBA scoring champ George "The Iceman" Gervin sparked both interest and a climb to division-title stature. The road to a championship, however, required the drafting of two of the biggest impact players of the last two decades. David Robinson's arrival in 1989–90 made a 35-game difference in one year, and Tim Duncan's debut was even better—an NBA record 36-game leap in 1997–98. Both added Rookie of the Year and MVP honors to the Spurs' resume. Their crowning achievement, though, was their dash to the 1999 championship, which helped atone for a long line of postseason failures by a franchise that has grown accustomed to life at or near the top of the regular-season standings. San Antonio has reached the playoffs in 13 of 14 seasons through 2002–03, when the Spurs added a second chamnpionship.

FRANCHISE RECORD			
	W	**L**	**Pct.**
Regular Season	1256	926	.576
Postseason	99	97	.505
NBA Finals	**1** (1999)		
NBA Championships	**1** (1999)		

SAN ANTONIO SPURS

1967–68 The Dallas Chaparrals are one of 11 original ABA teams.

1973–74 A group of San Antonio businessmen saves a franchise in turmoil, moving it to their town's HemisFair Arena and renaming it the Spurs. They acquire George Gervin in mid-season.

1976–77 The Spurs survive the ABA-NBA merger, leading their new league in scoring but finishing last in defense.

1977–78 Gervin nips David Thompson for the scoring title with a 63-point finale.

1979–80 Gervin wins his third straight scoring crown.

1982–83 The high-scoring Spurs win their division for the fifth time in six years, but the Lakers stop them in the Western Conference finals for the second straight season.

1983–84 Artis Gilmore tops the NBA in field-goal accuracy.

1987 After winning the NBA Draft lottery, the Spurs select David Robinson, then wait for "The Admiral" to fulfill his two-year Navy commitment.

1989–90 Robinson debuts and the Spurs make a 35-game jump in the standings.

1993–94 With 71 points in the final game, Robinson wins the NBA scoring title.

1994–95 MVP Robinson leads the Spurs to a league-best 62–20 record, but they fall to Houston in the conference finals.

1997–98 With Rookie of the Year Tim Duncan, the Spurs improve by 36 wins—breaking their own NBA record for biggest turnaround.

1998–99 After years of surprising playoff losses, the Spurs become the first former ABA team to win an NBA title. They beat the Knicks in five games.

2001–02 Duncan wins the MVP Award.

2002–03 Duncan repeats as MVP and the Spurs win a second championship in Robinson's final season.

UTAH JAZZ

If you can sum up a franchise with one play, it's the Utah Jazz and their pick-and-roll.

For two decades, defenders have known what's coming when guard John Stockton and forward Karl Malone go to work. And for two decades, those same defenders have been unable to stop it. Stockton is the NBA's all-time leader in assists, and no one can match his 19 years with the same team. Malone is a two-time MVP, the all-time NBA leader in free throws made and No. 2 on the career scoring list. Together for 18 years, they never missed the playoffs or posted a sub-.500 record. So much of the Jazz's identity has been crafted through this Hall of Fame tandem, one might be inclined to forget that the club had its share of earlier stars. The first player signed by the expansion New Orleans Jazz in 1974 was Pete Maravich, who was a college phenom at neighboring LSU. After the team's 1979 move to Utah, such standouts as Darrell Griffith, Adrian Dantley and defensive specialist Mark Eaton contributed to the team's growth. For all the records and awards, however, it's safe to call the Jazz the best NBA team never to have won a title. They had their hearts broken by Michael Jordan and the Chicago Bulls in both of their trips to the Finals in 1997 and '98.

FRANCHISE RECORD			
Formerly: New Orleans Jazz			
	W	**L**	**Pct.**
Regular Season	1279	1067	.545
Postseason	94	99	.487
NBA Finals	**2** (1997, 1998)		

UTAH JAZZ

1974–75   Local legend Pete Maravich becomes the first player on the expansion New Orleans Jazz roster, delighting crowds with his entertaining style.

1976–77   Maravich sets a team record with a 68-point game against the Knicks.

1979–80   The nickname no longer seems to fit when the Jazz move to Utah. Frank Layden takes over as GM.

1980–81   Utah's first draft pick in 1980, Darrell "Dr. Dunkenstein" Griffith, wins the Rookie of the Year Award.

1983–84   High-scoring Adrian Dantley leads the Jazz to their first winning record and playoff berth.

1984–85   In John Stockton's rookie year, it's Mark Eaton who shines, setting several NBA records for blocked shots and winning the Defensive Player of the Year Award.

1985–86   Utah builds a terrific tandem when it drafts Karl "The Mailman" Malone to be on the receiving end of Stockton's passes.

1988–89   After Layden's resignation, Jerry Sloan takes over as head coach—a post he will hold for more than a decade.

1992–93   Stockton and Malone win gold medals in the 1992 Olympics and are named co-MVPs of the 1993 All-Star Game, played in Salt Lake City.

1994–95   Stockton becomes the all-time NBA assists king.

1996–97   Malone wins the first of his two MVP Awards and Utah suffers the first of back-to-back Finals losses to the Bulls.

2000–01   Malone moves into second place on the all-time NBA scoring list, behind only Kareem Abdul-Jabbar.

2002–03   The Jazz reach the playoffs for the 20th consecutive season and notch their 18th straight winning record. Stockton extends his record to 19 seasons with the same team.

WESTERN CONFERENCE
PACIFIC

Golden State Warriors
Los Angeles Clippers
Los Angeles Lakers
Phoenix Suns
Portland Trail Blazers
Sacramento Kings
Seattle SuperSonics

GOLDEN STATE WARRIORS

One of the 11 charter members of the Basketball Association of America, which later became the NBA, the Philadelphia Warriors won the league's first championship under Eddie Gottlieb.

Back then, "Jumpin' Joe" Fulks led the way. In recent years, it has been youngsters like Antawn Jamison and Jason Richardson trying to re-establish a winning tradition in northern California. The Warriors won a second title in 1956, moved to San Francisco for the 1962–63 season and crossed the Bay in 1971, adopting the name Golden State in an effort to draw a wider audience. They even played some games in San Diego. The most memorable decade in franchise history was the 1960s, when Wilt Chamberlain and (later) Rick Barry carried the squad. Another great, Nate Thurmond, also emerged, but it was Barry's return that led to the Warriors' third and most recent title in 1975.

FRANCHISE RECORD			
Formerly: Philadelphia Warriors, San Francisco Warriors			
	W	**L**	**Pct.**
Regular Season	2043	2381	.462
Postseason	99	115	.463
NBA Finals	**6** (1947, 1948, 1956, 1964, 1967, 1975)		
NBA Championships	**3** (1947, 1956, 1975)		

GOLDEN STATE WARRIORS

1946–47 Scoring machine Joe Fulks leads the Philadelphia Warriors to the first BAA championship. Fulks' scoring average of 23.2 tops the league by six-plus points.

1955–56 Rookie Tom Gola joins veterans Paul Arizin and Neil Johnston and helps the Warriors to their second title.

1959–60 Wilt Chamberlain revives a Warriors team that has slipped. "The Stilt" posts scoring averages of 33-plus points in each of his first seven seasons, including 50.4 PPG and 25.7 RPG in 1961–62.

1960 On March 2, in a game against New York in Hershey, Pa., Chamberlain sets a record that might never be broken, scoring 100 points. He shoots 36-of-63 from the floor and 28-of-32 from the line.

1962 Two years after the Lakers' move to L.A., the Warriors head west to San Francisco and the Cow Palace.

1965 On January 15, Chamberlain is traded to the 76ers for three players and cash. The emergence of Rick Barry, a rookie in 1965–66, helps ease the pain felt by the fans.

1971 Plagued by low attendance, the Warriors take the name "Golden State" and move to Oakland before the 1971–72 season.

1974–75 In its third season since a court decision forced Barry to return to the Warriors after four years in the ABA, Golden State wins the third title in franchise history. Coach Al Attles does it with a deep bench and a team-first philosophy.

1990–91 The "Run TMC" trio of Tim Hardaway, Mitch Richmond and Chris Mullin helps Golden State to its best record in nine years.

1996–97 Golden State makes San Jose its temporary home when the Oakland Coliseum undergoes renovations.

LOS ANGELES CLIPPERS

A franchise that's undergone two city relocations, three arena switches and one name change began in 1970 with loads of promise as the Buffalo Braves.

With the legendary Jack Ramsay at the helm and Bob McAdoo playing a starring role, the Braves needed just four years to attain a winning record. The good times did not last long, however. Irving Levin moved the team to San Diego before the 1978–79 season, renamed it the Clippers and watched his charges repeatedly fall short of the playoffs. Nothing seemed to alter the team's direction, even with stars like Tom Chambers and Terry Cummings leading the way, new ownership in Donald T. Sterling and a 1984 move north to Los Angeles. On the bright side, the Clippers have set team attendance records since making the Staples Center in downtown L.A. their home in 1999–2000 and loading their roster with promising young players.

FRANCHISE RECORD			
Formerly: Buffalo Braves, San Diego Clippers			
	W	**L**	**Pct.**
Regular Season	952	1722	.356
Postseason	13	22	.371

LOS ANGELES CLIPPERS

1970   The Buffalo Braves join the NBA as one of three expansion teams, along with the Portland Trail Blazers and Cleveland Cavaliers.

1973–74   Under coach Jack Ramsay and NBA scoring leader Bob McAdoo, the Braves top .500 with a 42–40 record. They reach the playoffs for the first time.

1974–75   McAdoo wins the NBA Most Valuable Player Award after claiming his second straight scoring title with a 34.5 PPG average.

1975–76   Buffalo wins its first playoff series, eliminating Philadelphia in the first round. The Braves fall to Boston in the Eastern Conference semifinals.

1978   Boston Celtics owner Irv Levin, seeing an opportunity to put a team in his home state of California, swaps places with Braves owner John Y. Brown and takes the club to San Diego. He renames it the Clippers. One of the move's proponents is NBA attorney David Stern, who later becomes commissioner.

1978–79   Lloyd Free averages 28.8 PPG, second in the NBA, in the Clippers' first season in San Diego.

1981   In June, Beverly Hills real estate mogul Donald T. Sterling purchases the team.

1984   Los Angeles now has two NBA franchises. The Clippers head north to become the Lakers' crosstown rivals. Their first game in the L.A. Sports Arena is a 107–105 win over the New York Knicks.

1985   Hall of Famer Elgin Baylor is hired in April to serve as vice president of basketball operations.

1991–92   For the first time since its Braves days, the team reaches the NBA playoffs.

1999   The Clippers move to the Staples Center in downtown Los Angeles, triggering new club attendance records.

LOS ANGELES LAKERS

No team in the NBA owns more all-time victories or a higher winning percentage than the Lakers.

They have won 14 NBA championships in Minneapolis and Los Angeles and also captured league titles in the two years preceding the official NBA launch in 1949–50. Perhaps it's because Boston holds 16 NBA crowns—two more than the Lakers—that the Celtics are considered by many to be pro basketball's preeminent team. More likely, it's the fact the Lakers spent more than a decade unsuccessfully trying to unseat Boston in its heyday. If not for seven NBA Finals defeats at the hands of the Celtics in an 11-year span (1959–69), the Lakers clearly would be seen as the cream of the crop. For much of their history, they have been just that. The great George Mikan led six title teams (including one NBL and one BAA) in the late-1940s and 1950s. A 1960 move from Minneapolis to L.A. set the stage for Laker games to become Hollywood events. Wilt Chamberlain brought a title in 1972. Then Magic Johnson and Kareem Abdul-Jabbar formed the heart of the "Showtime" Laker teams that dominated the '80s with five championships. More recently, it was powerful center Shaquille O'Neal and high-flying Kobe Bryant who sparked L.A. to three straight titles beginning in 2000.

FRANCHISE RECORD		
Formerly: Minneapolis Lakers		
W	**L**	**Pct.**
Regular Season 2671	1648	.618
Postseason 366	241	.603
NBA Finals	**27** (1949, 1950, 1952, 1953, 1954, 1959, 1962, 1963, 1965, 1966, 1968, 1969, 1970, 1972, 1973, 1980, 1982, 1983, 1984, 1985, 1987, 1988, 1989, 1991, 2000, 2001, 2002)	
NBA Championships	**14** (1949, 1950, 1952, 1953, 1954, 1972, 1980, 1982, 1985, 1987, 1988, 2000, 2001, 2002)	

LOS ANGELES LAKERS

1947–48   The Minneapolis Lakers, starring George Mikan, win the National Basketball League title in their debut season.

1948–49   The Lakers claim the Basketball Association of America crown.

1949–50   The inaugural NBA title goes to—who else?—the Laker dynasty, as do three of the next four.

1958–59   After holding the worst record the year before, Rookie of the Year Elgin Baylor leads the Lakers to the Finals.

1960–61   The Lakers move to Los Angeles.

1961–62   Game 7 of the Finals sees the Celtics edge L.A. in overtime. The Lakers make the Finals seven times between 1959–69, each time losing to Boston.

1968–69   Wilt Chamberlain arrives via a trade. Still, Bill Russell and the Celtics get their usual win in the Finals.

1969–70   This time, it's Willis Reed and New York who break L.A. hearts, although Jerry West earns the nickname "Mr. Clutch" for his 60-foot Finals heave.

1971–72   The Lakers win 33 straight games and finally break through with a title.

1975–76   Two years after Chamberlain's retirement, the Lakers trade for Kareem Abdul-Jabbar.

1979–80   Rookie Magic Johnson kicks off the "Showtime" era with the first of two titles in three years.

1984–85   For the first time in nine Finals meetings, L.A. tops Boston for a championship.

1987–88   The Lakers make good on coach Pat Riley's promise of a second straight title—their fifth of the 1980s.

1991   Magic announces he has tested positive for the HIV virus.

1999–00   Phil Jackson is hired as coach and molds a team, starring Shaquille O'Neal and Kobe Bryant, into a champion. It's the first of three straight L.A. titles.

PHOENIX SUNS

The fact basketball has thrived in Phoenix is more than many would have predicted when Richard Bloch, the driving force behind the team's original ownership group, lobbied for an NBA expansion team.

It turns out the league made a wise move in granting one. The team has grown with its city over the last three decades and has built a strong fan base along the way, despite not having delivered an NBA championship. Some tremendous players have worn Phoenix jerseys—among them Connie Hawkins, Paul Westphal, Walter Davis, Tom Chambers, Kevin Johnson, Charles Barkley and Jason Kidd—and owner/CEO Jerry Colangelo has been a front-office staple from the start. However, big trades and player turnover have been a hallmark of the franchise, so it has been hard to predict where and when the next star will turn up. The Suns have made two trips to the Finals. Their 1976 loss to Boston was expected, and the series produced a triple-overtime classic that many consider the best game in league history. The Suns' 1993 Finals loss to Chicago was harder to take, since Phoenix owned the NBA's best record that season.

FRANCHISE RECORD			
	W	**L**	**Pct.**
Regular Season	1553	1285	.547
Postseason	97	110	.469
NBA Finals	**2** (1976, 1993)		

PHOENIX SUNS

1968–69 With 28-year-old Jerry Colangelo the GM and Johnny "Red" Kerr manning the bench, the Suns debut. Expansion draftee Dick Van Arsdale becomes "the original Sun."

1969–70 The Suns add Connie Hawkins and Paul Silas and, in just their second year, push the Lakers to seven games in a playoff series.

1970–71 Cotton Fitzsimmons starts the first of his three Suns coaching stints.

1973–74 John MacLeod is Phoenix's last head coaching hire for 13-plus years.

1975–76 Paul Westphal and Rookie of the Year Alvan Adams lead a "Sunderella" team to the Finals. Boston's three-overtime win in Game 5 is still considered by some the greatest game ever played.

1977–78 Walter Davis wins Rookie of the Year and joins Westphal in the All-Star Game.

1980–81 Phoenix claims its first division title but again comes up short in the playoffs.

1987–88 Colangelo takes over controlling interest in the team. Several trades ensue, including one that brings Kevin Johnson to Phoenix.

1988–89 K.J. and Tom Chambers lead a dramatic turnaround in which the Suns reach the Western Conference finals for the first of two straight years.

1992–93 The addition of Charles Barkley lifts the Suns to a 62-win season and trip to the Finals, where the Bulls prevail in six games.

1996–97 Barkley is traded and Jason Kidd arrives. The Suns start 0–13 but win 11 straight late in the year.

1998–99 Kidd leads the NBA in assists and triple-doubles.

2000–01 The Suns make the playoffs for the 13th straight time, a run that ends in 2001–02 after Kidd is traded for Stephon Marbury.

PORTLAND TRAIL BLAZERS

Although their supportive fans might clamor for a few more championships, there's no denying the fact the Portland Trail Blazers have been among the most successful clubs in the NBA since joining the league in a 1970 expansion.

Their very first trip to the playoffs, in 1977, produced a championship behind a pair of Hall of Famers: coach Jack Ramsay and center Bill Walton. Since then, the Blazers' consistency has been nothing short of remarkable. They have missed the playoffs only once since that title season. In fact, their string of 21 consecutive playoff appearances through the 2002–03 campaign is just one short of the NBA record set by Syracuse/Philadelphia from 1950–71. Along the way, "Blazermania" has applauded the likes of Walton, Geoff Petrie, Maurice Lucas, Clyde Drexler, Terry Porter, Buck Williams, Scottie Pippen and Rasheed Wallace—among others. Return trips to the Finals in 1990 and 1992 resulted in losses to Detroit and Chicago, respectively, and whet the appetite of Blazer fans for more. History says this much: Come playoff time, the Portland Trail Blazers will be there.

FRANCHISE RECORD			
	W	**L**	**Pct.**
Regular Season	1467	1207	.549
Postseason	91	103	.469
NBA Finals	**3** (1977, 1990, 1992)		
NBA Championships	**1** (1977)		

PORTLAND TRAIL BLAZERS

1970–71 The Trail Blazers become the rare expansion team that wins its first game, beating fellow expansion entry Cleveland 115–112. Geoff Petrie wins Rookie of the Year.

1971–72 Sidney Wicks gives the Blazers back-to-back Rookie of the Year honorees.

1976–77 With star center Bill Walton in his third season, the Blazers jump from a sub-.500 team to NBA champions. Jack Ramsay coaches the team that has added toughness in the shape of Maurice Lucas. They outlast the 76ers in six games.

1977–78 Walton wins the MVP Award but no repeat is in store.

1984 The Blazers drafted wisely one year earlier, selecting Clyde Drexler. This year, however, they bypass Michael Jordan with the No. 2 pick and select Sam Bowie.

1989–90 "Rip City" becomes Portland's moniker as the Blazers, with Buck Williams joining Drexler and Terry Porter, reach the NBA Finals before falling to Detroit.

1991–92 A second Finals trip in three years nets another hard-fought loss, this time to Jordan and the Bulls in six games.

1993–94 All-Star Clifford Robinson overtakes Drexler as the team's top scorer.

1995–96 The Blazers move from Memorial Coliseum to the Rose Garden.

1998–99 After six straight first-round exits, a balanced Blazer team advances to the Western Conference finals. Isaiah Rider leads five players averaging at least 11 PPG.

1999–00 Portland makes a return trip to the conference finals, taking the champion Lakers to the limit in a thrilling seven-game series.

2002–03 The Blazers make the playoffs for the 21st consecutive season—one shy of the NBA record.

SACRAMENTO KINGS

The onset of the 21st century marked a return to contention for the Kings, and not a moment too soon.

The team's first-round victory in 2001 was its first playoff series win in 20 years, and the last two campaigns have been even better. Before their recent surge, the Kings had to look back 50 years to recall the franchise's glory days, which took place all the way across the country in Rochester, New York. The Rochester Royals were one of 17 charter members of a new league that was created when the Basketball Association of America merged with the National Basketball League. They won the 1951 NBA title with a balanced team that included center Arnie Risen and perimeter standouts Bob Davies, Bobby Wanzer and Red Holzman. Several relocations later—from Cincinnati Royals to K.C.–Omaha and Kansas City Kings to their current home in Sacramento—no one would have predicted a half-century title drought for a club that started with such promise. The Kings appear to have weathered their laughingstock decades and have their sights set on championship days ahead.

FRANCHISE RECORD			
Formerly: Rochester Royals, Cincinnati Royals, Kansas City–Omaha Kings, Kansas City Kings			
	W	**L**	**Pct.**
Regular Season	2038	2281	.472
Postseason	70	94	.427
NBA Finals	**1** (1951)		
NBA Championships	**1** (1951)		

SACRAMENTO KINGS

1945–46 After claiming the National Basketball League crown in 1945, the Rochester Royals break the league's color barrier by signing Dolly King.

1950–51 The Royals win the NBA championship in the league's second season. Arnie Risen leads the team in scoring and rebounding.

1957–58 Owner Les Harrison moves the struggling team to Cincinnati.

1960–61 A territorial draft choice puts the Oscar Robertson in a Royals uniform. He runs away with Rookie of the Year honors.

1963–64 MVP Robertson and rebounding machine Jerry Lucas form a dynamite duo for the first of their six seasons together.

1969–70 Lucas is traded early in the year and Robertson goes to Milwaukee in April.

1972–73 The team relocates to Kansas City as the Kings. Nate "Tiny" Archibald becomes the first player to lead the NBA in scoring and assists in one season.

1978–79 Phil Ford wins Rookie of the Year and Cotton Fitzsimmons Coach of the Year as the Kings claim a division title.

1980–81 Kansas City reaches the Western Conference Finals but falls to Houston. The Kings will not win another playoff game for 15 years.

1985–86 Another relocation puts the Kings in Sacramento.

1989 Guard Ricky Berry, after a promising rookie season, commits suicide.

1994–95 Mitch Richmond wins All-Star Game MVP honors.

1995–96 Sacramento makes the playoffs for the first time in a decade.

1998–99 Adding Chris Webber, Jason Williams and Vlade Divac puts the club on the road to success.

2001–02 A 61–21 record produces the Kings' first division title in 23 seasons.

SEATTLE SUPERSONICS

All teams have their ups and downs, but the Sonics have experienced a little bit of everything since entering the NBA in a 1967 expansion.

Winning? Seattle captured the NBA championship in 1979 and won 60 or more games three times in the 1990s, ruling their division for a long stretch. Losing? The Sonics' long and frustrating string of playoff struggles includes a 1993–94 team that was the first No. 1 seed in NBA history to fall to a No. 8 seed (Denver) in the opening round. Offense? Some of the best shooters in the game have worn Seattle's green and yellow jersey, including record-setting 3-point aces Dale Ellis and "Downtown" Freddie Brown. Defense? It's how the franchise won its only title in '79, and more recent star Gary Payton (traded for Ray Allen in 2002–03) was the first guard since Michael Jordan to win a Defensive Player of the Year Award and made the NBA All-Defensive First Team a record eight straight times.

FRANCHISE RECORD			
	W	**L**	**Pct.**
Regular Season	1570	1350	.538
Postseason	101	105	.490
NBA Finals	**3** (1978, 1979, 1996)		
NBA Championships	**1** (1979)		

SEATTLE SUPERSONICS

1967–68 Coach Al Bianchi guides Seattle into the NBA. Its initial win comes against the other expansion team, the San Diego Rockets.

1969–70 Before the season, Lenny Wilkens is named player-coach.

1970–71 Wilkens wins All-Star MVP honors.

1971–72 Spencer Haywood signs in mid-year. After the season, the Sonics draft "Downtown" Fred Brown.

1974–75 Seattle makes the playoffs for the first time, topping Detroit.

1978–79 The Sonics hold foes to a league-low 103.9 PPG en route to an NBA title, topping Washington in five games one year after falling to the Bullets in seven. Gus Williams and Dennis Johnson lead the team in scoring and Jack Sikma patrols the paint.

1979–80 In the first year of the 3-point shot, Brown leads the NBA in accuracy.

1986–87 Dale Ellis, Tom Chambers and Xavier McDaniel become the first teammate trio in history to each average 23 PPG or better.

1992–93 George Karl, who had taken over as coach the previous season, steers the Sonics to one game short of the Finals.

1993–94 All-Stars Gary Payton and Shawn Kemp power the Sonics to the best record in the NBA (63–19), but No. 8 seed Denver shocks them in the first round.

1995–96 This time, Seattle backs up its great record (64–18) with a trip to the Finals, where Chicago wins in six. Payton is named Defensive Player of the Year.

1997–98 Vin Baker helps Seattle eclipse 60 wins for the third time in five seasons.

2000–01 Former Sonics great Nate McMillan is named head coach.

2002–03 Payton goes to Milwaukee in a deal that brings Ray Allen to Seattle.

THE PLAYERS

A–Z

KAREEM ABDUL-JABBAR

Full Name: **Kareem Abdul-Jabbar**
Date of Birth: **April 16, 1947, New York, New York**
Teams: **Milwaukee Bucks, Los Angeles Lakers**

Position: **Center**
Ht: **7-2**
Wt: **230**

"Kareem's sky hook was the most deadly and unstoppable weapon in any sport."—Former Lakers head coach Pat Riley.

Any discussion of the greatest centers in history has to include Kareem Abdul-Jabbar, who first gained fame as Lew Alcindor on the playgrounds of New York City and while powering UCLA to three consecutive NCAA championships. Though he converted to Islam and changed his name in 1971, his game remained easily recognizable and virtually unstoppable. With his 7-foot-2 frame and devastating "sky hook" that no one could block, Kareem towered over the opposition. Getting him the ball in the low post was as good as putting two points on the scoreboard.

"The first time I shot the hook, I was in fourth grade," he once recalled. "I was about 5 feet, 8 inches tall. I put the ball up and felt totally at ease with the shot. I was completely confident it would go in, and I've been shooting it ever since."

No one—perhaps in any sport—has perfected such a patented weapon with Abdul-Jabbar's results. After the three collegiate titles, he added an NBA championship with the Milwaukee Bucks in just his second pro season and won five more with the "Showtime" Los Angeles Lakers of the 1980s. His teams made the playoffs in 18 of his 20 seasons.

Along the way, Abdul-Jabbar set numerous individual records, some of which are likely to stand for a long time. He kept himself in marvelous shape despite two decades of wear and tear and retired at age 42 as the NBA's career leader in—among other categories—points, field goals, blocked shots, minutes and playoff scoring.

Kareem was the first man to play in 19 All-Star Games and the first to claim six league MVP Awards. He won scoring, rebounding and shot-blocking titles at various stages of his career. If it's possible to be underrated with those numbers and a spot in the Hall of Fame, Abdul-Jabbar was, never quite gaining the acclaim for his skills that centers like Bill Russell and Wilt Chamberlain earned before him.

CAREER TOTALS

	G	Pts	PPG	FGM	FG%	3ptM	3pt%	FTM	FT%	Reb	A	Stl	BS	TO
REG	1560	38387	24.6	15837	.559	1	.056	6712	.721	17440	5660	1160	3189	2527
POST	237	5762	24.3	2356	.533	0	.000	1050	.740	2481	767	189	476	447

NATE ARCHIBALD

Full Name: **Nathaniel Archibald**
Date of Birth: **September 2, 1948, New York, New York**
Teams: **Cincinnati Royals, Kansas City–Omaha Kings, Kansas City Kings, New York Nets, Buffalo Braves, Boston Celtics, Milwaukee Bucks**

Position: **Guard**
Ht: **6-1**
Wt: **158**

"All the individual accomplishments will be just a shadow when you talk about the NBA championship."—Nate "Tiny" Archibald on Boston's 1981 title.

It should come as no surprise that the first pair of NBA eyes to be impressed by Nate "Tiny" Archibald belonged to Bob Cousy, himself a legendary "little" man. Cousy was coaching the Cincinnati Royals when Archibald came out of Texas-El Paso in 1970, and the former Celtics great decided to take a second-round chance on the 6-foot-1, 160-pounder from the South Bronx housing projects.

Archibald proved to be better than even Cousy had dreamed. His ability to penetrate the lane, combined with pinpoint passing and great shooting range, made Tiny one of the best point guards of his time. His quickness gave defenders fits and was the key to everything he did on the hardwood.

"Tiny has it all," Cousy once said. "Instinct, vision and, most important, attitude—the unselfishness to give up the ball…There aren't six kids in the league who can do what he does." When the Royals moved to Kansas City–Omaha in 1972–73 and became known as the Kings, Archibald did something no one had ever done before, leading the NBA in scoring (34.0 per game) and assists (11.4) in the same season.

Archibald wound up calling six different cities home during his stellar 14-year career. When he joined the Celtics in a trade from Buffalo before the 1978–79 campaign, he was coming off an Achilles tendon injury and struggled to regain his form. Some thought he was washed up at age 30. His perseverance paid off in 1980–81, when Archibald was named MVP of the All-Star Game and quarterbacked the Celtics to the NBA championship—the lone title of his career.

Archibald was a six-time All-Star who guided Boston to the best record in the league for three straight seasons. He retired after one year with the Milwaukee Bucks (1983–84) and went to work on a passion he carried throughout his playing days, helping to run New York City community programs and shelters for underprivileged children.

CAREER TOTALS

	G	Pts	PPG	FGM	FG%	3ptM	3pt%	FTM	FT%	Reb	A	Stl	BS	TO
REG	876	16481	18.8	5899	.467	19	.224	4664	.810	2046	6476	719	81	1123
POST	47	667	14.2	235	.423	2	.118	195	.826	77	306	34	2	122

PAUL ARIZIN

Full Name: **Paul J. Arizin**	Position: **Forward**
Date of Birth: **April 9, 1928, Philadelphia, Pennsylvania**	Ht: **6-4**
Teams: **Philadelphia Warriors**	Wt: **198**

"His jump shot was perfect. There was no stopping it."
—Fellow Hall of Famer and former opponent Dolph Schayes on Paul Arizin.

History calls Paul Arizin's jump shot an innovation. Arizin called it an accident. "Some of our games were played on dance floors," he said, referring to the Philadelphia Catholic Club League games he would dominate. "It became quite slippery. When I tried to hook, my feet would go out from under me. So I jumped…The more I did it, the better I became. Before I knew it, practically all my shots were jump shots."

Arizin played basketball when the set shot was the norm, so his style was revolutionary. It was also very effective. Despite being cut from his high school team in Philadelphia, he honed his game at the club level and made the cut at Villanova, where he became an All-American, scored a record 85 points in a game and was selected NCAA Player of the Year by *The Sporting News* in 1949–50.

A territorial draft choice of the Philadelphia Warriors, "Pitchin' Paul" led the NBA in scoring in just his second season. He also emerged as a ball-hungry rebounder and was voted MVP of the 1952 All-Star Game. Despite standing just 6-foot-4 and being routinely guarded by taller players, none could handle Arizin's jump shot.

Two years of service in the Korean War as a U.S. Marine left Philadelphia without its best scorer in his prime, but Arizin made up for lost time upon his return. He sparked the Warriors to the best record in the NBA in 1955–56; his second season back, and culminated the year with a five-game championship win over Fort Wayne.

Arizin won his second scoring crown the following season and went on to become the third player to tally 15,000 career points, following Bob Cousy and Dolph Schayes to the milestone. When the Warriors moved to San Francisco in 1962, he decided to stay home, as he had for his entire Hall of Fame career. He finished his playing days in the Eastern Basketball League.

CAREER TOTALS

	G	Pts	PPG	FGM	FG%	3ptM	3pt%	FTM	FT%	Reb	A	Stl	BS	TO
REG	713	16266	22.8	5628	.421	-	-	5010	.810	6129	1665	-	-	-
POST	49	1186	24.2	411	.411	-	-	364	.829	404	128	-	-	-

CHARLES BARKLEY

Full Name: **Charles Wade Barkley**	Position: **Forward**
Date of Birth: **February 20, 1963, Leeds, Alabama**	Ht: **6-6**
Teams: **Philadelphia 76ers, Phoenix Suns, Houston Rockets**	Wt: **252**

"There will never be another player like me. I'm the ninth wonder of the world."—Charles Barkley.

As both an All-Star player and a popular NBA television analyst, Charles Barkley has long been one of basketball's loudest characters. His outspoken voice usually proclaims the truth—or at least something close to it. So when "Sir Charles" rates himself among the best forwards to have played the game, there's not much point in arguing.

The numbers bear him out, too. Some thought Barkley too small to be an inside force in the NBA when he came out of Auburn, in his home state of Alabama, with the nickname "Round Mound of Rebound." The doubters were way off base in his case. With athletic ability that defied his shape and a relentless hunger for the basketball, the 6-foot-6 (or shorter) Barkley averaged at least 20 points and 10 rebounds per game for 11 straight seasons after his 1984–85 rookie year with Philadelphia.

Seven-footers had nothing on this guy. They could not keep him from powering to the hoop for slam dunks and they were often overmatched on the glass by the undersized big man. Barkley led the NBA in rebounding in just his third year. He was voted MVP of the 1991 All-Star Game after hauling down 22 boards, the most since Wilt Chamberlain in 1967. He enjoyed his best year in 1992–93 after a trade to Phoenix, winning MVP honors, leading the Suns to the best record in the NBA (62–20) and powering his new team to the NBA Finals. The Suns fell to Chicago in six games despite Barkley's postseason averages of 26.6 points and 13.6 rebounds.

Along the way to retiring as one of four players in NBA history to collect 23,000 points, 12,000 boards and 4,000 assists, the 16-year veteran became known—for better or worse—as a man who was not afraid to speak his mind. "I love Charles because he's so honest," said former coach Chris Ford. "You can see a thought form in his head and them move right out of his mouth without stopping in between."

CAREER TOTALS

	G	Pts	PPG	FGM	FG%	3ptM	3pt%	FTM	FT%	Reb	A	Stl	BS	TO
REG	1073	23757	22.1	8435	.541	538	.266	6349	.735	12546	4215	1648	888	3376
POST	123	2833	23.0	1009	.513	64	.255	751	.717	1582	482	193	108	353

RICK BARRY

Full Name: **Richard F. Barry**	Position: **Guard**
Date of Birth: **March 28, 1944, Elizabeth, New Jersey**	Ht: **6-7**
Teams: **Oakland Oaks, Washington Capitals, New York Nets, San Francisco Warriors, Golden State Warriors, Houston Rockets**	Wt: **220**

"He's an intense competitor, whether it's basketball, golf, checkers or anything else. He just doesn't want to lose."
—Former coach Bill Sharman on Rick Barry.

Rick Barry was a defender's nightmare, and his own teammates could sympathize. The man wanted to win so badly; he could often be abrasive even to those who went to battle with him. If there was a battle on the hardwood, however, this was one weapon you wanted on your side.

Barry is the only player in history to win scoring crowns in the NCAA, ABA and NBA. He averaged more than 30 PPG four times in his 14 seasons, played in 12 All-Star Games and penciled his name at or near the top of most offensive statistical categories. His 90-percent free throw accuracy (NBA) ranks second all-time. The leader, Mark Price, had more than 1,800 fewer attempts. One year (1978–79), Barry missed only nine times.

Some called him a shooter, and he certainly excelled at the art. He considered himself a scorer more than a shooter, and no one would argue that, either. "I'm not a good shooter," he once said. "I'm a scorer, that's all… A good shooter is someone like Jerry West." The numbers tell a different story.

A New Jersey native, Barry starred at the University of Miami (Fla.), averaging a national-best 37.4 PPG as a senior. He earned Rookie of the Year honors with the San Francisco Warriors in 1966. His defection to the ABA after his second season resulted in two separate court disputes over contractual issues—one when he left the NBA and the other when he returned—but it was his play that was most memorable.

Barry was one of the best passing big men of all time. He averaged 5.1 APG in the NBA. He was also one of the best clutch players ever. His playoff scoring averages (33.5 in the ABA and 24.8 in the NBA) were better than his regular-season averages in both leagues, and he was named MVP of 1975 Finals after leading the Warriors to a sweep of Washington.

CAREER TOTALS

	G	Pts	PPG	FGM	FG%	3ptM	3pt%	FTM	FT%	Reb	A	Stl	BS	TO
REG	794	18395	23.2	7252	.449	73	.330	3818	.900	5168	4017	1104	269	574
POST	74	1833	24.8	719	.426	3	.250	392	.875	418	340	106	39	12

ELGIN BAYLOR

Full Name: **Elgin Gay Baylor**
Date of Birth: **September 16, 1934, Washington, District of Columbia**
Teams: **Minneapolis Lakers, Los Angeles Lakers**

Position: **Guard**
Ht: **6-5**
Wt: **225**

"I say without reservation that Elgin Baylor is the greatest cornerman who ever played pro basketball."—Bill Sharman, Baylor's former opponent and coach.

There's no doubt Elgin Baylor's name warrants mention in any discussion of history's NBA greats. His 14-year career with the Minneapolis and Los Angeles Lakers included 11 All-Star Games, eight trips to the Finals and 10 appearances on the All-NBA First Team. In some ways, however, Baylor was a victim of circumstance. Consider:

He was one of the first stars whose mid-air acrobatics made jaws drop; yet he played in an era before TV cameras captured such moves for round-the-clock highlight shows. He was a big-time scorer, from the time he was shattering records at Seattle University to his three straight NBA seasons averaging 34-plus PPG, yet Baylor never won a scoring title, largely because his career coincided with that of Wilt Chamberlain. Finally, the Celtics dynasty prevented Baylor from winning a championship.

For those who saw him play, however, none of those missing pieces on his resume overshadows Baylor's greatness. His ability to hang in the air that extra second to launch his shot or grab a rebound foreshadowed players like Julius Erving and Michael Jordan. "He never broke the law of gravity, but he's awfully slow about obeying it," a Lakers opponent reportedly said.

Baylor used his hang time, his accurate, low-trajectory jump shot and his determination around the rim to set several NBA records. He became the first player in league history to score 70 points in a game when he threw 71 at the Knicks in 1960. Chamberlain broke that record two years later with his 100-point outburst.

At one point in his career, Baylor also owned NBA marks for most points in a playoff game and in one half of a playoff game. In 1962–63, he became the first player in history to finish in the NBA's top five in four major statistical categories—scoring, rebounding, assists and free-throw accuracy. Nine games into the 1971–72 season, a knee injury forced Baylor to retire. Ironically, the Lakers won the championship that year.

CAREER TOTALS

	G	Pts	PPG	FGM	FG%	3ptM	3pt%	FTM	FT%	Reb	A	Stl	BS	TO
REG	846	23149	27.4	8693	.431	-	-	5763	.780	11463	3650	-	-	-
POST	134	3623	27.0	1388	.439	-	-	847	.771	1724	541	-	-	-

DAVE BING

Full Name: **David Bing** Date of Birth: **November 29, 1943, Washington, District of Columbia** Teams: **Detroit Pistons, Washington Bullets, Boston Celtics**	Position: **Guard** Ht: **6-3** Wt: **184**

"Maybe some other player does this better, and another player does that better. Nobody does as much as Dave does."
—Earl Lloyd, former player and Pistons scout, on Dave Bing.

It would have been easy to overlook Dave Bing in NBA annals. He did not retire with a slew of NBA records, and he never had the chance to play in a championship series. Yes, it would have been easy to overlook Bing, if not for one thing: Anyone who saw Bing play had to agree he was among the most special players in the history of the game.

It's difficult to fault Bing for spending most of his career with a Detroit Pistons team that could not surround him with the personnel to take full advantage of his skills. A product of the same Washington D.C. neighborhood that produced Elgin Baylor, Bing's scoring ability earned him All-America recognition at Syracuse University and the Pistons selected him second in the 1966 NBA Draft—behind only Cazzie Russell.

The jump to the pros did nothing to curtail Bing's ability to put the ball in the hole. He won the 1967 Rookie of the Year Award. The next season, he became the first backcourt player in 20 years to win an NBA scoring title. It seemed no one in the league was ready for Bing's uncanny fakes, which often had defenders jumping out of their hi-tops while he coolly waited for an opening. One small opening almost always equaled two points.

"Bing was an outstanding offensive player who could get his shot any time he wanted," said Matt Guokas, who frequently had the misfortune of drawing Bing as a defensive assignment.

Bing, hampered by a childhood injury to his left eye, was poked in a 1971–72 preseason game against the Lakers and nearly lost sight in his right eye as a result. Surgery to repair a partially detached retina preserved his career, although doctors warned him a return to the court would put him at great risk. His peripheral vision compromised, Bing managed to play through 1977–78, winning All-Star Game MVP honors in 1976.

	G	Pts	PPG	FGM	FG%	3ptM	3pt%	FTM	FT%	Reb	A	Stl	BS	TO
CAREER TOTALS														
REG	901	18327	20.3	6962	.441	-	-	4403	.775	3420	5397	483	89	216
POST	31	477	15.4	191	.423	-	-	95	.748	85	133	15	4	-

LARRY BIRD

Full Name: **Larry Joe Bird**
Date of Birth: **December 7, 1956, West Baden, Indiana**
Teams: **Boston Celtics**

Position: **Forward**
Ht: **6-9**
Wt: **220**

"Larry Bird just throws the ball in the air and God moves the basket underneath it."—Howie Chizek, Cleveland Cavaliers announcer, after a 1984-85 game.

"Larry Legend" earned his nickname almost from the first time he stepped on Boston's fabled parquet floor. Actually, you could argue that the pride of French Lick, Ind., earned legend status even before he became the pride of the Celtics, having led Indiana State to a memorable 1979 NCAA championship tussle with Magic Johnson and Michigan State.

His pro career was nothing short of brilliant. As Rookie of the Year, Bird's presence helped turn a 29–53 Boston team from the previous season into a 61–21 title contender. It was only a small sampling of what was to come. Over the course of his 13 seasons, Bird was the backbone of three Boston championship teams. He was also living proof that athletic greatness does not require the greatest raw athletic ability.

Bird was often knocked for being slow and unable to get off his feet. His response? Bird became the first non-center in NBA history to win three consecutive MVP Awards. And how many of America's premier athletes made 12 NBA All-Star appearances? Bird did. He also won four free throw crowns, two Finals MVP Awards and an Olympic gold medal as a member of the original Dream Team in 1992.

"A winner is someone who recognizes his God-given talents, works his tail off to develop them into skills and uses these skills to accomplish his goals," said Bird, who is considered by many to be the greatest forward of all time.

Bird's talents were vast. He needed only a split-second to flick his wrist and send a ball swishing through the net from virtually anywhere across the mid-court line. His 6-foot-9 frame allowed him to shoot over most defenders. As a passer, the only player of his era who did it better was perhaps Magic. He was a smart defensive player who exposed opponents' weaknesses. As a winner, this Hall of Famer had no peer in his day.

	G	Pts	PPG	FGM	FG%	3ptM	3pt%	FTM	FT%	Reb	A	Stl	BS	TO
CAREER TOTALS														
REG	897	21791	24.3	8591	.496	649	.376	3960	.886	8974	5695	1556	755	2816
POST	164	3897	23.8	1458	.472	80	.321	901	.890	1683	1062	296	145	506

KOBE BRYANT

Full Name: **Kobe Bryant**
Date of Birth: **August 23, 1978, Philadelphia, Pennsylvania**
Teams: **Los Angeles Lakers**

Position: **Guard**
Ht: **6-7**
Wt: **220**

"There are always going to be similarities, because that's just the way he plays. He is very versatile and a great leader."
—Michael Jordan on comparisons between Kobe Bryant and himself.

In the final match up between Kobe Bryant and Michael Jordan before Jordan's 2003 retirement, it was Bryant who dominated with 55 points in a Los Angeles Lakers victory. One fan held a sign that read, "Goodbye Michael, Hello Kobe."

Several players have been touted as "the next Jordan" over the last decade or so. Of course, all were destined to fall short against the man many consider to be the best who ever played. Only Bryant has stacked up so well that, as recently as the 2002–03 season, at least one columnist went so far as to suggest that Kobe might be even better than Jordan in the final tally.

It's all subjective, but it makes for an interesting argument. Bryant certainly looked as unstoppable as Jordan in his prime during 2002–03, when he ran off nine straight games with at least 40 points. It was the longest such string since Jordan's nine in a row in 1986–87. Hall of Fame center Wilt Chamberlain, with streaks of 14 and 10 consecutive 40-point games, is the only player who has surpassed nine.

Bryant was the youngest player ever to appear in an NBA game when, at 18 years, two months and 11 days, he took the floor for the Lakers straight out of Pennsylvania's Lower Merion High School in 1996–97. By 1998, he had become the youngest All-Star in NBA history. His daring drives, long-range shooting prowess and cool in the clutch made him the perfect complement to center Shaquille O'Neal on a Laker juggernaut that would claim the 2000, 2001 and 2002 NBA championships.

Then came 2002–03, when Bryant raised his game to another level and finished third in the MVP voting. He made a record nine consecutive 3-point shots in a game against Seattle. After his 55-point effort against the Wizards, O'Neal said: "That was a performance like I've never seen before, not even on PlayStation."

CAREER TOTALS

	G	Pts	PPG	FGM	FG%	3ptM	3pt%	FTM	FT%	Reb	A	Stl	BS	TO
REG	496	10658	21.5	3801	.456	417	.332	2639	.831	2458	2060	714	320	1339
POST	97	2155	22.2	779	.439	97	.349	500	.786	473	407	119	82	258

WILT CHAMBERLAIN

Full Name: **Wilton N. Chamberlain**
Date of Birth: **August 21, 1936, Philadelphia, Pennsylvania**
Teams: **Philadelphia Warriors, San Francisco Warriors,
Philadelphia 76ers, Los Angeles Lakers**

Position: **Center**
Ht: **7-1**
Wt: **270**

*"Wilt would still be the best center in the NBA, still be the dominant player
in the NBA."*—Former 76ers teammate Billy Cunningham on Wilt Chamberlain.

"Wilt the Stilt" was one of a kind. The sheer physical dominance with which he
played had never been witnessed before. Certainly, no defender had ever been
faced with the task of trying to slow such a powerful force. With the exception of Bill
Russell and the Celtics, none could.

Chamberlain was a high school legend in Philadelphia, and he was so
dominant as a Kansas collegian that rules changes (including the widening of the
lane and introduction of offensive goaltending) were enacted on account of him. It
turned out players in the NBA were no better equipped to stop him than their college
counterparts.

With his hometown Philadelphia Warriors in 1959–60, Chamberlain became the
first player in history to be named Rookie of the Year and MVP in the same season.
Of course, that was only the beginning. Over his 14-year career, Chamberlain was
a four-time MVP, 13-time All-Star, 11-time rebounding champion and seven-time
scoring leader. For good measure, Chamberlain even led the league in assists in
1967–68.

Those feats—accomplished with the Warriors, 76ers and Lakers—are
impressive enough, but it was on March 2, 1962, that Chamberlain did the
unthinkable. He scored 100 points in a 169–147 Warriors win over the Knicks in
Hershey, Pa., a record that he still holds. It appears to be safe for years to come.

Chamberlain averaged 50.4 PPG that season. His Hall of Fame career included
four games of 70 or more points and 118 of 50-plus. He was just as dominant on
the glass and led the NBA in field-goal percentage nine times. His motto: "Whatever
you do, large or small, do it well or don't do it at all."

If there's one knock on Chamberlain, it was his inability to derail Russell and the
Celtics' championship express. It was a matter of a great team outperforming a
great individual. However, Wilt did earn a pair of championship rings, with the 76ers
in 1967 and the Lakers in 1972.

CAREER TOTALS

	G	Pts	PPG	FGM	FG%	3ptM	3pt%	FTM	FT%	Reb	A	Stl	BS	TO
REG	1045	31419	30.1	12681	.540	-	-	6057	.511	23924	4643	-	-	-
POST	160	3607	22.5	1425	.522	-	-	757	.465	3913	673	-	-	-

BOB COUSY

Full Name: **Robert J. Cousy**
Date of Birth: **August 9, 1928, Queens, New York**
Teams: **Boston Celtics, Cincinnati Royals**

Position: **Guard**
Ht: **6-1**
Wt: **177**

"Cooz was the absolute offensive master. What Russell was on defense, that's what Cousy was on offense—a magician."
—Former Celtics teammate Tom Heinsohn on Bob Cousy.

Long before flashy was fashionable, Bob Cousy brought it to the Boston Garden. His style, honed on the playgrounds on Manhattan's east side, worked against him early. He was benched early in his All-America career at Holy Cross for choosing the sensational play over the routine one, but Cousy found his way onto the floor frequently enough to lead the school to three NCAA tournaments and the 1947 title.

Though he went on to quarterback the Boston Celtics to dynasty status in the 1950s and '60s, the team bypassed him in the 1950 draft. Cousy went to the Tri-Cities Black Hawks and was later traded to a Chicago Stags team that folded. As fate would have it, "Houdini of the Hardwood" wound up with the Celtics in a random drawing out of a hat.

Cousy's behind-the-back dribble, no-look passes and general razzle-dazzle were years ahead of his time. He led the NBA in assists eight straight times with averages that were unheard-of in the pre-shot clock years. It appeared as though the ball was attached to his hand as he triggered the Celtics' fast break—a style that set the team apart in those years. Said legendary boss Red Auerbach: "A coach would have to be dumb to have a man of his ability and not use the fast break."

The results were tangible. "Cooz" set up the offense for six Celtics championship teams, distributing to fellow Hall of Famer Bill Russell and a stellar supporting cast. He was no slouch in the scoring department himself either, averaging 21.7 PPG in his second season and amassing almost 17,000 career points. Cousy played in 13 straight All-Star Games—twice winning game MVP honors—and was named league MVP in 1957.

Cousy's final game, in 1963, was among his most memorable. At age 34, he dribbled out the clock against the Lakers and threw the ball high in the air as the Celtics wrapped up their fifth straight championship.

CAREER TOTALS

	G	Pts	PPG	FGM	FG%	3ptM	3pt%	FTM	FT%	Reb	A	Stl	BS	TO
REG	924	16960	18.4	6168	.375	-	-	4624	.803	4786	6955	-	-	-
POST	109	2018	18.5	689	.342	-	-	640	.801	546	937	-	-	-

DAVE COWENS

Full Name: **David W. Cowens**	Position: **Center**
Date of Birth: **October 25, 1948, Newport, Kentucky**	Ht: **6-9**
Teams: **Boston Celtics, Milwaukee Bucks**	Wt: **230**

"I never thought of myself as a superstar. I represent the working class of the NBA."—Dave Cowens.

Dave Cowens was the type of basketball player who brought his hardhat and lunch pail to work. That's not to say the man lacked great talent. On the contrary, he could run and jump better than most men his size, had a soft left-handed shooting touch and ranked among the best rebounders in the country during his college career at Florida State.

Still, most of Cowens' accomplishments were the result of his willingness to work—a trait Celtics GM Red Auerbach noticed before the 1970 NBA Draft and one that led him to select Cowens with the fourth pick. Some wondered whether Cowens, undersized at 6-foot-9, was up to the task of filling Bill Russell's shoes at center. Henry Finkel tried the year before and was routinely booed at the Boston Garden. Cowens, fans soon learned, could handle the heat.

"Big Red" might have tried too hard at first. Though he shared NBA Rookie of the Year honors with Geoff Petrie in 1970–71, he also led the league in fouls. Cowens made the first of his seven All-Star appearances the next season, serving notice with his tenacious defense, unselfish play and relentless attacking of the glass that opposing centers would have their hands full for the next decade. Most big men were not keen on playing perimeter defense. Cowens forced them to.

"I don't look for excuses when we lose and I don't buy excuses when we win," Cowens once said. Usually, his Celtics won. His presence in the lineup as a rookie helped Boston overcome a rare sub-.500 season, and it did not take long for the Celtics to return to the top of the NBA. Cowens was named MVP in 1973 and the following season he won the first of two championships in a three-year span. Cowens served as the Celtics' player-coach for one of his 11 seasons and took his first "full time" head-coaching job with Charlotte in 1996.

CAREER TOTALS

	G	Pts	PPG	FGM	FG%	3ptM	3pt%	FTM	FT%	Reb	A	Stl	BS	TO
REG	766	13516	17.6	5744	.460	1	.071	2027	.783	10444	2910	599	488	543
POST	89	1684	18.9	733	.451	0	.000	218	.744	1285	333	78	56	8

BILLY CUNNINGHAM

Full Name: **William J. Cunningham**	Position: **Forward**
Date of Birth: **June 3, 1943, Brooklyn, New York**	Ht: **6-7**
Teams: **Philadelphia 76ers, Carolina Cougars**	Wt: **220**

When you think about Billy's life, it is amazing. I don't know anything he has done that hasn't worked."—Former 76ers general manager Pat Williams.

Billy Cunningham easily could have made this book's list of greatest coaches. He was that good on the bench, having won nearly 70 percent of his games at the 76ers' helm (454–198) and guided the team to a 1983 NBA championship.

However, Cunningham first made his mark as a sensational player. Nicknamed "the Kangaroo Kid" for his amazing leaping ability, Cunningham learned how to score on the playgrounds of Brooklyn. He also learned how to win, developing a competitive fire that served him well both as a player and coach.

The 76ers, who had just added Wilt Chamberlain to their lineup, drafted the two-time All-American out of North Carolina in the first round in 1965, and Cunningham did not disappoint. He played a prominent role off the bench on the 1966–67 squad that won the NBA championship, but there was no keeping him out of the starting lineup for long. Cunningham began a string of four consecutive All-Star appearances the following season. He averaged a career-high 26.1 PPG in 1969–70.

Philadelphia was headed downhill, however, and Cunningham opted to sign with the ABA's Carolina Cougars after the 1971–72 campaign. How much did the 76ers miss his leadership? They set an all-time futility record (9–73) in his first year away. Meanwhile, Cunningham led the ABA in steals and won the league's 1972 MVP Award. He played one more year with the Cougars before returning to the 76ers in 1974. A serious knee injury brought his career to an end 20 games into the 1975–76 season.

"In a way the injury made things easy for me. I never had to agonize over that decision all athletes face," offered Cunningham, who finished with career averages of 21.2 points, 10.4 rebounds and 4.3 assists per game over 11 pro seasons. With no previous coaching experience, he took over the 76ers in 1977 and began a "second career" that was as successful as his first.

CAREER TOTALS

	G	Pts	PPG	FGM	FG%	3ptM	3pt%	FTM	FT%	Reb	A	Stl	BS	TO
REG	654	13626	20.8	5116	.446	-	-	3394	.720	6638	2625	115	45	-
POST	39	757	19.4	289	.427	-	-	179	.686	356	125	-	-	-

ADRIAN DANTLEY

Full Name: **Adrian Delano Dantley**	Position: **Guard**
Date of Birth: **February 28, 1956, Washington, District of Columbia**	Ht: **6-5**
Teams: **Buffalo Braves, Indiana Pacers, Los Angeles Lakers,**	Wt: **210**
Detroit Pistons, Dallas Mavericks, Milwaukee Bucks	

"He's our piranha. He'll eat you alive. He would score in a raging storm at sea."—Former Utah coach Frank Layden on Adrian Dantley.

Dantley was among the most prolific scorers of his generation, and his career .540 shooting percentage is among the best in NBA history by a non-center. If you needed a bucket, A.D. was your man. And while basketball has seen its share of scoring machines, what set Dantley apart was his ability to thrive from virtually anywhere on the floor.

Dantley's perimeter marksmanship was exceptional. His quick first step allowed him to get to the basket against almost any defender. His strength and determination made him a force around the hoop despite his height. "I can't figure out how a guy 6 foot 5 inches can score inside like that," Wilt Chamberlain once said. "Elgin Baylor didn't do that. Elgin had great hands. He'd score off the break, or drive. But he'd never do like Dantley—stay inside and grab balls, go up two or three times and score. That's incredible, especially with all those leapers around."

That combination of skills, instincts and determination was honed on the courts of Washington D.C. and at DeMatha High School in Maryland, where Dantley earned All-America status while leading the team to a 57–2 record. He was a two-time NCAA All-American in three years at Notre Dame, won a gold medal in the 1976 Olympics and earned 1977 NBA Rookie of the Year honors with the Buffalo Braves.

Three trades in the next two years eventually saw Dantley don a Jazz uniform. In it, he became the league's most dangerous scorer. He averaged 30-plus points per game in four straight seasons, winning a pair of scoring titles. He routinely made more trips to the free-throw line than anyone, leading the league five times in free throws made.

A 1986 trade to Detroit helped Dantley, a six-time All-Star, reach the NBA Finals for the only time in his career in 1988, but the Lakers kept him from winning a championship. A.D. retired in 1991 as the NBA's ninth-leading career scorer.

CAREER TOTALS

	G	Pts	PPG	FGM	FG%	3ptM	3pt%	FTM	FT%	Reb	A	Stl	BS	TO
REG	955	23177	24.3	8169	.540	7	.171	6832	.818	5455	2830	944	150	2503
POST	73	1558	21.3	531	.525	0	.000	496	.796	395	169	69	6	185

BOB DAVIES

Full Name: **Robert E. Davies**
Date of Birth: **January 15, 1920, Harrisburg, Pennsylvania**
Teams: **Brooklyn Indians, New York Gothams, Rochester Royals**

Position: **Guard**
Ht: **6-1**
Wt: **176**

"He had such uncanny control of the ball behind his back that it never concerned me. He made it look as easy as the conventional dribble."
—Former Seton Hall coach "Honey" Russell on Bob Davies and his behind-the-back dribble.

Leaping generations is an inexact science. Times change and styles change. There's really no accurate way to compare today's best basketball players with those who came along in the game's infancy 50-plus years ago. Suspend your disbelief a little bit, though, and you can almost hear pro basketball fans of the 1940s reacting to Bob Davies' style the way today's NBA followers "ooh" and "aah" at the moves of Allen Iverson.

Davies was known as the "Harrisburg Houdini" for the magical things he did with a basketball. Today, the behind-the-back dribble is a routine play even for pre-teen point guards. In the 1940s, that was hardly the case. In fact, few had ever witnessed the move before the 6-foot-1 Davies began using it to confound the opposition and electrify crowds as a two-time All-American at Seton Hall. He led the Pirates to 43 consecutive victories during one stretch, and his wizardry helped attract 18,403 fans—a record crowd at the time—to Madison Square Garden for a 1941 National Invitation Tournament game between Seton Hall and Rhode Island.

His exciting plays thrilled pro basketball fans as well and helped his teams to three championships. He began his pro career with Brooklyn and New York of the ABL, then led the Rochester Royals to back-to-back NBL titles in 1946 and '47. Davies was named league MVP in that second championship season, and he went on to lead his league in assists for six straight seasons.

Davies took the Royals to an NBA crown in 1951 as the league's second-biggest attraction behind George Mikan of Minneapolis. He once delivered a record 20 assists in a game and played in the first four NBA All-Star Games. Davies also enjoyed success in the coaching ranks and served a U.S. Navy stint during World War II. That dazzling dribble, however, remains his legacy.

CAREER TOTALS

	G	Pts	PPG	FGM	FG%	3ptM	3pt%	FTM	FT%	Reb	A	Stl	BS	TO
REG	462	6594	14.3	2292	.378	-	-	2010	.759	980	2250	-	-	-
POST	38	506	13.3	173	.341	-	-	160	.788	78	162	-	-	-

DAVE DeBUSSCHERE

Full Name: **David A. DeBusschere**
Date of Birth: **October 16, 1940, Detroit, Michigan**
Teams: **Detroit Pistons, New York Knicks**

Position: **Forward**
Ht: **6-6**
Wt: **227**

"He took away my first, second, third and fourth offensive move."
—Former star Connie Hawkins on Dave DeBusschere.

Dave DeBusschere's initials could not have been more fitting. For no one played defense quite like "Big D," who for a dozen years proved that hard work can win out over size and speed—even in the NBA.

Baseball might have been DeBusschere's best sport as a youth. He pitched his high school team to a Detroit city championship and his local youth team to a national junior title. He also won a state championship in basketball and starred in both sports at the University of Detroit. Faced with choosing one over the other upon his 1962 graduation, DeBusschere went with his instinct. He kept playing both, signing with the Chicago White Sox and the Detroit Pistons.

DeBusschere's four-year pro baseball career included a tour in the big leagues, but basketball eventually won out. NBA forwards wished he'd have stayed on the pitcher's mound. While he showed some promise offensively, defense became DeBusschere's calling card. He also stood out for his leadership, and in 1964 the Pistons named him player-coach at age 24, making him the youngest bench boss in NBA history.

Unfortunately for his coaching record, Detroit did not have much talent around him. DeBusschere did not have the same trouble after being traded to the Knicks in 1968. His clampdown defense turned out to be just what New York needed, and he was a driving force behind the team's NBA titles in 1970 and '73. DeBusschere earned NBA All-Defensive First Team honors every year from 1969 to '74. He was the rare player capable of shutting down his opponent, controlling the boards and, if the team needed it, scoring 20 points as well.

"I always knew he was an outstanding player, but not this good," Knicks head coach Red Holzman once said. DeBusschere played in eight All-Star Games. He later held front-office positions with the New York Nets and New York Knicks and served as commissioner of the ABA in its final season (1975–76).

CAREER TOTALS

	G	Pts	PPG	FGM	FG%	3ptM	3pt%	FTM	FT%	Reb	A	Stl	BS	TO
REG	875	14053	16.1	5722	.432	-	-	2609	.699	9618	2497	67	39	-
POST	96	1536	16.0	634	.416	-	-	268	.698	1155	253	7	4	-

CLYDE DREXLER

Full Name: **Clyde Austin Drexler**	Position: **Guard**
Date of Birth: **June 22, 1962, New Orleans, Louisiana**	Ht: **6-7**
Teams: **Portland Trail Blazers, Houston Rockets**	Wt: **222**

"Every athlete strives for excellence. And the excellence in professional sports is the championship ring."—Clyde Drexler.

Clyde Drexler spent much of his basketball career coming up just short of his ultimate goal. "Close but no cigar" could have been his legacy had it not been for a 1995 trade to Houston, where he finally added an NBA championship to a resume that was already overflowing with individual accolades, All-Star appearances and playoff trips.

"Clyde the Glide" first became a household name alongside Hakeem Olajuwon on the University of Houston's "Phi Slamma Jamma" teams that reached the NCAA Final Four in back-to-back seasons. They never won a title, but Drexler's leaping ability was the stuff of legend. He once dunked on a hoop set at 11 feet, 1 inch. Portland plucked Drexler with the 14th pick in the 1983 NBA Draft and, after a modest rookie campaign, he spent 10 straight years soaring to the bucket, draining jumpers, competing for scoring titles, making All-Star trips and generally re-writing the Trail Blazers' record book.

By the time of his trade to the Rockets, Drexler had become Portland's career leader in scoring, games, minutes, field goals, free throws, rebounds and steals. He had helped the Blazers to the NBA Finals in 1990 and 1992, losing to the Pistons and Bulls, respectively. Drexler's greatest triumph to that point had come as a member of the original "Dream Team" that cruised to a gold medal in the 1992 Olympics.

Then came 1994–95. Back in his old college town and reunited with Olajuwon after a mid-season trade to the Rockets, Drexler's lone NBA crown took shape quickly. He shed the distinction of being the player with the most playoff points never to have won a title, helping Houston sweep Orlando in the 1995 Finals despite being seeded sixth in the Western Conference.

Drexler finished his career three years later as one of just three players in NBA history to amass 20,000 points, 6,000 rebounds and 3,000 assists. His first non-playing job was as head coach at the University of Houston.

CAREER TOTALS

	G	Pts	PPG	FGM	FG%	3ptM	3pt%	FTM	FT%	Reb	A	Stl	BS	TO
REG	1086	22195	20.4	8335	.472	827	.318	4698	.788	6677	6125	2207	719	2977
POST	145	2963	20.4	1076	.447	141	.288	670	.787	1002	891	278	108	397

JOE DUMARS

Full Name: **Joe Dumars**
Date of Birth: **May 24, 1963, Natchitoches, Louisiana**
Teams: **Detroit Pistons**

Position: **Guard**
Ht: **6-3**
Wt: **195**

"When I first got drafted, my dad said, 'That's a pretty good job you've got there. Treat it with respect.' I think it was good advice."—Joe Dumars.

Joe Dumars was the model citizen on the "Bad Boys" Detroit Pistons teams that put fear into their NBA opponents in the late 1980s, winning championships in 1989 and '90. He was the quiet one: a man who reported for duty every night and made the opposing team's top guard work for every point he scored. No one did it better.

The son of a hard-working Louisiana truck driver, Dumars played college basketball in relative obscurity at McNeese State, averaging more than 22 points per game in his four seasons. The Pistons drafted him in the first round in 1985 and brought him off the bench early in his career. However, it soon became evident that Dumars' defense was too valuable to keep him out of the lineup.

Beginning in 1989, Dumars became a regular on the NBA All-Defensive Team. Bulls superstar Michael Jordan considered "Joe D" the best defender he faced. While players like Isiah Thomas, Bill Laimbeer and Dennis Rodman hoarded the headlines, Dumars did his job quietly and efficiently, and the Pistons became champions. "Joe had as much skill as anybody on that team," former teammate Vinny Johnson said. "He just didn't like talking about himself."

That did not mean Dumars went undecorated. He was a six-time All-Star and the MVP of the NBA Finals after the Pistons' 1989 championship run. He scored 33 points in Game 3 of the 1990 Finals, then was told after the game that his father had died earlier in the day. He was there for his family, and yet managed to help Detroit claim its second straight championship.

Dumars was the Pistons' career leader in games played and the 61st NBA player to reach 16,000 career points when he retired after 14 seasons. In 2000, the NBA's Sportsmanship Award he once won was renamed the Joe Dumars Award. That same year, he had his jersey retired and became Detroit's president of basketball operations.

CAREER TOTALS

	G	Pts	PPG	FGM	FG%	3ptM	3pt%	FTM	FT%	Reb	A	Stl	BS	TO
REG	1018	16401	16.1	5994	.460	990	.382	3423	.843	2203	4612	902	83	2084
POST	112	1752	15.6	646	.462	53	.358	407	.855	257	512	91	6	205

TIM DUNCAN

Full Name: **Timothy Theodore Duncan**
Date of Birth: **April 25, 1976, St. Croix, Virgin Islands**
Teams: **San Antonio Spurs**

Position: **Forward**
Ht: **7-0**
Wt: **260**

"Duncan just picks you apart. He passes, he runs, he defends, he rebounds, he scores. It's more beautiful than the way Shaq (Shaquille O'Neal) overpowers you."—Milwaukee coach George Karl on Tim Duncan.

Tim Duncan will never be the flashiest player in the NBA. In fact, he might be one of the least exciting superstars ever to win an MVP Award, which more often goes to those who leave fans wide-eyed with their moves. That's not Duncan. His game is all about doing everything the way it was meant to be done, and winning lots of games as a result.

Lakers center Shaquille O'Neal once called Duncan "the Big Fundamental." Duncan's sound fundamental skills in all areas of the game are rather amazing when you consider he did not play organized basketball until high school. He was a top swimmer growing up on the Virgin Islands, specializing in freestyle distance events. When Hurricane Hugo destroyed the local pool in 1989, the 7-footer switched sports.

Swimming's loss was basketball's gain. Duncan dominated his college competition, opting to stay all four years at Wake Forest to earn his degree. He also won the AP Player of the Year Award as a senior. San Antonio drafted Duncan No. 1 overall in 1997, and he was the only first-year player to make the 1998 All-Star Game en route to Rookie of the Year honors.

Duncan's maturity, both on and off the court, was remarkable. In no time at all he was leading the Spurs at both ends of the floor, unfazed by the rigors of battling NBA power forwards. His defense, rebounding, range and consistency around the hoop made him a coach's dream. "Trying to be fancy doesn't work for me," explained Duncan of his no-frills style.

Duncan is the first player since Larry Bird to be named to the All-NBA First Team in each of his first six seasons. Since joining the NBA, no player has notched more double-doubles. Duncan led the Spurs to only two championship in 1999 and 2003, earning two Finals MVP Awards. He was also named 2002 and 2003 regular-season MVP, becoming only the eighth player in history to win the award in consecutive seasons.

CAREER TOTALS

	G	Pts	PPG	FGM	FG%	3ptM	3pt%	FTM	FT%	Reb	A	Stl	BS	TO
REG	451	10324	22.9	3932	.510	16	.184	2444	.710	5548	1447	352	1129	1420
POST	72	1739	24.2	637	.505	2	.133	463	.707	936	286	53	221	240

ALEX ENGLISH

Full Name: **Alexander English**
Date of Birth: **January 5, 1954, Columbia, South Carolina**
Teams: **Milwaukee Bucks, Indiana Pacers, Denver Nuggets, Dallas Mavericks**

Position: **Forward**
Ht: **6-7**
Wt: **190**

"I'm not so flashy, not so boisterous. I'm low-key. My job is to do the job I'm supposed to do."—Alex English.

This English needed no translation. The definition of Alex English was scoring. See also, two points. In his case, it was quite all right to be known for one thing and one thing only. Because English mastered the art of scoring to such a degree that it carried him to the Basketball Hall of Fame, where he was inducted in 1997.

English was soft-spoken and thoughtful. He had poetry books published. His most beautiful verse, however, came in the creative moves he used to get near the basket and the touch he displayed in rippling the nets. English was the NBA's most prolific scorer in the 1980s, an eight-time All-Star who finished his career ranked seventh on the league's all-time scoring chart.

Alexander English was born in Columbia, S.C. and stayed home to play college basketball at South Carolina. He was not among the top prospects in the 1976 NBA Draft, waiting until the second round before Milwaukee called his name. At first, that round-two status seemed about right. English spent the bulk of his first two seasons coming off the Bucks' bench and was a modest-scoring starter for a year-and-a-half in Indiana before being traded to Denver—a move that altered the course of his career.

With the high-scoring Nuggets in the wide-open West, English became a star. He moved his lithe, 6-foot-7 frame to the hoop with such ease and hit his target consistently with an array of pull-up jumpers. The result was the NBA's first-ever string of eight consecutive 2,000-point seasons and a career in which he shot .507 from the floor.

English won a scoring title in 1982–83 (28.4 PPG), made eight straight trips to the All-Star Game and led the Nuggets to the playoffs nine years in a row. In addition to scoring more points than anyone in the league for a decade, English was a workhorse who rarely missed a game. He won the J. Walter Kennedy Citizenship Award in 1988.

CAREER TOTALS

	G	Pts	PPG	FGM	FG%	3ptM	3pt%	FTM	FT%	Reb	A	Stl	BS	TO
REG	1193	25613	21.5	10659	.507	18	.217	4277	.832	6538	4351	1067	833	2821
POST	68	1661	24.4	668	.503	0	.000	325	.862	371	293	47	32	142

JULIUS ERVING

Full Name: **Julius W. Erving**	Position: **Forward**
Date of Birth: **February 22, 1950, Roosevelt, New York**	Ht: **6-7**
Teams: **Virginia Squires, New York Nets, Philadelphia 76ers**	Wt: **206**

"Just as Babe Ruth changed baseball forever, I think that Julius changed basketball forever. Historians will recall his era as the pivotal point in the evolution of the game."—Former 76ers GM Pat Williams on Julius Erving.

As an athlete, a showman and a spokesman for his sport, Julius Erving was a cut above the rest. He was not only the best player of his time, he was also the superstar who took the game of basketball and raised it to new heights of popularity. At a time when the NBA needed a lift, "Dr. J" made a timely house call.

A high school friend in New York is credited with calling Erving "Doctor" for the first time, simply because Erving called him "the professor." Dr. J starred at Massachusetts for two years before signing with the Virginia Squires of the ABA. It was with that league's red, white and blue ball that Erving began captivating the masses with his grace on the basketball court. His mid-air changes of direction and flamboyant slam dunks became signature plays no one had seen before—at least the way Erving pulled them off.

"After my second year in Virginia," Erving once said, "I thought that there was a possibility that I could offer something unique." Indeed he did. His unique style and considerable skills proved nearly impossible to defend, as Erving led his second ABA team, the Nets, to two titles in three years. In five ABA seasons, he won the scoring title and MVP Award three times apiece.

When the ABA era ended in 1976, the NBA was thrilled to have him aboard—both as a player and an ambassador. The 76ers paid $3 million for his rights, which looked like a steal by the time he finished his Hall of Fame career as the all-time ABA/NBA scoring leader with more than 30,000 points over 16 seasons.

Erving won his only NBA MVP Award in 1981 and his 76ers broke through with a championship under his leadership in 1983, erasing years of postseason frustration with a 12–1 run through the playoffs.

CAREER TOTALS

	G	Pts	PPG	FGM	FG%	3ptM	3pt%	FTM	FT%	Reb	A	Stl	BS	TO
REG	836	18364	22.0	7237	.507	46	.261	3844	.777	5601	3224	1508	1293	2323
POST	141	3088	21.9	1187	.486	7	.194	707	.779	994	594	235	239	396

PATRICK EWING

Full Name: **Patrick Aloysius Ewing**	Position: **Center**
Date of Birth: **August 5, 1962, Kingston, Jamaica**	Ht: **7-0**
Teams: **New York Knicks, Seattle SuperSonics, Orlando Magic**	Wt: **255**

"Great competitor, ultimate warrior. ...The thing that comes to mind about him is I always see his face dripping with sweat, because every time he stepped on the court, he gave you everything he had."
—Former Pistons great Isiah Thomas on Patrick Ewing.

Upon his retirement in 2002, Patrick Ewing said he was disappointed to have finished his career without an NBA championship. It was clearly not for a lack of trying, for no player in New York Knicks history left more sweat—literally and figuratively—on the floor of Madison Square Garden.

Ewing was the greatest jump-shooting center in NBA history. He was almost automatic from either baseline. He retired as the Knicks' career leader in 11 statistical categories, including games, points, rebounds, steals and blocked shots. He led the team in scoring and blocks for 12 straight seasons and in rebounding eight times during that span. "In a way, he is the Knicks," said former teammate Allan Houston. "He's what this organization is all about."

Ewing was born in Jamaica and moved with his family to the United States at age 11. He became a high school All-American in Cambridge, Massachusetts, and gained fame as the driving force behind Georgetown's powerful teams of the mid-1980s. The All-American led the Hoyas to the 1984 NCAA championship and a runner-up finish the following year.

NBA accolades came early for this dominant big man. He won the 1986 Rookie of the Year Award and, in 1988, started a run of 10 straight trips to the All-Star Game (he made 11 trips in all). He led the Knicks to 60 wins in 1992–93 and to the Finals the following season, when they lost in seven games to Houston despite Ewing's Finals record 30 blocked shots.

Ewing spent 15 memorable seasons with the Knicks and one each with Seattle and Orlando before hanging up his sneakers in 2002. Though he never won an NBA title, he captured two Olympic gold medals—one as a collegian·in 1984 and another with the original 1992 Dream Team.

CAREER TOTALS

	G	Pts	PPG	FGM	FG%	3ptM	3pt%	FTM	FT%	Reb	A	Stl	BS	TO
REG	1183	24815	21.0	9702	.504	19	.152	5392	.740	11607	2215	1136	2894	3537
POST	139	2813	20.2	1104	.469	8	.348	597	.718	1435	275	122	303	345

WALT FRAZIER

Full Name: **Walter Frazier**	Position: **Guard**
Date of Birth: **March 29, 1945, Atlanta, Georgia**	Ht: **6-4**
Teams: **New York Knicks, Cleveland Cavaliers**	Wt: **205**

"It's Clyde's ball. He just lets us play with it once in a while."
—former Knicks teammate Willis Reed on Walt "Clyde" Frazier.

Frazier was one of the NBA's all-time snazzy dressers. In fact, it was a fancy derby he was wearing early in his career that prompted teammate Nate Bowman to nickname him "Clyde," after Warren Beatty's portrayal of Clyde Barrow in the movie "Bonnie and Clyde." Calling the Rolls Royce-driving Frazier stylish was an understatement.

On the court, he was every bit as artistic, and there was plenty of substance to go with that style. Frazier's ball-handling skills, scoring ability and tenacious defense sparked the New York Knicks for a decade. Frazier was the team's first-round draft choice in 1967, and his presence in the backcourt was felt almost immediately. In his third season, he quarterbacked the Knicks to their first NBA championship.

Most remember a limping Willis Reed's heroic Game 7 performance against the Lakers in that 1970 Finals, after missing the previous game with an injury. Every bit as important to the Knicks' victory was Frazier's 36-point, 19-assist, seven-rebound performance—one of the most impressive efforts in NBA Finals history.

"I always tried to hit the open man when I played," Frazier explained years later. "But that night, I was the open man. There's no doubt that '69–70 championship team was the highlight of my career. I think of that team every day."

There were more highlights for Frazier, to be sure. He led the Knicks back to the Finals in 1972, but they fell to Los Angeles. The next year, Frazier was paired with Earl Monroe in the backcourt and the Knicks regained the title with a five-game drubbing of the Lakers.

Frazier made seven straight trips to the NBA All-Star Game and was named MVP of the 1975 classic. He finished his career in Cleveland, but his Hall of Fame legacy will always reside with the Knicks, where he set numerous team records and has not lost his place as the best—and most stylish—guard in franchise history.

CAREER TOTALS

	G	Pts	PPG	FGM	FG%	3ptM	3pt%	FTM	FT%	Reb	A	Stl	BS	TO
REG	825	15581	18.9	6130	.490	0	.000	3321	.786	4830	5040	681	63	139
POST	93	1927	20.7	767	.511	-	-	393	.751	666	599	32	4	-

JOE FULKS

Full Name: **Joseph F. Fulks**
Date of Birth: **October 26, 1921, Marshall County, Kentucky**
Teams: **Philadelphia Warriors**

Position: **Forward**
Ht: **6-5**
Wt: **191**

"The greatest basketball player in the country."
—The Sporting News on Joe Fulks in 1949.

Long before Julius Erving, George Gervin and Alex English, it was Jumpin' Joe Fulks who gave professional basketball its first scoring machine. He is also credited with being the game's first modern jump shooter. While others used set shots and released the ball from eye level, the 6-foot-5 Fulks leaped high off the ground and released the ball over his head, making it almost impossible to block.

Fulks first shot with two hands, then mastered the one-handed jumper. His revolutionary style helped him earn small-college All-America recognition at Murray State in his native Kentucky. After a stint in the Marines during World War II, he returned to treat the Basketball Association of America—and later the NBA—to one of its first true superstars.

As a rookie in 1946–47, Fulks led the BAA in scoring (23.2 PPG) and carried the Philadelphia Warriors to the inaugural BAA title. He repeated as scoring champ the following season, and in 1949 his 63-point game against Indianapolis set a pro record that stood for a decade until Elgin Baylor came along.

Fulks was a dominant inside player who could score on hook shots with either hand, but it was his patented jump shot, which gained him notoriety and attracted large crowds to home and away gyms. He competed in the first two NBA All-Star Games. The Saturday Evening Post once dubbed him "the Babe Ruth of basketball." Fulks filled the nets for eight pro campaigns, averaging 16.4 PPG during the regular season and boosting his output to a 19-point average in the playoffs.

Fulks was enshrined in the Naismith Hall of Fame posthumously in 1977, but his life did not have a happy ending. He battled alcoholism for years and, after a drinking binge in 1976, was found dead of a shotgun blast in a Kentucky trailer home. The 23-year-old son of a woman Fulks had been dating was convicted of manslaughter and served half of a four-year sentence.

CAREER TOTALS

	G	Pts	PPG	FGM	FG%	3ptM	3pt%	FTM	FT%	Reb	A	Stl	BS	TO
REG	489	8003	16.4	2824	.302	-	-	2355	.766	1379	587	-	-	-
POST	31	588	19.0	192	.258	-	-	204	.782	28	11	-	-	-

KEVIN GARNETT

Full Name: **Kevin Garnett**	Position: **Forward**
Date of Birth: **May 19, 1976, Mauldin, South Carolina**	Ht: **6-11**
Teams: **Minnesota Timberwolves**	Wt: **220**

"He brings it every single time he steps on the floor. Everyone else follows suit."—Minnesota Timberwolves teammate Wally Szczerbiak on Kevin Garnett.

Talk about exclusive membership. Consider two clubs to which Kevin Garnett has earned admission. In 2002–03, Garnett became just the second player in history to string together four consecutive seasons averaging 20 points, 10 rebounds and five assists per game. Larry Bird, with five straight, is the only other man to accomplish the feat.

Garnett has also led his team, the Minnesota Timberwolves, in all five major statistical categories—points, rebounds, assists, steals and blocks—in a season. That was previously accomplished by just two NBA players: Dave Cowens of the 1977–78 Celtics and Scottie Pippen of the 1994–95 Bulls.

Those numbers state the obvious: Kevin Garnett has become one of the best all-around talent in the NBA, if not the best. His ability to score, pass, rebound and defend gives his opponents virtually no chance of containing him one-on-one. It seems the only remaining step in his burgeoning NBA career is to lead his team into championship contention.

Mr. Basketball is the honor bestowed upon the best high school player in a particular state. Garnett was so good, he won it in two states: South Carolina as an underclassman and Illinois as a senior. He was USA Today's Player of the Year in his final prep season at Chicago's Farragut Academy and was drafted fifth by the Timberwolves in 1995.

KG's youth worked against him at times, but his early growth was exponential. In 1997–98, he recorded his first triple-double and became the first Minnesota player to start in the All-Star Game. He notched his first 20–10–5 season two years later, in the midst of a string of 338 straight double-figure scoring games—eighth-longest in NBA history.

The 2002–03 campaign was Garnett's best yet. He was named MVP of the All-Star Game, hit career highs in most major statistical categories and finished second in the balloting for the MVP Award. Garnett led the NBA with six triple-doubles and an astounding 68 double-doubles.

CAREER TOTALS

	G	Pts	PPG	FGM	FG%	3ptM	3pt%	FTM	FT%	Reb	A	Stl	BS	TO
REG	611	11877	19.4	4824	.487	127	.308	2102	.756	6354	2650	848	1053	1568
POST	29	611	21.1	247	.462	7	.350	110	.748	365	144	39	47	86

GEORGE GERVIN

Full Name: **George Gervin**	Position: **Forward**
Date of Birth: **April 27, 1952, Detroit, Michigan**	Ht: **6-7**
Teams: **Virginia Squires, San Antonio Spurs, Chicago Bulls**	Wt: **184**

"You don't stop George Gervin. You just hope that his arm gets tired after 40 shots."—Former Lakers great Jerry West.

The "Iceman"—so nicknamed because he was cool under pressure—never experienced the heat of an NBA Finals game. Had he done so, this much is certain: George Gervin would have scored. Because, well, that's just what Gervin did.

One of the most prolific scorers in history grew up in a rough Detroit neighborhood. He befriended a janitor in high school who let him shoot baskets in the gym for hours on end. The only condition: Gervin had to sweep up when he was finished. It was a routine that helped keep Gervin off the streets while sharpening his offensive game.

His efforts paid off, and by the time the skinny kid reached college, he was a scoring machine in the making. His path to pro basketball did not follow the prescribed route. He was suspended from Eastern Michigan's team after hitting an opponent at a tournament, and Gervin joined the Eastern Basketball Association for $125 a week. That led to a contract with the ABA's Virginia Squires, and the Iceman was finally on his way.

Whether on long-range jumpers or his patented finger rolls, Gervin found a way to put the ball in the basket. It was a trend that continued after the San Antonio Spurs bought his contract and later joined the NBA. And it was never better evidenced than when Gervin won the first of his four NBA scoring titles in 1977–78.

Locked in a duel with Denver's David Thompson for most of the season, Gervin found himself needing to score at least 58 points in the season finale after Thompson had tallied an astounding 73 earlier the same day. After missing his first six shots against the Jazz, Gervin asked his teammates to give up their strategy of feeding him the ball at every opportunity. He quickly got hot, however, en route to a 63-point night.

Gervin scored 40-plus points a remarkable 64 times in the NBA and enjoyed 13 consecutive 1,000-point seasons.

CAREER TOTALS

	G	Pts	PPG	FGM	FG%	3ptM	3pt%	FTM	FT%	Reb	A	Stl	BS	TO
REG	791	20708	26.2	8045	.511	77	.297	4541	.844	3607	2214	941	670	2137
POST	59	1592	27.0	622	.508	0	.000	348	.821	341	186	69	51	187

ARTIS GILMORE

Full Name: **Artis Gilmore**	Position:**Center**
Date of Birth: **September 21, 1949, Chipley, Florida**	Ht: **7-2**
Teams: **Chicago Bulls, Kentucky Colonels, San Antonio Spurs, Chicago Bulls, Boston Celtics**	Wt: **246**

"There's just no one else like him in the league. He's devastating. He does devastating things."—Former teammate Dan Issel on Artis Gilmore's ABA success.

Big men knew they were in for a battle when their opponent was Artis Gilmore, and it became even clearer the next morning, when the aches and pains served as a reminder of an encounter with one of the strongest men ever to play the game.

Gilmore, who played at 7-foot-2 and 240 pounds, once picked up former Pittsburgh Steelers linebacker Jack Ham with one hand. On a basketball court, he was the definition of intimidation, swatting everything in sight and attacking the backboards in a way that defied his soft-spoken demeanor.

Few would have predicted stardom for "The Big A," who was raised on limited means among nine siblings in rural Florida and Alabama and started his college career at little-known Gardner-Webb in North Carolina. He played his final two seasons at Division I Jacksonville University, leading the nation in rebounding both years with an all-time record average of 22.7 per game.

It was enough to start a bidding war between the ABA and NBA, and the former league won with a 10-year, $2.5-million contract offer. Gilmore wasted little time emerging as a star. He was named Rookie of the Year and MVP in the same season (1971–72) and went on to lead the ABA in rebounding in four of his five years. He set career and single-season ABA records for blocked shots.

Gilmore went to the Chicago Bulls as the first pick of the 1976 ABA dispersal draft. While his 12 years in the NBA produced six All-Star trips and a career record for field-goal percentage (.599), his time with the Bulls was not always pleasant. Fans wanted a winner, and Gilmore did not enjoy great NBA success in the win-loss column until a 1982 trade to San Antonio.

By the time he retired following a return to the Bulls, a tour with the Celtics and an Italian League stint in 1988–89, Gilmore was one of 24 players to score 20,000 combined ABA/NBA points.

CAREER TOTALS													
	G	Pts	PPG	FGM	FG%	3ptM	3pt%	FTM	FT%	Reb	A	Stl	BS	TO
REG	909	15579	17.1	5732	.599	1	.077	4114	.713	9161	1777	470	1747	2347
POST	42	492	11.7	179	.568	0	-	134	.680	336	47	27	71	81

GAIL GOODRICH

Full Name: **Gail Charles Goodrich Jr.**

Date of Birth: **April 23, 1943, Los Angeles, California**

Teams: **Los Angeles Lakers, Phoenix Suns, New Orleans Jazz**

Position: **Guard**

Ht: **6-1**

Wt: **174**

"Gail Goodrich is the greatest all-around basketball player I've ever coached."—Legendary former UCLA head coach John Wooden.

Go ahead. Try telling Gail Goodrich there's something he can't do. Chances are, he will do it better than you ever could have imagined. At least, that's how he crafted a Hall of Fame career on the hardwood.

As a 6-foot-1 Los Angeles high school star, some thought he was too small to make an impact at the Division I college level, particularly when he opted for powerful UCLA. All Goodrich did under John Wooden was average more than 20 PPG in both his junior and senior years, leading the Bruins to back-to-back national titles as an All-American.

There were more doubters, however, who said his slight frame would never hold up to the rigors of an NBA schedule. Fourteen seasons later, Goodrich retired a five-time All-Star with a championship ring and his No. 25 jersey hanging in the rafters along with the Lakers' other all-time greats.

"If you told me I couldn't do something, I'd die trying to find a way to disprove you," Goodrich once said. "And someone once made the mistake of telling me that I was too small to play basketball."

Ironically, Goodrich initially struggled with the Lakers and was taken by Phoenix in the 1968 expansion draft. He thrived with the Suns, making the 1969 All-Star Game, and the Lakers re-acquired him in a 1970 trade. His left-handed shooting touch and knack for delivering the ball to the right place at the right time served him well on a team that starred the likes of Wilt Chamberlain and Jerry West.

Goodrich wound up leading the Lakers in scoring (25.9 PPG) in 1971–72, when the team—considered one of the best in NBA history—reeled off a record 33 straight victories and won 69 games overall en route to the championship. He was the club's top scorer again the following season for a return trip to the Finals and later served as the Lakers' captain (1974–76). Goodrich averaged 20-plus PPG six times in his NBA career.

CAREER TOTALS

	G	Pts	PPG	FGM	FG%	3ptM	3pt%	FTM	FT%	Reb	A	Stl	BS	TO
REG	1031	19181	18.6	7431	.456	-	-	4319	.807	3279	4805	545	72	390
POST	80	1450	18.1	542	.442	-	-	366	.819	250	333	7	1	-

HAL GREER

Full Name: **Harold E. Greer**	Position: **Guard**
Date of Birth: **June 26, 1936, Huntington, West Virginia**	Ht: **6-3**
Teams: **Syracuse Nationals, Philadelphia 76ers**	Wt: **176**

"Consistency. For me, that was the thing. I would like to be remembered as a great, consistent player."—Hal Greer.

Considering the consistency Hal Greer displayed throughout his career, one would have to conclude he was somewhat underrated. Those who coached him, played with him and watched him over his 15 pro seasons know full well how valuable he was to the Syracuse/Philadelphia franchise.

Harold "Hal" Greer hailed from Huntington, W. Va., where he became the first African-American scholarship athlete at Marshall. Despite earning All-America honors in 1958, the wiry, 6-foot-2 guard did not consider himself a great NBA prospect. In fact, he said he did not unpack his suitcase when the Syracuse Nationals chose him in the second round of the 1958 NBA Draft.

When Greer eventually did take his clothes out of his bag, he never had to re-pack for another franchise, staying with the team when it relocated to Philadelphia in 1963 as the 76ers. His quickness and deft jump shot proved to be a combination the club could not do without as it chased a championship.

That dream became a reality in 1966–67. With Wilt Chamberlain dominating the middle and the likes of Chet Walker and Billy Cunningham complementing Greer, the 76ers put together one of the best seasons in NBA history. They won 45 of their first 49 games and rolled to the NBA title, topping San Francisco in the Finals. Greer's postseason scoring average was 27.7—up from 22.1 during the season.

Greer was almost unstoppable from the top of the key. Former coach Alex Hannum once said he Greer would hit that shot "70 percent of the time." Greer scored 19 points in one quarter of the 1968 NBA All-Star Game, earning MVP honors in the process, and he competed in the NBA's midseason classic 10 times in his career.

Greer served as an assistant coach in his final season (1972–73). By the time he retired, he had appeared in more games (1,122) than anyone in NBA history and ranked among the top 10 in points, field goals made and attempted and minutes.

CAREER TOTALS

	G	Pts	PPG	FGM	FG%	3ptM	3pt%	FTM	FT%	Reb	A	Stl	BS	TO
REG	1122	21586	19.2	8504	.452	-	-	4578	.801	5665	4540	-	-	-
POST	92	1876	20.4	705	.425	-	-	466	.812	505	393	-	-	-

JOHN HAVLICEK

Full Name: **John J. Havlicek**
Date of Birth: **April 8, 1940, Martins Ferry, Ohio**
Teams: **Boston Celtics**

Position: **Guard/**
Forward
Ht: **6-5**
Wt: **203**

"John Havlicek is the measure of what it means to be a Celtic."
—Legendary Boston coach Red Auerbach.

John Havlicek was known for many things. He won an NCAA championship with Ohio State in 1960. He was a member of eight Boston Celtics championship teams. He helped define the "sixth man" role by coming off the bench for most of his first six years in the NBA. He was a 13-time All-Star, a regular on the All-Defensive Team and the first player in history to score 1,000 points in 16 consecutive seasons.

Perhaps more than anything, fans remember Havlicek's "motor," which never stopped running and was, above all else, the key to his success. Havlicek described it like this: "A lot of people say 'John Havlicek never gets tired.' Well, I get tired. It's just a matter of pushing myself. I say to myself, 'He's as tired as I am. Who's going to win the mental battle?'" More often than not, "Hondo" won the battle.

Both the Celtics and the NFL's Cleveland Browns drafted Havlicek. He chose basketball, and he played a key reserve role on four championship teams in his first four seasons. In addition to his "tireless" defense, Havlicek was a deft passer, a clutch scorer and a fine ball-handler who, at 6-foot-5, could play guard or forward. His versatility made him an invaluable asset on a club that measured success not in wins, but in championships.

It's entirely fitting that the defining play of Havlicek's career involved a steal rather than a bucket. His deflection of Hal Greer's inbounds pass in the 1965 Eastern Conference finals preserved a one-point Boston win over Philadelphia and was immortalized in Johnny Most's "Havlicek stole the ball!" call over the radio waves.

The Celtics won another title that year—one of Havlicek's six rings in the 1960s. He was also a leader on Boston's 1974 and 1976 title teams, earning Finals MVP honors for the 1974 club. He retired in 1978 as the NBA's all-time leader in games and was among the top 10 in minutes and points.

CAREER TOTALS

	G	Pts	PPG	FGM	FG%	3ptM	3pt%	FTM	FT%	Reb	A	Stl	BS	TO
REG	1270	26395	20.8	10513	.439	-	-	5369	.815	8007	6114	476	117	204
POST	172	3776	22.0	1451	.436	-	-	874	.836	1186	825	60	16	-

CONNIE HAWKINS

Full Name: **Cornelius L. Hawkins**	Position: **Forward**
Date of Birth: **July 17, 1942, Brooklyn, New York**	Ht: **6-8**
Teams: **Pittsburgh Rens, Pittsburgh Pipers, Minnesota Pipers, Phoenix Suns, Los Angeles Lakers, Atlanta Hawks**	Wt: **219**

"He was Julius before Julius. He was Elgin before Elgin. He was Michael before Michael. He was simply the greatest individual player I have ever seen."—Longtime NBA coach Larry Brown on Connie Hawkins.

Connie Hawkins once said that if he did not break the laws of gravity, he was slow to obey them. However, he could not defy NBA mandates quite so readily. A legend on the playgrounds of Brooklyn who first dunked a basketball at age 11 in a public school game, Hawkins was a freshman at Iowa in 1961 when a New York City gambling investigation linked him to a known "fixer." Though Hawkins was never directly implicated or even accused of any wrongdoing, the NBA decided it could ill-afford such publicity.

As a result, Hawkins would spend his early pro days touring with the Harlem Globetrotters and starring in the fledgling American Basketball League. And few stars shone brighter than the 6-foot-8 forward with giant hands who could jump out of the gym and power the ball through the hoop in ways never before seen. Hawkins specialized in the spectacular, and no one could stop him.

When the ABA welcomed him in its inaugural season (1967–68), Hawkins won MVP honors and led the Pittsburgh Pipers to the championship. After one more ABA season, when further evidence of Hawkins' innocence in the earlier gambling probe came to light, the NBA lifted its ban and allowed Hawkins to join its ranks.

By that time, of course, many of Hawkins' best years were behind him. He was 27 when he played his first NBA game. He still made four straight trips to the NBA All-Star Game and became the first member of the Phoenix Suns named to the All-NBA First Team when he averaged 24.6 PPG in 1969-70.

If Hawkins held any resentment against the NBA, he did not show it, saying he was happy to be playing against the world's best players. He closed out his seven-year NBA career with the Lakers and Hawks and, in 1992, was rewarded for his entire career with induction to the Hall of Fame.

CAREER TOTALS

	G	Pts	PPG	FGM	FG%	3ptM	3pt%	FTM	FT%	Reb	A	Stl	BS	TO
REG	499	8233	16.5	3013	.467	-	-	2207	.785	3971	2052	244	150	-
POST	12	232	19.3	83	.395	-	-	66	.815	137	57	7	1	-

ELVIN HAYES

Full Name: **Elvin E. Hayes**
Date of Birth: **November 17, 1945, Rayville, Louisiana**
Teams: **San Diego Rockets, Houston Rockets, Baltimore Bullets, Capital Bullets, Washington Bullets, Houston Rockets**

Position: **Center/ Forward**
Ht: **6-9**
Wt: **235**

"My father always taught me to be strong and have dignity, to not have to bow down or to have anyone run over you."—Elvin Hayes.

Few opponents ran over Elvin Hayes in his Hall of Fame basketball career. One of the best shooting big men in NBA history, "the Big E" led the league in five categories as a rookie in 1968–69 and kept his momentum going, making the All-Star Game in each of his first 12 seasons.

While Hayes certainly made a sudden impact, it was not like he came out of nowhere. He first mastered his unstoppable turnaround jump shot in high school in Rayville, La., and more than 100 colleges came calling. Hayes chose the University of Houston, where he became one of the most widely publicized college players of all time. His 39-point, 15-rebound game in a win against Lew Alcindor and mighty UCLA in 1968—still called the "game of the century" by some—drew 52,000-plus fans to the Astrodome and ended the Bruins' 47-game win streak.

It's no wonder the San Diego Rockets made Hayes the top overall choice in the 1968 NBA Draft, though he was undersized for a center at 6-foot-9 and would wind up playing power forward as well. The Rockets expected his mere presence to sell tens of thousands of tickets in Houston when the franchise relocated in 1971. When it didn't work out as planned, Hayes was traded to the Baltimore Bullets in 1972. He earned Finals MVP honors when the Bullets, now in Washington, won the NBA title in 1978.

Despite giving up a few inches to many of his opponents, Hayes twice led the NBA in rebounding. He tallied 54 points in a 1968 game against Detroit and he once grabbed a record 11 offensive boards in an NBA Finals game (1979) against Seattle. When he retired in 1984, he had played more minutes than anyone in NBA history and was third in scoring, games and blocked shots. He was inducted into the Hall of Fame in 1989.

CAREER TOTALS

	G	Pts	PPG	FGM	FG%	3ptM	3pt%	FTM	FT%	Reb	A	Stl	BS	TO
REG	1303	27313	21.0	10976	.452	5	.147	5356	.670	16279	2398	864	1771	1358
POST	96	2194	22.9	883	.464	0	-	428	.652	1244	185	97	222	124

SPENCER HAYWOOD

Full Name: **Spencer Haywood** Date of Birth: **April 22, 1949, Silver City, Mississippi** Teams: **Denver Rockets, Seattle SuperSonics, New York Knicks,** **New Orleans, Los Angeles Lakers, Washington Bullets**	Position: **Forward** Ht: **6-8** Wt: **228**

"Haywood could become the greatest forward ever to play the game. He has no glaring weakness."
—Former Kings coach Bob Cousy on Spencer Haywood, then in his third NBA season.

Spencer Haywood was many things to professional basketball. First and foremost, he was a remarkable talent—a dominating rebounder with a deft shooting touch whose quickness made him virtually impossible to defend. However, Haywood would also become known as something of a revolutionary. Some even considered him a renegade.

You see, Haywood played only two stellar seasons at the University of Detroit before taking his game to the pros. He signed with Denver of the ABA and enjoyed one of the greatest campaigns in the history of pro basketball. He led the league in scoring (30.0), rebounding (19.5) and minutes and won both Rookie of the Year and MVP honors in 1969–70.

At the time, the NBA prohibited players from joining the league until four years after their high school graduation date. Sonics owner Sam Schulman defied the rule and signed Haywood anyway, forcing the U.S. Supreme Court to make a landmark decision. The ruling was in Haywood's favor. The NBA was found to be in violation of the Sherman Antitrust Act, and beginning in 1971 college underclassmen could enter the draft if they could show evidence of "hardship" to the NBA office.

Despite being considered a villain in many arenas for his battle against the league—"They thought I was going to destroy the college game," he said—Haywood thrived on the court. He made the All-NBA First Team twice and the All-Star Game four times in his five seasons with Seattle. He later played with the Knicks, Jazz, Lakers and Bullets, making a fifth All-Star trip and amassing a combined NBA/ABA average of 20.3 points and 10.3 boards per game.

With help from Kareem Abdul-Jabbar and a rookie Magic Johnson, his one season in Los Angeles (1979–80) netted Haywood a championship ring. He later beat a drug problem and wrote an autobiography entitled "Spencer Haywood: The Rise, The Fall, The Recovery."

CAREER TOTALS

	G	Pts	PPG	FGM	FG%	3ptM	3pt%	FTM	FT%	Reb	A	Stl	BS	TO
REG	760	14592	19.2	5790	.465	1	.125	3011	.800	7038	1351	355	629	716
POST	33	441	13.4	172	.448	0	.000	97	.789	188	41	13	36	45

TOM HEINSOHN

Full Name: **Thomas W. Heinsohn**	Position: **Forward**
Date of Birth: **August 26, 1934, Union City, New Jersey**	Ht: **6-7**
Teams: **Boston Celtics**	Wt: **220**

"If I was going to get beat up, I wanted to be indoors where it was warm."
—Tom Heinsohn, on why he picked basketball over football at Holy Cross.

Tom Heinsohn was somewhat overshadowed in his playing career by such Celtics teammates as Bill Russell, Bill Sharman and Bob Cousy. When you consider he helped Boston win eight NBA championships in the span of a decade, you can understand why such overshadowing was not a concern of this rugged forward from Jersey City, New Jersey.

Heinsohn knew the value of hard work and earned everything he accomplished, both on the basketball court and off. He was a high school All-American and could have chosen a football career at the college level. Basketball won out, and by his senior season the 6-foot-7 forward had set a Holy Cross scoring record while also dominating the boards.

A territorial pick of the Celtics in 1956—the same year Russell joined the team —Heinsohn nearly gave up his pro basketball dream amid speculation he might not make the team. He stuck with it, however, and his outstanding debut season combined with Russell's 24-game absence to compete in the Olympics helped Heinsohn claim the Rookie of the Year Award.

More important, Heinsohn's 37-point outburst against St. Louis in Game 7 of the 1957 NBA Finals sparked the Celtics to a double-overtime victory and the first championship of their remarkable run. Two years later, the team began a run of eight in a row, with Heinsohn playing a valuable role through his retirement in 1965.

In addition to being a six-time All-Star and team leader, Heinsohn doubled as an artist and one of the biggest pranksters in the Boston locker room. "No matter how important the game is," Cousy once said, "he'll get one of the guys in some give-and-take that relaxes the tension."

It's no wonder then, that Boston owner Red Auerbach gave his former standout a chance to coach the Celtics. After refusing Auerbach's offer three years earlier, Heinsohn took the reins in 1969–70 and guided the team to a pair of championships.

CAREER TOTALS

	G	Pts	PPG	FGM	FG%	3ptM	3pt%	FTM	FT%	Reb	A	Stl	BS	TO
REG	654	12194	18.6	4773	.405	-	-	2648	.790	5749	1318	-	-	-
POST	104	2058	19.8	818	.402	-	-	422	.743	954	215	-	-	-

DAN ISSEL

Full Name: **Daniel P. Issel**
Date of Birth: **October 25, 1948, Batavia, Illinois**
Teams: **Kentucky Colonels, Denver Nuggets**

Position: **Forward**
Ht: **6-9**
Wt: **240**

"Dan was the perfect pro player."—Former coach Hubie Brown on Dan Issel.

Search high and low. Analyze today's pro basketball players and those of past decades. You will be pressed to find a harder-working player than Dan Issel, who on talent alone would not have ranked among the all-time greats.

His nickname, "the Horse," was well earned. The durable Issel missed a mere 24 games in his 15-year pro career. His work ethic, though, was not simply a means to an end—a tool to help him compete against quicker, bigger and more physical centers and power forwards in the ABA and NBA. Issel came by his approach naturally, shooting buckets for hours on end as an Illinois youth and molding himself into the University of Kentucky's all-time scoring leader under legendary coach Adolph Rupp.

When professional ball became an option for the All-American, he chose the ABA over the NBA and signed with the Kentucky Colonels. Issel, a terrific perimeter-shooting big man, led the league in scoring in his first season, edging Rick Barry for 1971 Rookie of the Year honors.

Issel was named league MVP and won another scoring crown the following year, then led the Colonels to the 1975 ABA title. In six ABA seasons (he joined the NBA as a member of the Denver Nuggets in 1976–77), Issel amassed 12,823 points. He wound up topping that total over nine NBA seasons—all with the Nuggets—though his string of making every All-Star Game ended when he left his initial league.

That's not to say Issel struggled against NBA competition. On the contrary, his new opponents were not sure how to handle a big man who would outwork them for every loose ball and force them to defend the perimeter. Issel was deceptively mobile and he could shoot on the move as well as anyone. Said ex-teammate Alex English: "He had this one fake, the head fake, and they would always go for it."

Issel's pro totals exceed 20,000 points and 10,000 rebounds, putting him in rare company. He later went on to become an NBA head coach.

CAREER TOTALS

	G	Pts	PPG	FGM	FG%	3ptM	3pt%	FTM	FT%	Reb	A	Stl	BS	TO
REG	718	14659	20.4	5424	.506	19	.253	3792	.797	5707	1804	698	396	1281
POST	53	1029	19.4	402	.496	2	.500	223	.829	393	145	42	24	93

ALLEN IVERSON

Full Name: **Allen Ezail Iverson**	Position: **Guard**
Date of Birth: **June 7, 1975, Hampton, Virginia**	Ht: **6-0**
Teams: **Philadelphia 76ers**	Wt: **165**

"Allen appeals to a lot of people for different reasons. There are single mothers out there who like to see him with his kids. There are people who come to the games because they like the way he plays. There are Hip Hop kids who like the way he dresses."

—Former Georgetown coach John Thompson on Allen Iverson.

"The Answer." It's a fitting nickname for a player who has prompted his share of questions over the course of his young career. A poster boy for the Hip Hop generation who ran with a tough crowd as a Virginia youth, is adorned with tattoos, has experienced legal run-ins and once cut a controversial rap music CD, Iverson is not your father's NBA superstar. Give him a basketball, though, and you have your answer.

There is no questioning his ability. Listed (perhaps generously) as a 6-footer, he was named MVP in 2000–01 after leading the NBA in scoring and steals per game. He won another scoring crown and the second of three straight steals titles the following season. Iverson is a regular among the league leaders in points, thefts and minutes, placing him among the most feared players in the game today.

Esquire magazine once called Iverson "one of the 21 most important people of the 21st century." Certainly, his popularity among urban youths had something to do with that. As a basketball player, his coaches might be quick to agree. For as Iverson goes, so go the Philadelphia 76ers.

The former Georgetown All-American and top pick in the 1996 NBA Draft has been everything Philadelphia expected he might be—a lightning-quick guard who is almost impossible to defend one-on-one. Without inside help, no one can keep him from getting to the hoop, and he can drain long-range shots all night if you concede even a step. He hits off-balance jumpers as easily as open ones and is a feisty defender, too.

Iverson's 55-point effort against New Orleans was among the most memorable moments of the 2003 playoffs. "That was right up there with (Michael) Jordan's (playoff record) 63," Hornets coach Paul Silas noted.

CAREER TOTALS

	G	Pts	PPG	FGM	FG%	3ptM	3pt%	FTM	FT%	Reb	A	Stl	BS	TO
REG	487	13170	27.0	4669	.420	632	.312	3200	.760	1997	2722	1158	107	1738
POST	57	1743	30.6	618	.396	103	.326	404	.758	247	328	126	11	178

MAGIC JOHNSON

Full Name: **Earvin Johnson Jr.**	Position: **Guard**
Date of Birth: **August 14, 1959, Lansing, Michigan**	Ht: **6-9**
Teams: **Los Angeles Lakers**	Wt: **220**

"I don't think there will ever be another 6-9 point guard who smiles while he humiliates you."—Former Lakers teammate James Worthy on Magic Johnson.

Put this one near the top of the list of nicknames that fit perfectly. "Magic." Earvin Johnson certainly was. At 6-foot-9, Magic was the tallest point guard in NBA history. He was also perhaps the greatest point guard of all time, making pinpoint passes that others would not have considered trying while leading the Lakers to five titles in the 1990s.

The nickname "Magic" first surfaced while Johnson was leading Everett High in Lansing, Mich., to a state championship. It held true at hometown Michigan State, where he won an NCAA title against Larry Bird and Indiana State in 1979. The Lakers, thanks to a compensation package with Utah three years earlier, had the first pick in the 1979 draft and were delighted to take the big point guard with the contagious smile.

Johnson paid dividends right away. When Kareem-Abdul Jabbar was injured in Game 6 of the 1980 NBA Finals, a rookie Magic switched from point guard to center and totaled 42 points, 15 assists and seven rebounds in one of the best playoff performances ever. It led to the first of his five championship rings and three Finals MVP Awards. He also earned league MVP honors five times.

It wasn't just his size that helped Magic revolutionize the point guard position. It was the way he surveyed the floor, his ability to deliver accurate passes both on the fast break and out of a halfcourt set, and his expert choreographing of "Showtime"—the Lakers' high-octane offense that dominated the league for most of a decade.

Johnson broke Oscar Robertson's career assist record but was overtaken by Utah's John Stockton in 1995. Magic also delivered some shocking news on his way out, announcing in 1991 that he had tested positive for the HIV virus. He returned to win MVP honors in the 1992 All-Star Game, coached the Lakers for 16 games in 1994 and made a brief comeback in 1995–96.

CAREER TOTALS

	G	Pts	PPG	FGM	FG%	3ptM	3pt%	FTM	FT%	Reb	A	Stl	BS	TO
REG	906	17707	19.5	6211	.520	325	.303	4960	.848	6559	10141	1724	374	3506
POST	190	3701	19.5	1291	.506	51	.241	1068	.838	1465	2346	358	64	696

NEIL JOHNSTON

Full Name: **Donald Neil Johnston**
Date of Birth: **February 4, 1929, Chillicothe, Ohio**
Teams: **Philadelphia Warriors**

Position: **Forward**
Ht: **6-8**
Wt: **218**

"When I played, I was the Warriors' rebounder, but believe me I wasn't big enough the past few years. When you're 6-8, you're just average."
—Neil Johnston during his tenure as Warriors coach.

Neil Johnston was no average player, though baseball—not basketball—was his first love. After two relatively modest basketball seasons at Ohio State, he gave up his final two years of college eligibility to sign a professional baseball contract with the Philadelphia Phillies, with dreams of becoming a big-league ace.

Johnston pitched for three years in the Phillies' minor-league system, but a sore arm slowed his progress and it soon became clear the 6-foot-8 athlete was better off on the hardwood than the mound. It was especially clear to Philadelphia Warriors coach Eddie Gottlieb, who recognized Johnston's vast potential and signed him in 1951.

Some might have wondered what Gottlieb was thinking when Johnston averaged just six points per game in his debut season. Any doubters received their answer the next year, when Johnston began a run of three consecutive NBA scoring crowns with averages well over 20 PPG. He also won the rebounding title in 1954–55, becoming the first player in league history to lead in both categories in the same campaign.

Though Johnston downplayed his rebounding abilities in later years, that 1954–55 season also saw him corral 39 boards in one game against Syracuse—one of the top efforts in the history of the NBA. His accurate hook shot, relentless style and willingness to sacrifice for the good of the team earned him six trips to the All-Star game and four consecutive All-NBA First Team selections in the 1950s. Those traits also helped him become a champion.

In 1955–56, Johnston teamed up with fellow Hall of Famers Paul Arizin and Tom Gola in leading the Warriors to the best record in the NBA and a championship. They needed just five games to stop Fort Wayne in the Finals. After suffering a career-ending knee injury, Johnston went on to coach the Warriors, Pittsburgh of the ABL and Wilmington of the EBL.

CAREER TOTALS

	G	Pts	PPG	FGM	FG%	3ptM	3pt%	FTM	FT%	Reb	A	Stl	BS	TO
REG	516	10023	19.4	3303	.444	-	-	3417	.768	5856	1269	-	-	-
POST	23	344	15.0	121	.390	-	-	102	.734	257	75	-	-	-

SAM JONES

Full Name: **Samuel Jones**
Date of Birth: **June 24, 1933, Wilmington, North Carolina**
Teams: **Boston Celtics**

Position: **Guard**
Ht: **6-4**
Wt: **205**

"He's always in shape and ready to play, and nobody works any harder at basketball than he does."—Legendary Celtics coach Red Auerbach on Sam Jones.

With a common name like Sam Jones, it would have been easy to get lost on the star-studded Boston Celtics. That's particularly true when one of your teammates goes by the name K.C. Jones. That Sam Jones stood out anyway is a testament to his talent, his work ethic and the vital role he played in helping the Celtics claim 10 NBA championships in 12 years.

Jones was actually upset when Boston drafted him out of little-known North Carolina Central College with the eighth overall pick in 1957. The Celtics had just won a title and had 11 veterans returning, so Jones gave himself little hope of making the team. He also had a teaching offer on the table, and it was only after the high school turned down his request for a $500 pay increase that Jones decided to give the NBA a try.

His athletic ability helped Jones make the cut. Auerbach marveled at how he could run up and down the court without getting winded. Jones' unselfishness with the ball and hustle on defense also impressed the Celtics, but with Bill Sharman and Bob Cousy in the backcourt, it would take a while for Jones to break into the starting five.

That happened in 1960–61, when injuries took Sharman out of the lineup. Jones blossomed with his extra playing time. His use of the glass had some calling him the "master of the bank shot," and his penchant for raising his scoring output in the playoffs earned him another nickname: Mr. Clutch.

Jones averaged 20.6 PPG in the 1962 playoffs and 23.8 in the following postseason, sparking Boston to championships each time. After a brilliant performance against the Philadelphia Warriors in a seven-game 1962 Eastern finals, Wilt Chamberlain called Jones the Celtics' best player. Jones enjoyed his best regular-season scoring production (25.9) in 1964–65. He retired a five-time All-Star in 1969 and fulfilled his teaching aspirations in the coaching profession.

CAREER TOTALS

	G	Pts	PPG	FGM	FG%	3ptM	3pt%	FTM	FT%	Reb	A	Stl	BS	TO
REG	872	15411	17.7	6271	.456	-	-	2869	.803	4305	2209	-	-	-
POST	154	2909	18.9	1149	.447	-	-	611	.811	718	358	-	-	-

MICHAEL JORDAN

Full Name: **Michael Jeffrey Jordan**
Date of Birth: **February 17, 1963, Brooklyn, New York**
Teams: **Chicago Bulls, Washington Wizards**

Position: **Guard**
Ht: **6-6**
Wt: **216**

"I think he's God disguised as Michael Jordan."
—Former Celtics great Larry Bird after a 63-point playoff effort by Jordan.

There is no definitive answer, of course, whenever you compare players from different eras and different positions. So when you consider the wide agreement among basketball followers that Michael Jordan is the greatest player in NBA history, you know you're referring to a once-in-a-lifetime talent.

Jordan retired for a third and final time after the 2002–03 season with the highest scoring average (30.1 PPG) in NBA history, six championship rings, 10 scoring titles, five MVP awards and the admiration of everyone who ever saw him play. "I beat him one-on-one a couple of times his freshman year," said former college teammate James Worthy. "I knew he had the potential to be an All-Star, but I never dreamed he was going to take it to this level. I didn't think he would dominate and just 'be' the league."

Jordan's brilliant story is best told in chapters. Chapter 1 is the inspirational story of a Wilmington, North Carolina youth who once gets cut from his high school varsity team, only to work tirelessly, earn prep and college All-America honors and hit the winning jump shot as a North Carolina freshman in the 1982 national title game.

In Chapter 2, "Air" Jordan arrives in the NBA as a gravity-defying dunk artist and scoring machine. A No. 3 overall draft choice, he wins 1985 Rookie of the Year honors and refines his game to benefit the team. He wins his first MVP Award in 1991 and leads the Bulls to three straight titles before his abrupt retirement in 1993.

Chapter 3 includes Jordan's failed attempt to play big-league baseball, his 1994 NBA comeback and another run of three straight titles. Jordan was named Finals MVP after all six Bulls championships and retired for a second time in 1998. Though one hesitates to call anything a "final" chapter with Jordan, his competitive zeal brought him out of the Washington Wizards' front office and into their jersey for two more seasons—a remarkable ending to an unparalleled career.

CAREER TOTALS

	G	Pts	PPG	FGM	FG%	3ptM	3pt%	FTM	FT%	Reb	A	Stl	BS	TO
REG	1072	32292	30.1	12192	.497	581	.327	7327	.835	6672	5633	2514	893	2924
POST	179	5987	33.4	2188	.487	148	.332	1463	.828	1152	1022	376	158	546

JASON KIDD

Full Name: **Jason Fredrick Kidd**	Position: **Guard**
Date of Birth: **March 23, 1973, San Francisco, California**	Ht: **6-4**
Teams: **Dallas Mavericks, Phoenix Suns, New Jersey Nets**	Wt: **212**

"The guys who play with him and are on the receiving end of his unselfishness never will (take him for granted). They know they're playing with royalty."—Nets coach Byron Scott on Jason Kidd.

Jason Kidd is the premier playmaker in the NBA. Some might like to throw the word "arguably" in that previous sentence. Not here. Through the 2002–03 season, Kidd had led the league in assists in four of five years (he was second in 2001–02). His run of three assist titles in a row during that span has been matched by only three players—John Stockton, Oscar Robertson and Bob Cousy—in NBA history.

Of those three greats, Kidd's game leans more toward Robertson's than Stockton's or Cousy's. He is a triple-double waiting to happen, a player capable of dominating a game in the scoring column, on defense and on the boards in addition to his expertise in all the traditional point guard roles: running an offense, leading the fastbreak and distributing the ball to the right shooters at the right times.

Growing up, Kidd was no better than the second-best point guard in Oakland, California. That's because Gary Payton was four years older. Payton served as a mentor, of sorts, for Kidd, letting him join the older players in pick-up games and teaching him toughness and competitiveness at a young age. "He opened my eyes to some different things," Kidd recalled.

Kidd did quite well on his own, too. He earned 1992 High School Player of the Year honors and was a two-year college star at California before Dallas selected him second in the 1994 NBA Draft. Kidd shared 1995 Rookie of the Year honors with Grant Hill, and in his second year set a Mavericks record with 25 assists in a game. His multiple 700-assist, 500-board seasons placed him in an elite class with Robertson and Magic Johnson.

Kidd spent three years with Dallas and five with Phoenix before joining New Jersey for 2001–02. In his first two years with the Nets, the perennial All-Star became the team's career leader in triple-doubles.

CAREER TOTALS

	G	Pts	PPG	FGM	FG%	3ptM	3pt%	FTM	FT%	Reb	A	Stl	BS	TO
REG	653	9630	14.7	3464	.404	750	.325	1952	.776	4157	6120	1380	211	2225
POST	62	1071	17.3	389	.400	75	.270	218	.790	442	562	121	18	215

KARL MALONE

Full Name: **Karl Anthony Malone** Date of Birth: **July 24, 1963, Summerfield, Louisiana** Teams: **Utah Jazz**	Position: **Forward** Ht: **6-9** Wt: **256**

"I've done things that 90 percent of the people who knew me when I started said I wouldn't do. I proved something to myself—that with hard work and some God-given ability, you can achieve a lot."—Karl Malone.

Karl Malone finished the 2002–03 season trailing only Kareem Abdul-Jabbar on the all-time NBA scoring chart. The gap is closing quickly, too. "The Mailman" has delivered in a powerful way for close to two decades, and even at age 40 he can teach lessons to rising stars half his age. He is the NBA's all-time leader in free throws made and attempted—two of the eight major statistical categories in which he ranks among the top four.

The chiseled Malone joined the Jazz in the first round of the 1985 NBA Draft after playing three seasons at Louisiana Tech, a college known more for women's basketball success than for men's. Little did Utah realize it had selected a player who would perform consistently at the highest level for the Jazz into the 21st century.

It became obvious quickly that Malone was something special. His sheer strength inside, exquisite touch on mid-range jumpers and ability to keep up with guards on the fastbreak were unique. If Malone did not redefine the power forward position, he certainly came close to perfecting it. It's safe to say no player in NBA history has been on the receiving end of more pick-and-roll buckets than Malone, whose finishing ability helped career teammate John Stockton become the NBA's all-time assists king.

About the only goal Malone has yet to achieve is an NBA title. His 17 consecutive seasons (through 2002–03) averaging 20-plus PPG equaled Abdul-Jabbar's NBA record, and not even Kareem can match the Mailman's record run of 11 consecutive 2,000-point seasons. Malone is an 11-time All-NBA First Team choice, 14-time All-Star selection, two-time MVP (1997 and '99) and two-time Olympic gold medallist (1992 and '96).

Though the ultimate prize has been elusive, Malone led the Jazz to back-to-back NBA Finals in 1997 and 1998. Each time, Michael Jordan and the Chicago Bulls prevailed.

CAREER TOTALS

	G	Pts	PPG	FGM	FG%	3ptM	3pt%	FTM	FT%	Reb	A	Stl	BS	TO
REG	1434	36374	25.4	13335	.517	85	.275	9619	.742	14601	5085	2035	1125	4421
POST	172	4519	26.3	1645	.463	6	.167	1223	.740	1877	538	234	133	503

MOSES MALONE

Full Name: **Moses Eugene Malone**
Date of Birth: **March 23, 1955, Petersburg, Virginia**
Teams: **Utah Stars, St. Louis Spirit, Buffalo Braves, Houston Rockets, Philadelphia's 76ers, Washington Bullets, Atlanta Hawks, Milwaukee Bucks, San Antonio Spurs**

Position: **Center**
Ht: **6-10**
Wt: **260**

"He would position himself so magnificently for rebounds…He knew where the ball was going. And he would go get it and stick it back in."
—Hall of Fame center Bill Walton on Moses Malone.

Malone was among the first players to successfully make the jump directly from high school basketball to the pros, a path that has become much more common in recent years. If no one in the Virginia high school ranks could stop the 6-foot-10 kid from Petersburg High from having his way, they could at least take solace in the fact few ABA or NBA big men could do it either.

Malone made an instant impact. He averaged 18 points and 14 rebounds in the first of his two ABA seasons before entering the NBA in 1976 with Buffalo. The Braves traded him after just two games to Houston, where in 1978–79 Malone led the league in rebounding (17.6) and won the first of his three MVP Awards. Two years later, he powered the Rockets to the 1981 NBA Finals.

Malone's small hands prevented him from "palming" a basketball, but they did not restrict him from making a huge impact on the boards. Some said he missed inside shots on purpose to pad his offensive rebounding numbers. No one could ever prove this, and even if they could, Malone's teams could hardly be upset. The ball wound up in the basket eventually.

From the time the NBA began distinguishing between offensive and defensive rebounds in 1973–74 until Malone retired after 19 NBA seasons, no one grabbed more offensive boards. Only Robert Parish had more on the defensive end. Moses also retired as the NBA's career leader in free throws made.

His lasting legacy, however, was built in Philadelphia. Needing an inside presence to complement star forward Julius Erving and a talented backcourt of Andrew Toney and Mo Cheeks, the 76ers traded for Malone before the 1982–83 season. The results: a 65–17 regular season and 12–1 run through the playoffs for the championship. Malone was named MVP of both the regular season and the Finals.

CAREER TOTALS

	G	Pts	PPG	FGM	FG%	3ptM	3pt%	FTM	FT%	Reb	A	Stl	BS	TO
REG	1329	27409	20.6	9435	.491	8	.100	8531	.769	16212	1796	1089	1733	3804
POST	94	2077	22.1	750	.479	1	.143	576	.762	1295	136	84	151	215

EARL "THE GOAT" MANIGAULT

Full Name: **Earl Manigault**
Date of Birth: **1944, Harlem, New York**
Teams: **Not applicable**

Position: **Guard**
Ht: **6-2**
Wt: **Not available**

"It would have to be Goat—Earl 'the Goat' Manigault."
—Kareem Abdul-Jabbar, when asked on the day of his retirement to name the best player against whom he had played.

Basketball is the ultimate city game. Nowhere is that more true than on the playgrounds of New York, where some of the all-time greats first honed their skills and gained their reputations. Many of those Big Apple greats go on to become NBA stars. Pickup games in the 1960s produced the likes of Lew Alcindor, Earl "The Pearl" Monroe and Connie Hawkins, to name a few.

Then there was Earl "the Goat" Manigault. Though he never played in the NBA, some say he might have been the greatest of them all. Just 6-foot-2, Manigault was said to have plucked quarters off the top of a backboard thanks to a vertical leap exceeding 50 inches. No one in Harlem's famed Rucker League played bigger than "Goat"—not Alcindor, not Hawkins, not Jackie Jackson or Herman "the Helicopter" Moore. Manigault's drives to the basket were unstoppable, especially in the wide-open style of play preferred on the blacktop, and he is credited with inventing and mastering several new ways to dunk a basketball. Crowds packed the courts to watch him dazzle.

College scouts also came en masse to watch Manigault work his magic. He could have had his pick of campuses were it not for one tricky detail: He hadn't graduated from high school. After two-plus years at the Laurinburg Institute in North Carolina, he enrolled at Johnson C. Smith University but lasted only one semester. A dispute with his coach over playing time had Manigault packing his bags and returning to his Harlem comfort zone.

Drugs ultimately cost Manigault any later chances to play pro basketball. He began using heroin, was jailed in 1969–70 for drug possession and again in 1977–79 for a failed robbery attempt. Perhaps even more impressive than his basketball skills was his conquering of his drug habit. Manigault became a counselor who helped steer inner-city youngsters away from drugs before his death (heart failure) in 1998.

PETE MARAVICH

Full Name: **Peter P. Maravich**
Date of Birth: **June 22, 1947, Aliquippa, Pennsylvania**
Teams: **Atlanta Hawks, New Orleans Jazz, Utah Jazz, Boston Celtics**

Position: **Guard**
Ht: **6-5**
Wt: **200**

"Shooting is nothing. Anybody can shoot. The big charge is putting on a show for the crowd."—Pete Maravich.

"Pistol Pete" Maravich was an artist. The hardwood was his canvas, the basketball his tool of the trade. Players long before him had dribbled behind the back and between the legs, dished out no-look passes and thrown circus shots through the hoop. However, no one put the entire package together quite like the man whose every move seemed more dazzling than the one before.

If Maravich played like he grew up in a gym, it's because he did. His father, Press, had been a pro guard in the 1940s and later coached Pete at LSU. Pete spent countless hours shooting hoops and dribbling a ball around his Pennsylvania town. His efforts paid off. Maravich, a 6-foot-5 whiz, turned heads as a North Carolina high schooler and, in just three years at LSU, rewrote college basketball's record books.

He averaged between 43 and 45 points per game in each of his college seasons, leading the NCAA in scoring in all three of his All-America seasons. In addition to establishing the all-time NCAA scoring record, he netted 50-plus points a record 28 times and was selected 1970 Player of the Year.

The Atlanta Hawks recognized his star power and drafted him third overall in 1970, behind Bob Lanier and Rudy Tomjanovich. Maravich posted a 23.2-point average as a rookie while keeping fans on the edges of their seats. He earned his first All-Star trip in his third season, when he averaged a career-high 6.9 assists per game. "Nobody did the stuff that Maravich was doing," Isiah Thomas once said of a player he followed as a youth.

Maravich was traded to the Jazz in 1974 and spent the height of his career in New Orleans. He made the All-NBA First Team in 1976 and '77, tallying 68 points in a '76–77 game en route to a career-best 31.1 average. Maravich finished his career with Boston in 1979–80, his only season with the three-point shot. He made 10 of 15 from long range.

CAREER TOTALS

	G	Pts	PPG	FGM	FG%	3ptM	3pt%	FTM	FT%	Reb	A	Stl	BS	TO
REG	658	15948	24.2	6187	.441	10	.667	3564	.820	2747	3563	587	108	530
POST	26	487	18.7	190	.423	2	.333	105	.784	95	98	3	0	9

BOB McADOO

Full Name: **Robert McAdoo**
Date of Birth: **September 25, 1951, Greensboro, North Carolina**
Teams: **Buffalo Braves, New York Knicks, Boston Celtics, Detroit Pistons, New Jersey Nets, Los Angeles Lakers, Philadelphia 76ers**

Position: **Center**
Ht: **6-9**
Wt: **214**

"McAdoo's game was just offensive brilliance. He was just a phenomenal, flat-out scorer. He could score at will."—Hall of Fame center Bill Walton on Bob McAdoo.

One of the best shooting big men of all time, Bob McAdoo learned how to play two things well as a youth in Greensboro, North Carolina.—the saxophone and basketball. He played the former in his high school marching band and with a local blues group. As for the latter, his 2000 Hall of Fame induction says it all.

McAdoo was a prep high jump standout in addition to starring on the basketball court. His athletic ability served him well as he worked his way from junior college to an All-America season at the University of North Carolina, and ultimately to the NBA.

The Buffalo Braves selected McAdoo, who bypassed his senior season, second overall in the 1972 NBA Draft. Coach Jack Ramsay was not convinced a 6-foot-9 rookie was suited for the rigors of the center position, so McAdoo initially tried to earn minutes at forward. After a half-season of struggling, however, he was moved to the middle and wound up winning Rookie of the Year honors.

McAdoo's second season proved the success was no fluke. He led the NBA in scoring (30.6 PPG) and field-goal accuracy (.547), made the first of his five All-Star trips and led the Braves to their initial playoff berth. When told the following season—an MVP year—that Ramsay had said he could become the greatest big man to play the game, McAdoo responded, "I think I'm the greatest already."

For three straight seasons, McAdoo was the NBA's top scorer. Other centers might have been taller and stronger, but none could match McAdoo's skills facing the basket and on the fastbreak. A falling-out with Buffalo management triggered a trade to New York—the first of a series of trades—and his game was never as dominant again.

McAdoo played for the Celtics, Pistons, Nets, Lakers and 76ers to finish his 14 NBA seasons and later spent six seasons in Italy. His crowning moment came as a reserve with the champion 1981–82 Lakers.

CAREER TOTALS

	G	Pts	PPG	FGM	FG%	3ptM	3pt%	FTM	FT%	Reb	A	Stl	BS	TO
REG	852	18787	22.1	7420	.503	3	.081	3944	.754	8048	1951	751	1147	1223
POST	94	1718	18.3	698	.491	2	.250	320	.724	711	127	72	151	2

TRACY McGRADY

Full Name: **Tracy Lamarr McGrady Jr.**
Date of Birth: **May 24, 1979, Bartow, Florida**
Teams: **Toronto Raptors, Orlando Magic**

Position: **Guard**
Ht: **6-8**
Wt: **210**

"This guy has established himself as not only one of the great players in today's game, but as a historical-level player who will be on every NBA all-time team for eternity."—Hall of Famer and NBA television analyst Bill Walton.

No less an authority than Shaquille O'Neal said it's Tracy McGrady's combination of talent and humility that makes him a treat to watch. "T-Mac is one of my favorite players because he's very unselfish, he's a very humble kid and plays hard all the time," said the Lakers' star center.

That is not to imply, however, that McGrady lacks self-confidence. After a 43-point outburst against Detroit in the first playoff game of 2003, McGrady commented, "When I'm feeling good on the basketball court and the jumpers are falling for me, you're pretty much at my mercy."

If opponents were not aware of that already, they learned it the hard way in 2002–03, when T-Mac stormed through the NBA like he owned it. The 6-foot-8 guard who spent most of his first three years struggling to get off the Toronto Raptors bench carried the Orlando Magic to the playoffs almost single-handedly, winning the NBA scoring title with a 32.1-point average.

McGrady scored 20 or more points in 45 consecutive games during one stretch of the season, and in 50 of his team's final 52 contests. He was named NBA Player of the Week three times—more than any other player in 2002–03—and finished fourth in the MVP balloting. "I've just grown up," McGrady said matter-of-factly.

McGrady, a former high school Player of the Year at Mount Zion Christian in North Carolina, did have some growing up to do. That's because he was just 18 years old when Toronto made him the ninth overall draft choice in 1997. He showed flashes of brilliance with the Raptors, but he started less than half the time before his 2000 trade to Orlando.

McGrady blossomed with the Magic. He won the 2001 Most Improved Player Award and averaged 25-plus PPG in each of his first three years with the team.

CAREER TOTALS

	G	Pts	PPG	FGM	FG%	3ptM	3pt%	FTM	FT%	Reb	A	Stl	BS	TO
REG	420	8542	20.3	3138	.453	375	.361	1891	.748	2713	1637	550	528	888
POST	18	530	29.4	184	.435	25	.313	137	.783	119	97	26	21	57

KEVIN McHALE

Full Name: **Kevin Edward McHale**	Position: **Forward**
Date of Birth: **December 19, 1957, Hibbing, Minnesota**	Ht: **6-10**
Teams: **Boston Celtics**	Wt: **225**

"We didn't know how to match up with McHale. We were stuck between a rock and a hard place. He had the best post moves probably of any player I can remember."—Former 76ers head coach Billy Cunningham on Kevin McHale.

Coaches teaching low-post offense still use replays of Kevin McHale as Exhibits A, B and C of how to play. The square-shouldered McHale covered more ground on his pivot foot than perhaps any player in history. His vast array of scoring moves around the basket baffled opponents and provided the perfect complement to the perimeter prowess of longtime teammate Larry Bird.

Like Bird, McHale took the road from small-town hero to Celtics star. Like many Minnesotans, he was a hockey fan first. Growing to 6-foot-10 as a Hibbing High School student on the Iron Range, however, made basketball the logical choice. Kevin won Mr. Basketball honors as a senior and accepted a scholarship offer from Minnesota.

For two years, McHale and Mychal Thompson gave Minnesota a frontcourt tandem of future NBAers. By the time McHale graduated, he was second on the Gophers' all-time scoring and rebounding charts. A blockbuster trade before the 1980 NBA draft brought Robert Parish from Golden State to Boston along with the Warriors' No. 3 pick, which allowed the Celtics to select McHale. A championship lineup had taken shape.

At first, McHale was employed as a sixth man, making strong contributions off the bench for Boston's 1981 championship team. He became the first back-to-back winner of the NBA Sixth Man Award in 1984 and '85, winning another title in '84. He became a regular starter in 1985–86, a season that produced a third championship ring.

The following season was his best. McHale made the All-NBA First Team for the only time in his career after becoming the first player ever to shoot better than 60 percent from the field and 80 percent from the free-throw line in the same campaign. Only a foot injury suffered in the 1987 Finals slowed McHale, although he continued to make annual All-Star visits through 1991.

CAREER TOTALS

	G	Pts	PPG	FGM	FG%	3ptM	3pt%	FTM	FT%	Reb	A	Stl	BS	TO
REG	971	17335	17.9	6830	.554	41	.261	3634	.798	7122	1670	344	1690	1893
POST	169	3182	18.8	1204	.561	8	.381	766	.788	1253	274	65	281	326

REGGIE MILLER

Full Name: **Reginald Wayne Miller**
Date of Birth: **August 24, 1965, Riverside, California**
Teams: **Indiana Pacers**

Position: **Guard**
Ht: **6-7**
Wt: **195**

"He's kind of like a superhero. He's going to do something to save the day, whether it's one basket or 15 baskets."
—Teammate Jermaine O'Neal on Reggie Miller's traditionally elevated level of play in the postseason.

No one in NBA history has made more 3-point baskets than Reggie Miller, and few can match the wiry guard for quantity of clutch shots in a career. For the better part of 16 seasons, it has been "Miller Time" whenever Indiana has needed a big bucket.

Reginald Wayne Miller was born in Riverside, California with a hip deformity that caused severely splayed feet. He wore leg braces for the first four years of his life. Some doctors wondered whether he would ever walk on his own. Reggie not only walked, he had to sprint to keep up with his athletic siblings, including big sister Cheryl, once the premier women's basketball player in the country.

Undeterred by chants of "Cheryl's better!" during his UCLA career, Reggie became a star in his own right. He finished his college career as the second-leading scorer in Bruins history, behind only Kareem Abdul-Jabbar, and Indiana drafted him 11th overall in 1987.

By his third season, it was apparent Miller was destined to exceed the expectations of those who thought he was too scrawny to star in the NBA. He posted the first of his record 14 consecutive years with 100 or more made 3-pointers.

Miller became the first Pacer ever to start in an NBA All-Star Game in 1994–95. He made the All-NBA Third Team that same season and repeated the feat in two of the next three years. He consistently finishes at or near the top of the league in free-throw accuracy (.885 career).

It was in the 1994 playoffs, though, that Miller truly emerged by leading the Pacers to their first-ever series wins and taking on the Knicks (and their most vocal fan, Spike Lee) in a memorable Eastern Conference finals. Miller later took the Pacers to the 2000 NBA Finals. "He's one of the greatest playoff performers in the history of the game," Celtics star Paul Pierce noted.

CAREER TOTALS

	G	Pts	PPG	FGM	FG%	3ptM	3pt%	FTM	FT%	Reb	A	Stl	BS	TO
REG	1243	23505	18.9	7667	.474	2330	.398	5841	.886	3838	3746	1390	283	2264
POST	115	2618	22.8	834	.453	275	.399	675	.888	339	292	118	30	208

EARL MONROE

Full Name: **Vernon Earl Monroe** Date of Birth: **November 21, 1944, Philadelphia, Pennsylvania** Teams: **Baltimore Bullets, New York Knicks**	Position: **Guard** Ht: **6-3** Wt: **189**

"God couldn't go one-on-one with Earl."—Former teammate Ray Scott on Earl Monroe.

Earl Monroe was the most exciting basketball player of his era, and perhaps of all time. Even the most creative of modern-day scorers and playmakers would not have outshone "The Pearl" when it came to inventing new ways to put the ball in the hoop or set up his teammates. "If I don't know [what I'm going to do with the ball]," Monroe once said, "I'm quite sure the guy guarding me doesn't know either."

On the playground courts of a rough South Philadelphia neighborhood, Monroe needed every ounce of creativity to get his shots against older, bigger and burlier foes. Juking his opponents out of their sneakers became his trademark. Bill Bradley once called him "the ultimate playground player." At Winston-Salem State in North Carolina—a school he led to a Division II national title—a local sportswriter once described Monroe's points as "Earl's Pearls." The name stuck.

Monroe, drafted second overall, won Rookie of the Year honors with the Baltimore Bullets in 1967–68. A 56-point game against the Lakers left little doubt about his ability to thrive in the NBA with a "playground" style. His bump-and-spin moves to the hoop and unorthodox shooting stroke were good enough to lead the Bullets from cellar-dwellers to division champs in his second season.

By 1971, Monroe had the Bullets in the Finals, where they lost to Lew Alcindor and the Milwaukee Bucks. The Pearl's most memorable playoff moments, though, came against Walt Frazier and the Knicks. Each time they squared off, the Monroe-Frazier match-up was the marquee attraction.

Imagine the stir in Baltimore, then, when Monroe was traded to the hated Knicks in November 1971. It took Monroe a while to adjust to being only half of a most amazing backcourt duo. Once he and Frazier developed a chemistry, there was little opponents could do to stop them. They beat the Lakers for the 1973 championship. Monroe continued to thrive through the late 1970s and retired with a bum knee in 1980.

CAREER TOTALS

	G	Pts	PPG	FGM	FG%	3ptM	3pt%	FTM	FT%	Reb	A	Stl	BS	TO
REG	926	17454	18.8	6906	.464	0	-	3642	.807	2796	3594	473	121	305
POST	82	1471	17.9	567	.439	-	-	337	.791	266	264	18	11	6

DIKEMBE MUTOMBO

Full Name: **Dikembe Mutombo**	Position: **Center**
Date of Birth: **June 25, 1966, Kinshasa, Zaire**	Ht: **7-2**
Teams: **Denver Nuggets, Atlanta Hawks, Philadelphia 76ers, New Jersey Nets**	Wt: **265**

"He's a 7-foot-2 guy, but I think he has a bigger heart. He's the perfect role model."—New Jersey Nets teammate Jason Kidd on Dikembe Mutombo.

One of the greatest defensive players in NBA history has spent his entire career on the offensive in his native land. Dikembe Mutombo, who spent the first 21 years of his life in the Democratic Republic of Congo, has been a champion of its people. He has donated millions of dollars and countless hours toward making life more tolerable in a land where poverty prevails, in addition to his charitable efforts in the United States and elsewhere around the globe.

"I love basketball. I'm doing what I love to do, and I'm in a position where I can help people," said the 7-2 center who speaks four languages and five African dialects. Those evaluating Mutombo's impact on his sport might argue that his native tongue is defense.

Mutombo's statue ought to adorn the Defensive Player of the Year Award. He has won that NBA honor four times since finishing his Georgetown University career as Big East Defensive Player of the Year in 1991. Mutombo once blocked a record 31 shots in a five-game NBA playoff series and was just the seventh player in league history to reach the 2,500-block plateau for his career.

This is no one-dimensional player, either. Mutombo topped the NBA in rebounding average as recently as the 1999–2000 campaign and has been a three-time league leader in total boards. Mutombo started his career with 12 straight seasons averaging double digits in the rebounding column. It should come as no surprise, then, that he has seven All-Star appearances on his resume.

Critics have knocked his offense, but Mutombo netted 16-plus PPG as a rookie with Denver in 1991–92. A decade later, he enjoyed perhaps his most memorable season as the key inside player on a Philadelphia team that reached the 2001 NBA Finals before falling to the Lakers. He also spent five years with the Atlanta Hawks. The 2002–03 season was his first with New Jersey.

CAREER TOTALS

	G	Pts	PPG	FGM	FG%	3ptM	3pt%	FTM	FT%	Reb	A	Stl	BS	TO
REG	864	10511	12.2	3737	.520	0	.000	3037	.680	10470	1183	411	2873	1972
POST	76	857	11.3	284	.514	0	.000	289	.701	858	73	35	224	138

SHAQUILLE O'NEAL

Full Name: **Shaquille Rashaun O'Neal**	Position: **Center**
Date of Birth: **March 6, 1972, Newark, New Jersey**	Ht: **7-1**
Teams: **Orlando Magic, Los Angeles Lakers**	Wt: **335**

"No, I couldn't cover Shaq. I never put myself in situations that aren't manageable."

—Hall of Fame center Willis Reed, when asked if he would like to try defending Shaquille O'Neal.

There are irresistible forces and immovable objects. Shaquille O'Neal is both, wrapped in a 7-foot-1, 300-something-pound package of talent that no one has yet figured out how to defend. There might not be a way. Shaq was once asked how he would guard himself. His answer? "I wouldn't. I would just go home. I'd fake an injury or something."

His first two names, Shaquille Rashaun, mean "Little Warrior" in Arabic. At least the second part matches. Shaq's combination of size, skill and will has made him a dominant player at every level. He wore size-17 shoes at age 13. Because his stepfather was in the U.S. Army, Shaq moved several times as a child. He discovered basketball in Germany and later powered his San Antonio high school team to a Texas state title.

After three seasons, two All-America campaigns and a national college Player of the Year Award at LSU, O'Neal was the top draft choice of the Orlando Magic in 1992. He was an instant NBA star for both his game and his playful off-court style, prompting some to dub him the "gentle giant."

With the 1993 Rookie of the Year dominating the middle and developing a vast arsenal of low-post moves, Orlando took off. The Magic made the Finals in 1994–95, when Shaq won the first of his two league scoring titles. His signing with the Lakers as a free agent before the 1996–97 season was huge news, and a colossal boost to L.A. basketball.

Shaq's impact could hardly have been greater. In 1999–2000, he won his second scoring title, a league MVP Award and his first championship. The Lakers repeated as champs in each of the next two seasons, with O'Neal winning Finals MVP honors all three times. In addition to his basketball exploits, Shaq continues to rate among the most recognizable entertainment icons. He owns his own record label and has several movie credits to his name.

CAREER TOTALS

	G	Pts	PPG	FGM	FG%	3ptM	3pt%	FTM	FT%	Reb	A	Stl	BS	TO
REG	742	20475	27.6	8116	.577	1	.050	4242	.542	9012	2113	526	1936	2139
POST	136	3821	28.1	1476	.558	0	-	869	.531	1749	437	85	313	420

HAKEEM OLAJUWON

Full Name: **Hakeem Abdul Olajuwon**
Date of Birth: **January 21, 1963, Lagos, Nigeria**
Teams: **Houston Rockets, Toronto Raptors**

Position: **Center**
Ht: **7-0**
Wt: **255**

"He didn't want to let his teammates down and he didn't want to let the fans or coaches down. To me, that's the consummate winner."
—Former college and pro teammate Clyde Drexler on Hakeem Olajuwon.

"Nigerian Nightmare" and "Hakeem the Dream." Olajuwon was a terror to opposing centers every time he took the floor yet remained one of the most gentlemanly players of his era. Thoughtful, charity-minded, fluent in English, French and four Nigerian dialects, and—make no mistake—among the most fearsome big men the game has ever seen.

Olajuwon's first sports were soccer and handball. He had very limited exposure to basketball when the 7-footer from Lagos arrived at the University of Houston. Suffuce it to say he was a quick learner. Patrolling the paint for the "Phi Slamma Jamma" Cougars, Olajuwon played in three straight NCAA Final Fours.

"People asked me if he'd improve in the pros," recalled his college coach, Guy Lewis. "I said, 'Yes, he's just learning the game.' He went from being a fairly non-player to the best basketball player in the world."

The Houston Rockets chose Olajuwon first overall in the 1984 NBA Draft, two spots ahead of Michael Jordan. They have no regrets. Olajuwon was initially paired with fellow 7-footer Ralph Sampson in a "Twin Towers" lineup, but Hakeem soon separated himself as the team's dominant player and one of the league's elite.

In 17 seasons with the Rockets, Olajuwon made 12 All-Star appearances, won league MVP accolades in 1994, was a two-time Defensive Player of the Year and led the club to back-to-back championships in 1994 and '95. He was named Finals MVP both times.

Hakeem's fallaway, turnaround jumper, which came to be known as the "Dream Shake," simply could not be stopped. He averaged at least 20 PPG in each of his first 13 seasons and scored at a 25.9 clip in the playoffs. Olajuwon was perhaps even more dominant on defense. He was the first player ever to amass 2,000 blocks and 2,000 steals, and he retired in 2002 as the all-time leader in blocked shots with 3,830.

CAREER TOTALS

	G	Pts	PPG	FGM	FG%	3ptM	3pt%	FTM	FT%	Reb	A	Stl	BS	TO
REG	1238	26946	21.8	10749	.512	25	.202	5423	.712	13748	3058	2162	3830	3667
POST	145	3755	25.9	1504	.528	4	.222	743	.719	1621	458	245	472	424

ROBERT PARISH

Full Name: **Robert Lee Parish**	Position: **Center**
Date of Birth: **August 30, 1953, Shreveport, Louisiana**	Ht: **7-2**
Teams: **Golden State Warriors, Boston Celtics, Charlotte Hornets, Chicago Bulls**	Wt: **230**

"He's probably the best medium-range shooting big man in the history of the game."—Hall of Fame center and former teammate Bill Walton on Robert Parish.

He wore number "00" and was merely the third-best player on the most dominant frontcourt in NBA history. But make no mistake, Robert Parish, "the Chief," belongs in any debate about the most accomplished centers in NBA annals.

A native of Shreveport, Louisiana, Parish stayed home and starred at tiny Centenary College, averaging better than 21 points and 16 rebounds per game in a four-year career. Still, no one would have called this 7-footer a "sure thing" when Golden State selected him in the first round of the 1976 NBA Draft.

In fact, Parish's career got off to a non-descript start. His scoring averages of 9.1 and 12.5 in his first two seasons gave no indication he would become a 23,000-point man by the end of his 21-year career. Parish also retired holding the sixth spot on the NBA career rebounding and shot-blocking lists.

It was a 1980 trade to Boston that helped his career take flight. That same year, the Celtics drafted Kevin McHale out of Minnesota. Along with Larry Bird, who had won the 1980 Rookie of the Year Award, Boston had assembled a frontcourt that no team before or since could match. Their first season together produced a 1981 NBA title.

Parish soon became known for his accurate and unblockable jumper. "The guy held the ball straight up. I couldn't block it with a broom," opposing center Mike Gminski once said. Parish finished second to Bird in the 1982 MVP voting. He helped Boston claim two more titles in 1984 and '86 and built a string of seven consecutive All-Star appearances. He once played in 116 consecutive playoff games.

While Bird and McHale retired in the early 1990s, Parish played with the Celtics until age 40. He became the NBA's career leader in games played with Charlotte in 1995–96 and won a fourth championship ring as a seldom-used reserve with Chicago in his last season (1996–97).

CAREER TOTALS

	G	Pts	PPG	FGM	FG%	3ptM	3pt%	FTM	FT%	Reb	A	Stl	BS	TO
REG	1611	23334	14.5	9614	.537	0	.000	4106	.721	14715	2180	1219	2361	3183
POST	184	2820	15.3	1132	.506	0	.000	556	.722	1765	234	145	309	365

GARY PAYTON

Full Name: **Gary Dwayne Payton**	Position: **Guard**
Date of Birth: **July 23, 1968, Oakland, California**	Ht: **6-4**
Teams: **Seattle SuperSonics, Milwaukee Bucks**	Wt: **180**

"In my mind, Gary is one of the top five competitors ever to play the game of basketball. He leads by that, and then you put his defense into that, his passing skills into it, and his ability to win."
—Milwaukee coach George Karl on Gary Payton.

Few players can match Gary Payton in two notable areas: defense and "trash-talking." And although the latter, in and of itself, has never punched anyone's ticket for the Hall of Fame, it has been an integral part of the Payton package for 13 NBA seasons.

G.P. is willing to say just about anything on the court to rattle an opposing point guard. The reason it works, however, is because it's accompanied by relentless physical pressure that earned Payton the nickname "the Glove." His quick hands, fast feet and in-your-face style made him a member of the NBA All-Defensive First Team nine consecutive years from 1993–94 to 2001–02.

Belief in himself has never been a problem for Payton, the author of a book entitled "Confidence Counts." He grew up in a rough Oakland, California neighborhood, played on the same high school team with NBA-bound Greg Foster and went north for an All-America career at Oregon State. It's a rare college star who arrives in the NBA with a defensive reputation like Payton's, but he proved it was warranted after being drafted second overall by Seattle in 1990.

Payton was not your typical rookie. Instead of being pushed around, he did the pushing. He started all 82 games in his first season, earning All-Rookie Second Team honors, and it soon became clear he was the Sonics' backbone. His breakout season came in 1993–94, when he earned the first of his nine All-Star trips (through 2002–03) and became an All-Defensive First Team regular.

As Payton grew, so did the Sonics. He won the Defensive Player of the Year Award and led the team to the NBA Finals in 1996. He also won his first of two Olympic gold medals that year. Payton spent 12 years in Seattle before a 2003 trade to the Milwaukee Bucks.

CAREER TOTALS

	G	Pts	PPG	FGM	FG%	3ptM	3pt%	FTM	FT%	Reb	A	Stl	BS	TO
REG	1027	18757	18.3	7513	.469	937	.321	2794	.727	4326	7590	2147	241	2563
POST	100	1779	17.8	705	.452	105	.343	264	.700	430	624	164	24	236

BOB PETTIT

Full Name: **Robert L. Pettit**
Date of Birth: **December 22, 1932, Baton Rouge, Louisiana**
Teams: **Milwaukee Hawks, St. Louis Hawks**

Position: **Forward**
Ht: **6-9**
Wt: **215**

"Bob made 'second effort' a part of the sport's vocabulary. He kept coming at you more than any man in the game."—Former Celtics center Bill Russell on Bob Pettit.

Bob Pettit's career in organized basketball did not get off to a rousing start. He was cut from his high school team as a freshman and sophomore before his father provided an assist by erecting a hoop in their Baton Rouge, Louisiana, back yard. Wise move.

Bob Jr. finally made the team as a junior and, in his senior year, led the school to its first state title in more than 20 years. He took his relentless work ethic to LSU and earned All-America honors twice. Pettit also benefited from a growth spurt that brought him to 6-foot-9 by the time the Hawks drafted him in the first round in 1954.

Any doubts about Pettit's ability to hold up against NBA big men were erased immediately by his 1955 Rookie of the Year Award. He averaged 20.4 points and 13.8 rebounds per game and earned the first of his 10 straight All-NBA First Team honors. In his 11 pro seasons, Pettit never failed to make the All-Star Game and was its MVP four times.

He did it not with supreme ability in any one area, but rather with a style that never settled for second-best. If there was a rebound available, he grabbed it. If there was an inch of room through which he could launch his shot, he tossed it through the hoop. His defensive intensity was a coach's dream. "He always played to win," said former teammate and Hawks player-coach Alex Hannum.

Pettit led the NBA in scoring (25.7) and rebounding (16.2) and won the 1956 MVP Award in his second season. He won it again in 1959, but it was the 1957–58 campaign that would go down as his most memorable because of what the Hawks accomplished as a team. Behind a 50-point Game 6 by Pettit, St. Louis avenged a 1957 Finals loss to the Celtics and knocked off the champs in a six-game Finals.

CAREER TOTALS

	G	Pts	PPG	FGM	FG%	3ptM	3pt%	FTM	FT%	Reb	A	Stl	BS	TO
REG	792	20880	26.4	7349	.436	-	-	6182	.761	12849	2369	-	-	-
POST	88	2240	25.5	766	.418	-	-	708	.774	1304	241	-	-	-

SCOTTIE PIPPEN

Full Name: **Scottie Pippen**	Position: **Forward**
Date of Birth: **September 25, 1965, Hamburg, Arkansas**	Ht: **6-8**
Teams: **Chicago Bulls, Houston Rockets, Portland Trail Blazers**	Wt: **228**

"Guarding Scottie Pippen is what us small forwards like to call 'Mission Impossible.' If you guard him tight he's going to break your ankles. If you guard him loose he's going to drain 3 after 3 over you."—NBA star Glen Rice.

Perhaps no player in NBA history has experienced the ups and downs of fame and obscurity like Scottie Pippen. Once an unknown NAIA player at the University of Central Arkansas, the graceful and athletic forward surprised many by growing into an NBA star and six-time champion with the Chicago Bulls.

For all his accomplishments, however, there are some who still think of Pippen only as Michael Jordan's sidekick. Those who do so ignore a mountain of evidence that confirms Pippen's place among the best all-around forwards to have played the game—not to mention the struggles of virtually everyone who has tried to defend him.

It wasn't Pippen's gaudy scoring and rebounding averages as a college senior that attracted a handful of NBA scouts, but rather his success in the 1987 pre-draft camps. Though Seattle selected him fifth overall, it was the Bulls who were most enamored and worked out an off-season trade for his services.

Pippen became a starter in his third season and made the first of his seven trips to the All-Star Game. Even bigger honors were on the horizon. With Jordan beginning to master the team-oriented approach of coach Phil Jackson and Pippen having his way with opposing small forwards who could not handle his quick drives, improving jumper and tenacious defense, Chicago became the NBA's dominant team.

The Bulls won three straight championships from 1991 to '93, with Pippen notching a triple-double in Game 6 of the 1993 Finals, and three more titles from '96 to '98. Jordan was Finals MVP all six times, but was by no means a one-man show. In fact, after M.J.'s first retirement, Pippen powered the Bulls to within one game of the 1994 Finals. The 1992 Olympic gold medalist spent one season with Houston prior to joining Portland before the 1999–2000 campaign.

CAREER TOTALS

	G	Pts	PPG	FGM	FG%	3ptM	3pt%	FTM	FT%	Reb	A	Stl	BS	TO
REG	1155	18804	16.3	7376	.473	965	.327	3105	.704	7426	6085	2286	938	3228
POST	208	3624	17.5	1335	.444	200	.303	772	.724	1583	1048	395	185	602

WILLIS REED

Full Name: **Willis Reed Jr.**
Date of Birth: **June 25, 1942, Hico, Louisiana**
Teams: **New York Knicks**

Position:**Center/**
Forward
Ht: **6-9**
Wt: **238**

"His past exploits while injured are well known to the public, but they are merely a small indication of the tremendous 'heart' that he exhibited throughout his basketball career."

—Former teammate Bill Bradley in a letter endorsing Willis Reed's Hall of Fame election.

The story is among the best-known in basketball, but pardon us for reminiscing a bit about Willis Reed's performance in the 1970 NBA Finals. Reed, the Knicks' captain, had been nearly unstoppable against the Lakers in the first four games, but a deep thigh injury in Game 5 had New York fans wondering whether victory was possible. After sitting out Game 6, Reed limped to the court for the finale, hit the first two Knicks buckets and the team rode the momentum to a 113–99 triumph. Reed's value to the Knicks, in that game and others, cannot be overstated.

After a dominant small-college career at Grambling (including an NAIA championship), the small-town Louisiana product landed in the big city when the Knicks chose him in the second round of the 1964 NBA Draft. Reed turned out to be a steal, scoring 46 points in a game against the Lakers and becoming the first Knick to win Rookie of the Year honors. The best was yet to come.

Though it took the team a few years to assemble championship-level talent around him and despite the fact Reed often played out of position at power forward, he was not to be denied, even when he battled the likes of Chamberlain, Russell and Abdul-Jabbar. Reed proved to be a big-time scorer, rebounder and leader whose seven All-Star appearances (in his 10-year career) were well deserved.

Reed, by then a full-time center, was named regular-season MVP and Finals MVP in the memorable 1969–70 season, when he went from respected to legendary in the Big Apple. He was not finished, however. Reed and the Knicks captured another title—and Reed a second Finals MVP Award—with a five-game win against the Lakers in 1973. Reed retired during the following season and became the first Knicks player to have his uniform number retired.

CAREER TOTALS

	G	Pts	PPG	FGM	FG%	3ptM	3pt%	FTM	FT%	Reb	A	Stl	BS	TO
REG	650	12183	18.7	4859	.476	-	-	2465	.747	8414	1186	12	21	-
POST	78	1358	17.4	570	.474	-	-	218	.765	801	149	2	0	-

OSCAR ROBERTSON

Full Name: **Oscar P. Robertson**

Date of Birth: **November 24, 1938, Charlotte, Tennessee**

Teams: **Cincinnati Royals, Milwaukee Bucks**

Position: **Guard**

Ht: **6-5**

Wt: **213**

"Oscar is without a doubt the greatest basketball player I have ever played against."—Jerry West on Oscar Robertson.

Oscar Robertson did not invent the triple-double. He simply played that way. The fact he made the difficult-to-attain statistical feat seem somewhat routine is a testament to his abilities as perhaps the most complete player of all time.

The NBA caught a glimpse of what was coming when the former University of Cincinnati star averaged 30.5 points, 10.1 rebounds and 9.7 assists per game as a rookie with the Cincinnati Royals. He was not about to settle for almost making history, so the following year he did the unthinkable. Increasing his output in each category, the "Big O" averaged double figures in each of the three main statistical categories, a feat that may never be duplicated.

Robertson, a three-time college scoring champion and 1960 Olympic gold medalist, set an NBA career assists record (9,887) that lasted nearly two decades. He made the All-NBA First Team nine years in a row, earned the league's MVP Award in 1964 and was named MVP of the All-Star Game three times. Robertson won the 1967–68 scoring title and led the NBA in assists eight times. The stats, however, do not do justice to the Robertson story.

Oscar's moves were legendary. Long before school children recounted the graceful acrobatics of Julius Erving, marveled at the point guard skills of 6-foot-9 Magic Johnson or tried to "be like Mike" on playgrounds across America, it was Robertson who made jaws drop with his creative passes in mid-air, unstoppable fadeaway jump shot and willingness to make whatever big play needed to be made.

Said former Celtics guard Bill Sharman: "Robertson was a big man with the moves of a really tremendous little man." Jerry West called Robertson "the closest player I have ever seen to being perfect."

Although Robertson spent most of his 14 seasons on Cincinnati and Milwaukee teams that were far from title contenders, he did not retire without a championship, helping the Bucks to the 1971 crown in the twilight of his great career.

	G	Pts	PPG	FGM	FG%	3ptM	3pt%	FTM	FT%	Reb	A	Stl	BS	TO
						CAREER TOTALS								
REG	1040	26710	25.7	9508	.485	-	-	7694	.838	7804	9887	77	4	-
POST	86	1910	22.2	675	.460	-	-	560	.855	578	769	15	4	-

DAVID ROBINSON

Full Name: **David Maurice Robinson**
Date of Birth: **August 6, 1965, Key West, Florida**
Teams: **San Antonio Spurs**

Position: **Center**
Ht: **7-1**
Wt: **250**

"He's done everything the right way, the unselfish way. He could have left this (San Antonio) market when it wasn't a great market to be in. He turned it into a viable franchise."—San Antonio Spurs teammate Steve Smith on David Robinson.

David Robinson did not finish his career in 2002–03 with the most points, the most rebounds, the most blocks or the most championships in NBA history. He never felt the need to make the outrageous statement or the razzle-dazzle dunk that would earn him top billing on the nightly highlight shows. What he did, for 14 NBA seasons, was carry himself with class while doing his job to the best of his considerable ability.

If "the Admiral" played with a military-like efficiency, it's for good reason. Robinson was a two-time All-American at the U.S. Naval Academy and won several Player of the Year honors while leading the nation in blocks as a senior. After fulfilling his two-year service obligation, the No. 1 draft choice and remarkably polished two-way player was the unanimous winner of the 1990 Rookie of the Year Award.

This was not your typical young center feeling his way around the NBA. In just his second season, Robinson won the league rebounding title and was the only player among the top 10 in four major statistical categories. The following season (1991–92), he won a shot-blocking crown and Defensive Player of the Year accolades. He was named 1995 league MVP.

A 7-footer who could run, shoot, rebound and defend was quite a find. One with a head like Robinson's was truly unique. He became only the second player (along with Kareem Abdul-Jabbar) to win scoring, rebounding and shot-blocking titles. The Admiral spent his entire career with San Antonio, earning 10 trips to the All-Star Game and leading the Spurs to their most successful seasons.

The capper came in 1998–99, when with Tim Duncan joining him in the middle the Spurs rolled to a 15–2 postseason record and the first of their two NBA titles (the second coming in his final action in 2003). Some called them "the most gentlemanly" champions in history. Just as Robinson would have scripted it.

CAREER TOTALS

	G	Pts	PPG	FGM	FG%	3ptM	3pt%	FTM	FT%	Reb	A	Stl	BS	TO
REG	987	20790	21.1	7365	.518	25	.250	6035	.736	10497	2441	1388	2954	2417
POST	123	2221	18.1	768	.479	1	.100	684	.708	1301	280	151	312	280

DENNIS RODMAN

Full Name: **Dennis Keith Rodman**	Position: **Forward**
Date of Birth: **May 13, 1961, Trenton, New Jersey**	Ht: **6-8**
Teams: **Detroit Pistons, San Antonio Spurs, Chicago Bulls, Los Angeles Lakers, Dallas Mavericks**	Wt: **220**

"I've been homeless. I've worked at 7–Eleven. I'm a real person, with real experiences, not some image that somebody in the NBA office created."
—Dennis Rodman.

For better and for worse, there has never been another NBA personality like Dennis Rodman. There has never been another player like him, either.

Setting aside his off-court shenanigans, Rodman clearly belongs in elite company in any discussion of the top rebounders and defensive standouts who have ever played the game. He led the NBA in rebounding a record seven years in a row despite standing only 6 feet, 8 inches tall. Only 7-foot center Wilt Chamberlain, with 11, won more carom titles than Rodman, perhaps the best rebounding forward of all time.

Then there was his defense. Named the NBA's Defensive Player of the Year in 1990 and '91, Rodman set the tone at that end of the floor for the Detroit Pistons' "Bad Boy" teams that won back-to-back championships. Rodman is a seven-time member of the NBA All-Defensive First Team and earned three more championships ('96, '97 and '98) with the Chicago Bulls.

At first, Rodman's was the kind of success story that makes people stand up and cheer. He never played high school basketball and was working the overnight shift as a janitor in the Dallas-Fort Worth airport before deciding that an eight-inch growth spurt since high school made a basketball career possible. Rodman was a big scorer and rebounder at Cooke County Junior College and Southeastern Oklahoma State before the Pistons made him a 1986 second-round draft choice.

During their 1988–89 title season, Rodman was the Pistons' sixth man and led the NBA in field-goal percentage. The following year, he captured his first Defensive Player of the Year Award and a second title. Soon, however, Rodman began making headlines for the wrong reasons. His erratic off-court behavior and abrasive comments turned off teammates, coaches and fans.

Rodman continued leading the NBA in rebounding with San Antonio and Chicago, helping the Bulls to the final three of their six titles in the 1990s. He later played for the Lakers and Mavericks.

CAREER TOTALS

	G	Pts	PPG	FGM	FG%	3ptM	3pt%	FTM	FT%	Reb	A	Stl	BS	TO
REG	911	6683	7.3	2766	.521	82	.231	1069	.584	11954	1600	611	531	1484
POST	169	1081	6.4	442	.490	7	.149	190	.540	1676	205	106	97	258

BILL RUSSELL

Full Name: **William F. Russell**
Date of Birth: **February 12, 1934, Monroe, Louisiana**
Teams: **Boston Celtics**

Position: **Center**
Ht: **6-10**
Wt: **220**

"Russell single-handedly revolutionized this game simply because he made defense so important."—Boston coach Red Auerbach on Bill Russell.

"Defense wins championships." It's true in almost every sport, and no one proved its accuracy in basketball better than Boston Celtics center Bill Russell. Standing just over 6 feet, 9 inches tall, he was far from the biggest center of his time. When it came to winning, however, no one in the game has ever stood taller than Russell.

He led the University of San Francisco to 55 consecutive wins and two NCAA championships, before winning an Olympic gold medal in 1956. The Boston Celtics had assembled a talented offensive team, and coach/GM Red Auerbach felt Russell could bring the defense and rebounding his team needed to become a champion. He was right. Russell's tenacity in holding opposing big men in check and keeping them off the boards were the final ingredients in the building of a dynasty.

One could make a statistical case that Russell was the best defensive center of all-time. He led the NBA in rebounding five times and retired as the second-leading rebounder in league history. He once grabbed 51 boards in a game. It was one of seven times he hauled down 40 or more. He was a 12-time All-Star and won five league MVP Awards.

However, there is only one statistic that truly matters when discussing Russell. He powered the Celtics to 11 NBA championships in 13 seasons, numbers that are not likely to be duplicated by any athlete in any era. Lamented former Lakers forward "Hot Rod" Hundley: "If we played Boston four-on-four, without Russell, we probably would have won every series. The guy killed us. He's the one who prevented us from achieving greatness."

Russell's tussles with fellow Hall of Fame center Wilt Chamberlain were the stuff of legend. While the taller Chamberlain was the better scorer and carried more impressive individual statistics, Russell and the Celtics were his Achilles heel. Russell served as Boston's player-coach for the last three years of his career, steering the team to championships in the final two.

CAREER TOTALS

	G	Pts	PPG	FGM	FG%	3ptM	3pt%	FTM	FT%	Reb	A	Stl	BS	TO
REG	963	14522	15.1	5687	.440	-	-	3148	.561	21620	4100	-	-	-
POST	165	2673	16.2	1003	.430	-	-	667	.603	4104	770	-	-	-

DOLPH SCHAYES

Full Name: **Adolph Schayes**	Position:**Forward/**
Date of Birth: **May 19, 1928, New York, New York**	**Center**
Teams: **Syracuse Nationals, Philadelphia 76ers**	Ht: **6-8**
	Wt: **219**

"Until (Dolph) Schayes came along, all the good long shooters were little weasels who couldn't get close to the basket often enough to score in any other way."—Former Knicks coach Joe Lapchick.

Dolph Schayes was "old school," even for his era. And that's saying something, considering he came into the NBA in the league's inaugural season. You see, even after the one-handed jump shot came into fashion, Schayes continued to ripple the nets with two-handed set shots from remarkable distances. At 6-foot-8, he was just as capable of scoring from 30 feet away as he was from scoring in the lane.

Schayes, a Bronx schoolboy standout, became a 1948 All-American at New York University. He was a hot commodity of both the Basketball Association of America and the rival National Basketball League. The latter won out when the Syracuse Nationals offered more money than the New York Knickerbockers.

Schayes' size, shooting ability and tenacious rebounding made him one of pro basketball's first stars. His second season was the NBA's first, thanks to a merger of the NBL and BAA. Schayes began a string of 12 consecutive seasons as Syracuse's leading scorer, and the team took flight. He led the Nationals to the first NBA Finals (1950), but they fell to the Minneapolis Lakers.

In addition to spending more than a decade as one of the league's best overall players, Schayes was one of its top free-throw shooters. He practiced with a 14-inch diameter rim inside the regulation 18-inch hoop, a method that helped him hit a career .849 percentage. He was also among the most durable players ever, once appearing in a record 764 consecutive games (including playoffs) before a broken cheekbone ended the run.

Schayes and the Nats earned a Finals rematch with Minneapolis in 1954, but lost again to the George Mikan-led Lakers. Finally, in 1955, Schayes won his only title—the first of the shot-clock era—when the Nats outlasted Fort Wayne in seven games. Schayes retired as the NBA's all-time leader in several categories, including points, games and free throws made and attempted.

CAREER TOTALS

	G	Pts	PPG	FGM	FG%	3ptM	3pt%	FTM	FT%	Reb	A	Stl	BS	TO
REG	996	18438	18.5	5863	.380	-	-	6712	.849	11256	3072	-	-	-
POST	97	1887	19.5	582	.390	-	-	.723	.825	1051	257	-	-	-

BILL SHARMAN

Full Name: **William W. Sharman**	Position: **Guard**
Date of Birth: **May 25, 1926, Abilene, Texas**	Ht: **6-1**
Teams: **Washington Capitals, Boston Celtics, Los Angeles Jets**	Wt: **185**

"Bill was tough... You did not drive by him. He got into more fights than Mike Tyson. You respected him as a player."—Former opponent Jerry West on Bill Sharman.

It almost wasn't fair. The Boston Celtics already had Bob Cousy working his magic in the backcourt, so why would they need sharpshooter Bill Sharman? When they traded for him in 1951, a terrific tandem was in place. And when star center Bill Russell joined the mix later that decade, the opposition was truly in over its head.

Sharman was a two-sport star at the University of Southern California. He signed a minor-league baseball contract with the Brooklyn Dodgers in 1950, the same year he was drafted in the second round by the Washington Capitals. The Caps folded within a year and Fort Wayne gained his rights, but the aforementioned trade brought Sharman to Boston and paired him with Cousy in one of basketball's legendary backcourts.

Though he played minor-league baseball for five years, it was on the hardwood where Sharman was destined to make his name. His in-your-face defensive style earned league-wide respect (and a few enemies in opposing jerseys), and he was one of the premier shooters in the game. Sharman led the league seven times in free-throw accuracy, sinking better than 88 percent over his 11-year career. He set a record by making 56 in a row during 1958–59, when he converted at a .932 clip for the season.

Just as important was Sharman's leadership. Never one to back down from a challenge, he played a major role in lifting the Celtics to championship status. Sharman and Cousy had the Celtics near the top in the East, but Syracuse usually had their number in the playoffs. Then along came Russell in 1966–67, and Boston finally had the interior presence it needed to complement its guard play.

The result: NBA championships in four of Sharman's final five seasons. He earned titles in 1957, '59, '60 and '61. He later coached teams to championships in the ABL, ABA and NBA, the last one with the Lakers in 1972.

CAREER TOTALS

	G	Pts	PPG	FGM	FG%	3ptM	3pt%	FTM	FT%	Reb	A	Stl	BS	TO
REG	711	12665	17.8	4761	.426	-	-	3143	.883	2779	2101	-	-	-
POST	78	1446	18.5	538	.426	-	-	370	.911	285	201	-	-	-

JOHN STOCKTON

Full Name: **John Houston Stockton**
Date of Birth: **March 26, 1962, Spokane, Washington**
Teams: **Utah Jazz**

Position: **Guard**
Ht: **6-1**
Wt: **175**

"You're not going to find another John Stockton. He does everything the right way."—Former 76ers star point guard Mo Cheeks.

His longtime teammate, Karl Malone, goes by the nickname "Mailman." Stockton resembles an NBA superstar about as much as your average businessman. For two full decades, however, the Utah Jazz point guard delivered more assists than any player—athletic-looking or otherwise—who ever dribbled a basketball. "If you wanted to learn and study how to approach the game," noted Jazz coach Jerry Sloan, "he's the consummate guy to follow."

Aside from his eye-popping statistics, Stockton deserves recognition for his durability alone. His 19 seasons with Utah through 2002–03 are an NBA record for service with a single franchise, and he played in each of Utah's games in 17 of those campaigns. He is only the seventh man in history to play in the NBA at age 41.

Of course, Stockton has done more than play. He has played the point guard role in textbook fashion, earning 10 trips to the All-Star Game. "He's playing against guys who are 21 and still beating them," said teammate Matt Harpring in 2003. Stockton owns the NBA records for career steals and assists, and neither mark is in danger of falling any time soon. His .517 career field-goal accuracy is among the best ever among guards.

Few would have predicted that level of success for the scrawny point guard out of Gonzaga. On the whole, Jazz fans were less than thrilled when their team drafted him 16th overall in 1984. The following year, they picked Malone out of Louisiana Tech, and the best pick-and-roll combination in basketball history was off and running.

Stockton and Malone were teammates on the 1992 and '96 gold medal-winning U.S. Olympic teams. They were co-MVPs of the 1993 All-Star Game in Salt Lake City and, more significantly for Jazz fans, they led the team to the NBA Finals in 1997 and '98, falling both times to the Bulls. Stockton ranks second all-time in postseason assists (behind Magic Johnson) and stands fourth in playoff steals.

CAREER TOTALS

	G	Pts	PPG	FGM	FG%	3ptM	3pt%	FTM	FT%	Reb	A	Stl	BS	TO
REG	1504	19711	13.1	7039	.515	845	.384	4788	.826	4051	15806	3265	315	4244
POST	182	2436	13.4	855	.473	111	.326	615	.810	608	1839	338	50	517

ISIAH THOMAS

Full Name: **Isiah Lord Thomas III**	Position: **Guard**
Date of Birth: **April 30, 1961, Chicago, Illinois**	Ht: **6-1**
Teams: **Detroit Pistons**	Wt: **185**

"He might have been the best player in history if he were five inches taller."
—Former Pistons coach Chuck Daly on Isiah Thomas.

Don't let that baby face fool you. Underneath it was a killer instinct that few players could match, their height notwithstanding. Combine it with abilities that garnered Isiah Lord Thomas III the title of "best little man in basketball," and it's not surprising that he led his teams to NCAA and NBA championships on his way to the Hall of Fame.

Thomas grew up poor in Chicago, the youngest of nine children. The story of his mother, Mary, raising her family alone later inspired a 1990 television movie. Thomas found their path out of poverty through basketball. He played for Bob Knight at Indiana, guiding the Hoosiers to the 1981 national championship. Some said he was too small, at 6-foot-1, to be effective in the NBA. How wrong they were.

Leaving college after two seasons (but not before promising his mother he would go back to earn his degree—a vow he later fulfilled), Thomas was drafted second overall in 1981 by a Pistons team that had won just 21 games the year before. He quickly became their floor general, made the first of his 12 straight trips to the All-Star Game and started turning Detroit's fortunes around.

Detroit became a playoff team under coach Chuck Daly in the mid-1990s and reached the Finals in 1988, falling to the Lakers in seven games. Thomas and the Pistons swept L.A. in the rematch a year later, then made it back-to-back titles in 1990.

The Pistons' rugged, defensive style earned them the nickname "Bad Boys." Bruisers like Rick Mahorn, Bill Laimbeer and Dennis Rodman indeed fit the bill. But so did Thomas, no matter how innocent he might have looked. An opposing coach once called him the "baby-faced assassin" for the way he could smile before taking you down.

"It's not a battle of skills," Thomas once said of the NBA playoffs. "It's a battle of wills." In any such battle, Thomas was just the man you wanted on your side.

CAREER TOTALS

	G	Pts	PPG	FGM	FG%	3ptM	3pt%	FTM	FT%	Reb	A	Stl	BS	TO
REG	979	18822	19.2	7194	.452	398	.290	4036	.759	3478	9061	1861	249	3682
POST	111	2261	20.4	825	.441	81	.346	530	.769	524	987	234	38	369

DAVID THOMPSON

Full Name: **David Thompson**
Date of Birth: **July 13, 1954, Shelby, North Carolina**
Teams: **Denver Nuggets, Seattle SuperSonics**

Position: **Guard**
Ht: **6-4**
Wt: **195**

"For him to be 6-foot-4 and do what he did was totally amazing."
—Former North Carolina State teammate Tom Burleson on David Thompson.

Perhaps it was too much, too soon. In his early 20s, David Thompson had the world in the palm of his hand. Quite literally, he had reached heights on a basketball court no one had hit before. There are video clips and photos of Thompson soaring over defenders to the hoop, his head level with the rim and his outstretched arms looking as though they could set the ball on top of the backboard.

So what happened? "I just didn't have the will power," Thompson said of a drug habit that probably cost him the chance to be called one of the top dozen players in the history of the game. It was a shame because Thompson, who was born with so little, had accomplished so much in a short period of time.

Thompson and his 10 siblings grew up in a shack on an unpaved road in rural North Carolina. He began writing a rags-to-riches story at North Carolina State, where his high-flying style and unstoppable scoring powered the Wolfpack to the 1974 national title and earned him acclaim as one of the greatest players in NCAA history.

The top 1975 draft choice in two different leagues, Thompson chose the ABA over the NBA and signed with the Denver Nuggets in what turned out to be the league's last year. Thompson made the most of it, winning Rookie of the Year and All-Star Game MVP accolades. He enjoyed similar success in the NBA, maintaining his 26-point ABA scoring average over the next eight seasons, including a 1977–78 campaign on which he lost the scoring title to George Gervin on the final day. Thompson finished with a stunning 73-point game, but Gervin's 63-point finale gave him a slight edge for the season.

At age 23, Thompson's $4 million, five-year contract with the Nuggets made him the highest-paid athlete in the history of team sports. However, injuries and a worsening drug problem took their toll over his final years.

CAREER TOTALS

	G	Pts	PPG	FGM	FG%	3ptM	3pt%	FTM	FT%	Reb	A	Stl	BS	TO
REG	509	11264	22.1	4213	.504	23	.277	2815	.778	1921	1631	459	407	1129
POST	27	619	22.9	249	.462	1	.333	120	.745	115	101	24	27	63

NATE THURMOND

Full Name: **Nathaniel Thurmond**	Position: **Center**
Date of Birth: **July 25, 1941, Akron, Ohio**	Ht: **6-11**
Teams: **San Francisco Warriors, Golden State Warriors, Chicago Bulls, Cleveland Cavaliers**	Wt: **231**

"When I score on Nate, I know I've done something. He sweats and he wants you to sweat, too."—Kareem Abdul-Jabbar on Nate Thurmond.

Nate Thurmond has to be considered one of the most well-rounded centers in NBA history. His numbers certainly speak to that assertion. Over 14 pro seasons, Thurmond averaged a matching 15.0 points and 15.0 rebounds per game. And some might add that, on a scale from 1 to 10, Thurmond's defense was a 15 as well.

"I scored my fewest points against him," Knicks Hall of Fame center Willis Reed once offered. "When the ball went away from most guys, you were open. When the ball went away against Nate, he went with you."

Thurmond played during the Bill Russell and Wilt Chamberlain era, so it's no wonder he sometimes gets overlooked in discussions of the game's great pivot men. Those who saw him play, however, are likely to tell you Thurmond's shooting touch made him a more skilled offensive player than Russell and his shot-blocking and rebounding tenacity provided a better defensive repertoire than Chamberlain's.

Thurmond played on the same Akron, Ohio high school team as Gus Johnson and gave a hint of double-doubles to come during an All-America career at Bowling Green, averaging a little over 17 points and 17 rebounds per game. When he entered the NBA as the third overall draft choice in 1963, he did so as a power forward for the Warriors, whose starting center was Chamberlain.

Although most of the points and rebounds were going Wilt's way, Thurmond managed to make the NBA All-Rookie team with the first of his double-digit rebounding seasons. His early promise was no small factor in the Warriors' decision to trade Chamberlain midway through the 1964–65 season. After the trade, Thurmond took off.

During a nine-year stretch beginning with that '64–65 campaign, Thurmond never averaged less than 16.3 PPG. He enjoyed six straight seasons with a rebounding average of at least 17.7. In a 1974 overtime game against Atlanta, Thurmond became the first player in NBA history to record a quadruple-double.

CAREER TOTALS

	G	Pts	PPG	FGM	FG%	3ptM	3pt%	FTM	FT%	Reb	A	Stl	BS	TO
REG	964	14437	15.0	5521	.421	-	-	3395	.667	14464	2575	125	553	-
POST	81	966	11.9	379	.416	-	-	208	.621	1101	227	11	51	-

WES UNSELD

Full Name: **Westley S. Unseld**
Date of Birth: **March 14, 1946, Louisville, Kentucky**
Teams: **Baltimore Bullets, Capital Bullets, Washington Bullets**

Position: **Center**
Ht: **6-7**
Wt: **249**

"I didn't do anything pretty. My contributions were more in the intangibles, but they were the type of things that help to lead a team."—Wes Unseld.

Wes Unseld is making a comeback of sorts. Recently, his Washington Bullets' red, white and blue jersey has been one of the hottest-selling "retro" uniforms online and in sporting goods stores. It's a fashion statement Unseld himself has trouble understanding, and the several-hundred-dollar price tag also perplexes him.

If the trend—albeit two decades after his retirement—helps young basketball fans emulate the head and heart of the man who wore the jersey, the new ones will be worth every penny. Though he stood just 6-foot-7, Unseld was one of the biggest overachievers in the history of the game.

That's not to say the man was short on talent. He led his high school team to two state titles and stayed home to star at Louisville, where his prolific scoring (20.6 for his career) and rebounding (18.9) earned him All-America honors. Only Elvin Hayes went higher in the 1968 NBA Draft. The two would later become teammates. In the rugged Unseld, Washington had selected a leader for years to come.

The Bullets made a 21-game improvement in 1968–69 with rookie Unseld in the pivot. He became the first player since Wilt Chamberlain to be named Rookie of the Year and MVP in the same season. His presence at both ends of the floor made Washington an instant contender. The Bullets had never previously enjoyed a winning season; with Unseld, they made 12 straight trips to the playoffs and had 10 winning records.

Despite chronic knee problems, Unseld battled for 13 seasons—all with Washington—on even terms with some of the all-time great centers. He did all the little things well, from outlet passing to positioning for rebounds and on defense. He competed in five All-Star Games and topped the 10,000 mark in career points and boards. Unseld and Hayes, a fellow Hall of Famer, powered the Bullets past Seattle in the 1978 NBA Finals.

CAREER TOTALS

	G	Pts	PPG	FGM	FG%	3ptM	3pt%	FTM	FT%	Reb	A	Stl	BS	TO
REG	984	10624	10.8	4369	.509	3	.500	1883	.633	13769	3822	628	367	579
POST	119	1260	10.6	513	.493	0	.000	234	.608	1777	453	67	55	69

BILL WALTON

Full Name: **William T. Walton**	Position: **Center**
Date of Birth: **November 5, 1952, La Mesa, California**	Ht: **6-11**
Teams: **Portland Trail Blazers, San Diego Clippers, Los Angeles Clippers, Boston Celtics**	Wt: **230**

"He had a great insight into the game. ... Had Bill not been injured, he'd have been the best center ever in the NBA, no doubt in my mind."
—Former coach Jack Ramsay on Bill Walton.

Folks stopped trying to figure out Bill Walton a long time ago. As a player, he had precious little to say once the final horn sounded. As a popular television analyst, Walton is rarely at a loss for words on any subject. This much of the mystery is certain: Walton was quite possibly the greatest college player ever, and his injury-shortened pro career was outstanding while it lasted.

Walton was, above all else, a winner. His high school team captured back-to-back California state titles and won the final 49 games of Walton's career. At UCLA, the 6-11 center rewrote the NCAA record books. He dominated the middle, carrying the Bruins to national titles in 1972 and '73 and most of their record 88 consecutive wins.

Walton earned at least one national Player of the Year honor in each of his three UCLA seasons and tasted defeat only four times. He scored, rebounded, defended and got up and down the floor better than anyone his size. His brightest moment came in the '73 national title game, when he made 21 of 22 shots and totaled 44 points and 13 rebounds in the Bruins' victory over Memphis State.

There was no reason to believe Walton could not propel Portland toward a title when it made him the top overall draft choice in 1974. Again, he did not disappoint. In just his third season, Walton led the league in rebounding and blocked shots and took the Blazers to their lone NBA crown. Their four straight wins erased a 2–0 Finals deficit against the 76ers in 1977.

Walton, the Finals MVP, won the league's regular-season MVP award the following season. Despite chronic knee and foot injuries, he later won an NBA Sixth Man Award in 1985–86, when he added a second NBA title to his resume with the Boston Celtics before retiring to a broadcasting career.

CAREER TOTALS

	G	Pts	PPG	FGM	FG%	3ptM	3pt%	FTM	FT%	Reb	A	Stl	BS	TO
REG	468	6215	13.3	2552	.521	0	.000	1111	.660	4923	1590	380	1034	865
POST	49	528	10.8	230	.525	0	.000	68	.673	444	145	32	83	36

JERRY WEST

Full Name: **Jerry A. West**	Position: **Guard**
Date of Birth: **May 28, 1938, Cheylan, West Virginia**	Ht: **6-3**
Teams: **Los Angeles Lakers**	Wt: **179**

"He was the captain of the all-clutch team."

—Hall of Fame coach Jack Ramsay on former Laker legend Jerry West.

His nicknames were almost as plentiful as his talents. Mr. Clutch. Mr. Outside (to Elgin Baylor's Mr. Inside). And the hard-to-forget "Zeke from Cabin Creek" (although West's humble roots were actually Cheylan, West Virginia). One thing everyone can agree to call him is one of the greatest guards to ever touch a basketball.

West, whose silhouette adorns the official NBA logo, was the consummate perfectionist. As far as he was concerned, none of his shots should be missed, none of his passes should go astray and none of his decisions should backfire. In most cases, the shots went in, the passes set up easy buckets for his teammates and the decisions led to victory for the Los Angeles Lakers.

Practicing year-round on a dirt- or snow-covered court in West Virginia— sometimes shooting until blood ran from his fingers—West developed impeccable control of the ball and a jumper that rarely needed help from the rim. He was the first player in state history to score 900 points in a prep season, leading his school to a title as a senior. He was a two-time All-American at West Virginia University and a member of the gold medal-winning 1960 U.S. Olympic team.

There was little doubt West would enjoy professional success when the Lakers, with Baylor patrolling the middle, drafted him first overall in 1960. What West accomplished over 14 seasons, however, went beyond even his own standards. He made the All-Star Game every year, led the team in scoring seven times and averaged 30-plus PPG in four seasons, including a 31.3 average in 1965–66. He steered L.A. to nine Finals appearances.

The late Chick Hearn, the Lakers' longtime broadcaster, said West took losses harder than anyone he had ever known. It pained West greatly that he suffered eight losses in the Finals, including six to the Celtics. West would not be denied. He finally capped his career with a title in 1972 when the Lakers topped the Knicks in five games.

CAREER TOTALS

	G	Pts	PPG	FGM	FG%	3ptM	3pt%	FTM	FT%	Reb	A	Stl	BS	TO
REG	932	25192	27.0	9016	.474	-	-	7160	.814	5366	6238	81	23	-
POST	153	4457	29.1	1622	.469	-	-	1213	.805	855	970	0	0	-

PAUL WESTPHAL

Full Name: **Paul Westphal**	Position: **Forward/**
Date of Birth: **November 30, 1950, Torrance, California**	**Guard**
Teams: **Boston Celtics, Phoenix Suns, New York Knicks, Seattle SuperSonics**	Ht: **6-4**
	Wt: **195**

"I admired Jerry West growing up in L.A. But the real significance was that when I was drafted by the Celtics, they'd retired so many (numbers) that they didn't have any left."—Paul Westphal, when asked why he wore No. 44.

Paul Westphal helped the Boston Celtics win an NBA championship in just his second year in the NBA (1973–74). What the well-rounded shooting guard is most remembered for, though, is his success in leading Phoenix to prominence in the late 1970s.

Actually, fans of California high school basketball remember Westphal for his accomplishments a decade earlier. No one could defend Redondo Beach Aviation High's scoring machine. His 32.5-point average as a senior in 1968 earned him Player of the Year honors in California. One publication went so far as to name him Los Angeles/Orange County "Prep Basketball Player of the Century."

It was with much fanfare that Westphal arrived at USC, where he earned All-America accolades twice in three years and led the Trojans to a 24–2 record in 1970–71—with the only losses coming to rival UCLA. At 6-foot-4, he could swish picture-perfect jump shots over most opposing guards and his court awareness made everyone around him better.

Those talents appealed to the mighty Celtics, who chose Westphal with the 10th pick in the 1972 NBA Draft. Westphal was a quality role player during the '74 title season, but a trade to Phoenix one year later thrust him into a starring role. Westphal and the Suns ran all the way to the their first Finals appearance in 1976, but they were defeated by his former team.

Westphal led the Suns in scoring for five consecutive seasons. He also played for New York and Seattle before returning to the Suns to close out a career in which he shot better than 50 percent from the field and 82 percent from the free-throw line. In overcoming a broken foot with the Knicks, Westphal won the NBA's 1983 Comeback Player of the Year Award. He returned to the Finals in 1993 as the Suns' head coach.

CAREER TOTALS

	G	Pts	PPG	FGM	FG%	3ptM	3pt%	FTM	FT%	Reb	A	Stl	BS	TO
REG	823	12809	15.6	5079	.504	55	.275	2596	.820	1580	3591	1022	262	1117
POST	107	1337	12.5	553	.481	6	.207	225	.789	153	353	89	23	89

LENNY WILKENS

Full Name: **Leonard Wilkens**	Position: **Guard**
Date of Birth: **October 28, 1937, Brooklyn, New York**	Ht: **6-1**
Teams: **St. Louis Hawks, Seattle SuperSonics, Cleveland Cavaliers, Portland Trail Blazers**	Wt: **185**

"When I was in college, I never had any idea of playing pro ball. So to achieve in this world gives me a good feeling."—Lenny Wilkens.

The Hall of Fame has only two men honored as both player and coach. One is John Wooden. The other is Lenny Wilkens. Clearly, Wilkens has come a long way since his decision not to go out for basketball in his sophomore and junior years of high school in Brooklyn. "I didn't think I was good enough," he said. And every bit as impressive as the basketball journey he has taken is the class he has demonstrated along the way.

Wilkens wasn't ready to give up the game after his high school freshman season. He simply felt he needed more practice, so he sharpened his skills in New York's Catholic Youth Organization leagues. It was good friend Tommy Davis, who went on to pitch big-league baseball for the Dodgers, who talked Wilkens into returning to his high school team in his final semester.

Providence College took note and offered Wilkens a scholarship. In the last two of his three varsity seasons, the heady guard pushed the Friars to the NIT semifinals and finals, gaining acclaim for his feisty defense. He was an All-American as a senior. Though he had never seen an NBA game in person and was not sure he wanted to play pro ball, Wilkens was drafted in the first round by the St. Louis Hawks in 1960.

Soon, whatever doubts he had about his ability disappeared. Wilkens started as a rookie for a Hawks team that reached the 1961 NBA Finals, falling in five games to the Celtics. His exceptional playmaking and emerging scoring ability earned him the first of his nine All-Star trips in 1963.

Wilkens later played for Seattle, Cleveland and Portland. He served as player/coach for both the Sonics and Blazers, beginning his march toward the all-time record for coaching victories. When he retired as a player in 1975 to direct all his efforts toward coaching, Wilkens ranked second on the NBA's career assists chart.

CAREER TOTALS

	G	Pts	PPG	FGM	FG%	3ptM	3pt%	FTM	FT%	Reb	A	Stl	BS	TO
REG	1077	17772	16.5	6189	.432	-	-	5394	.774	5030	7211	174	26	-
POST	64	1031	16.1	359	.399	-	-	313	.769	373	372	-	-	-

DOMINIQUE WILKINS

Full Name: **Jacques Dominique Wilkins**
Date of Birth: **January 12, 1960, Sorbonne, France**
Teams: **Utah Jazz, Atlanta Hawks, Los Angeles Clippers, Boston Celtics, San Antonio Spurs, Orlando Magic**

Position: **Forward**
Ht: **6-8**
Wt: **224**

"Everybody said, 'This guy's a great player, a great player, a great player.' And you go watch him play and he's even better than you thought he was."
—Former University of Georgia coach Hugh Durham on Dominique Wilkins.

Some players bring a unique artistry to dunking a basketball. Dominique Wilkins was a Picasso. He was the first player to regularly perform the "windmill" dunk in games, and it was merely one of his several eye-popping moves that earned him the nickname "Human Highlight Film." His combination of grace and power in the air made the high-scoring Wilkins one of the NBA's marquee attractions in the 1980s and '90s.

Wilkins was born in Paris, where his father was stationed in the Air Force, and starred in the high school gyms of North Carolina. He led his school to a 55–1 record and two state titles in his final two years before enrolling at the University of Georgia. Bulldogs coach Hugh Durham said he knew Wilkins was special when, as a freshman, he leaped high for an overthrown pass that was sailing toward the stands and turned the miscue into an unfathomable dunk.

After three seasons and a 21.6-point college scoring average, 'Nique was ready to make NBA fans do double-takes. He was drafted third overall by Utah in 1982 and, unwilling to play for the Jazz, was traded to Atlanta for Freeman Williams, John Drew and cash. The Hawks got a bargain. Wilkins averaged 17.5 PPG as a rookie, then started an amazing string of 11 consecutive seasons averaging 20 points or better.

Wilkins won an NBA scoring title (30.3) in 1986 and finished second to Michael Jordan three times in his career. His Slam Dunk Contest showdowns with Jordan were classics in creativity. Wilkins' most memorable career performance came against Boston in Game 7 of the 1988 Eastern Conference semifinals. Wilkins and Larry Bird went on a bucket-for-bucket scoring spree in the fourth quarter. 'Nique netted 16 of his 47 points that frame, but Bird answered with 20 on 9-of-10 shooting and the Celtics prevailed.

CAREER TOTALS

	G	Pts	PPG	FGM	FG%	3ptM	3pt%	FTM	FT%	Reb	A	Stl	BS	TO
REG	1074	26668	24.8	9963	.461	711	.319	6031	.811	7169	2677	1378	642	2669
POST	56	1423	25.4	515	.429	27	.281	366	.824	375	143	73	35	153

JAMES WORTHY

Full Name: **James Ager Worthy**	Position: **Forward**
Date of Birth: **February 27, 1961, Gastonia, North Carolina**	Ht: **6-9**
Teams: **Los Angeles Lakers**	Wt: **225**

"I don't think there has been or will be a better small forward than James. ... When he was in his prime, I can guarantee you, there wasn't anybody who could touch him."—Ex-Lakers coach Pat Riley on James Worthy.

If your team was playing for a title, James Worthy was a man you wanted in your lineup. His nickname, Big Game James, was earned honestly as a leader on North Carolina's 1982 national championship team and as a standout on three NBA championship Lakers squads. "James Worthy was one of the top ten (or) top five players in playoff history," former teammate Magic Johnson said the day Worthy retired in 1994.

Worthy was a high school All-American before his decorated college career with the mighty Tar Heels. That 1981–82 team featured one of the top collections of talent ever to play college basketball, with Sam Perkins and a freshman named Michael Jordan joining Worthy, the co-national Player of the Year. Worthy came up with the clinching steal in the title game and was named MVP of the Final Four.

The Lakers had won the NBA title that year, after which they selected Worthy with the No. 1 pick they had acquired in a trade with Cleveland two years earlier. If Worthy was surrounded by talent in college, his pro experience followed form. He backed up Jamaal Wilkes on a team that also featured Johnson, Norm Nixon and Kareem Abdul-Jabbar.

Not to be outdone, Worthy soon joined them as an NBA superstar. He became a starter in 1983–84 and fit perfectly into the Lakers "Showtime" style of fastbreak basketball. His baseline spin move was virtually unstoppable and his clutch play helped Los Angeles claim championships in '85, '87 and '88.

Worthy's career playoff average of 21.1 points per game topped his regular-season mark by 3.5 points. His most important postseason effort came in the deciding game of the '88 Finals. Against the Pistons, he recorded a triple-double with 36 points, 16 boards and 10 assists as the Lakers took the title and Worthy earned Finals MVP honors.

CAREER TOTALS

	G	Pts	PPG	FGM	FG%	3ptM	3pt%	FTM	FT%	Reb	A	Stl	BS	TO
REG	926	16320	17.6	6878	.521	117	.241	2447	.769	4708	2791	1041	624	1859
POST	143	3022	21.1	1267	.544	14	.209	474	.727	747	463	177	96	298

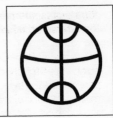

THE
COACHES
A–Z

RED AUERBACH

Full Name: **Arnold J. "Red" Auerbach**

Date of Birth: **September 20, 1917, Brooklyn, New York**

Teams Coached: **1946–47 to 1948–49 Washington Capitols, 1949–50 Tri-Cities Blackhawks, 1950–51 to 1965–66 Boston Celtics**

"Strategy is something anyone can learn, but not all coaches take the time to understand a man's personality."—Red Auerbach.

The image of Red Auerbach puffing a cigar while watching his team put the wraps on another NBA championship could easily serve as the Boston Celtics' logo. Few people have put their stamp on a franchise the way Auerbach did while building and maintaining one of the greatest professional sports dynasties of all time.

The man who cast such an imposing shadow over the NBA was once an undersized scoring leader at George Washington College. After a stint in the Navy, Auerbach began his coaching career with the Basketball Association of America's Washington Capitals and won two division titles in three years. He coached the Tri-Cities Black Hawks in 1949–50 before the Celtics hired him for $10,000 annually. It turned out to be some bargain for Boston.

Auerbach was a demanding coach who believed in an up-tempo style. He was not the easiest man to play for, but his players respected him and it showed in their work habits. The 1950–51 Celtics led the NBA in assists and finished above .500 for the first time. The 1954–55 club became the first in NBA history to average 100-plus points per game. Of course, this was only the beginning.

The Celtics won 10 division titles and nine NBA championships between 1956 and Auerbach's final season as head coach in 1966, establishing themselves as one of the greatest dynasties in sports. "An acre of performance is worth a whole world of promise," Auerbach once said. His players performed. Led by center Bill Russell, Boston took the NBA championship in each of its Hall of Fame coach's last eight seasons on the bench.

Red's legacy did not end there, however. He stayed on as the Celtics' general manager through 1984 and became team president after that. He added a 1980 NBA Executive of the Year Award to his 1965 Coach of the Year honor. During his 34 years as general manager, Auerbach's Celtics won an unmatched 16 NBA titles.

COACHING RECORD			
	W	**L**	**Pct.**
Regular Season	938	479	.662
Postseason	99	69	.589
NBA Championships	**9** (1957, 1959, 1960, 1961, 1962, 1963, 1964, 1965, 1966)		

LARRY BROWN

Full Name: **Lawrence Brown**

Date of Birth: **September 14, 1940, Brooklyn, New York**

Teams Coached: **1976–77 to 1978–79 Denver Nuggets, 1981–82 to 1982–83 New Jersey Nets, 1988–89 to 1991–92 San Antonio Spurs, 1991–92 to 1992–93 Los Angeles Clippers, 1993–94 to 1996–97 Indiana Pacers, 1997–98 to 2002–03 Philadelphia 76ers**

"He's the best coach in the world. I've told you that a million times."
—76ers star Allen Iverson on his former head coach, Larry Brown.

Star player Allen Iverson and Hall of Fame coach Larry Brown had their share of well-publicized run-ins while trying to spark the Philadelphia 76ers to a title. This much is certain, though—each believes the other is among the all-time best at what he does.

Brown grew up in Brooklyn, New York, but has spent much of his life on the move. There are running jokes about the length of time he'll wait before unpacking his bags at each new coaching stop. There are no such jokes about his ability to turn each new team into a winner. Brown became the first coach in NBA history to guide six different clubs to the playoffs. In his 31 years as a professional and college head man, he has enjoyed a remarkable 27 winning seasons.

Brown was not a spectacular player, but he was a solid one. He was also a smart one—the kind who seemed cut out for coaching even early in his career. He was a three-time ABA All-Star and a member of Oakland's 1969 ABA championship team. He once dished out a record 23 assists in a game.

Brown's pro coaching career began in his old league, the ABA, with the Carolina Cougars and Denver Nuggets. He won three ABA Coach of the Year Awards before the Nuggets became an NBA franchise in 1976. Brown returned to the college ranks in 1979, leading UCLA to the national title game in his first season with the Bruins. He later won an NCAA championship in 1987–88, the last of his five seasons at the Kansas helm.

The pursuit of an NBA crown has been Brown's passion since then. He enjoyed two 50-win seasons apiece with San Antonio and Indiana and he even led the struggling Clippers to back-to-back winning seasons. Brown was named 2001 Coach of the Year when his Iverson-led 76ers reached the Finals before falling to the Los Angeles Lakers.

COACHING RECORD

	W	L	Pct.
Regular Season	879	685	.562
Postseason	69	72	.489

CHUCK DALY

Full Name: **Charles J. Daly**
Date of Birth: **July 20, 1930, St. Mary's, Pennsylvania**
Teams Coached: **1981–82 Cleveland Cavaliers, 1983–84 to 1991–92 Detroit Pistons, 1992–93 to 1993–94 New Jersey Nets, 1997–98 to 1998–99 Orlando Magic**

"He worked his way to the top, from high school to college to (the NBA). Nobody ever handed Chuck anything."
—Former Chuck Daly assistant coach Ron Rothstein.

It's no wonder Chuck Daly became such a popular coach among his NBA players and colleagues. It's easy to root for a guy who started his coaching career making $3,600 a year in the rural Pennsylvania high school ranks after finishing his playing days at Bloomsburg State College and St. Bonaventure University.

Daly's hard work and perseverance paid off. His rise up the college ranks included an assistant coaching job at Duke, two years as head coach at Boston College and a six-year stint at Pennsylvania that included four Ivy League titles. He paid his NBA dues as well, serving as an assistant with Philadelphia, a struggling head coach with Cleveland (9–32) and a broadcaster for the 76ers before the Detroit Pistons gave Daly his second head coaching position in 1983. This time, Daly made sure he stuck around.

The Pistons had not enjoyed back-to-back winning seasons since moving to Motown from Fort Wayne in 1957. Under the sharp-dressed Daly, they posted nine consecutive winning seasons and made nine straight trips to the playoffs. Their climb culminated with NBA championships in 1989 and '90, as Daly became just the fifth head coach in league history to engineer a repeat.

He did it by molding some of the NBA's loudest personalities—players like Dennis Rodman, Isiah Thomas, Rick Mahorn, John Salley and Bill Laimbeer—into a cohesive, defensive-minded unit. Daly's understanding of star players again shone through in the 1992 Olympics, when he guided the original "Dream Team" to its dominant gold medal run. "I'm basically a teacher and a basketball coach," he once said. "That's what I am. That's what I do."

Daly left the Pistons in 1992 and guided the New Jersey Nets for two seasons, after which he was inducted into the Hall of Fame. He later came out of retirement to coach the Orlando Magic for two years, hanging up his whistle for good in 1999.

COACHING RECORD			
	W	**L**	**Pct.**
Regular Season	638	437	.593
Postseason	75	51	.595
NBA Championships	**2** (1989, 1990)		

BILL FITCH

Full Name: **Billy Charles Fitch**

Date of Birth: **May 19, 1934, Davenport, Iowa**

Teams Coached: **1970–71 to 1978–79 Cleveland Cavaliers, 1979–80 to 1982–83 Boston Celtics, 1983–84 to 1987–88 Houston Rockets, 1989–90 to 1991–92 New Jersey Nets, 1994–95 to 1997–98 Los Angeles Clippers**

"I owe a lot to Bill Fitch. He taught me just how much mental, as well as physical, toughness was needed to win a championship."
—Former Celtics center Robert Parish.

To say Bill Fitch taught many lessons in an NBA head coaching career that spanned a quarter century would be a massive understatement. His impact on the league in the 1970s, '80s and '90s is difficult to quantify. During his final season in 1997–98, Sports Illustrated ran a "Six Degrees of Bill Fitch" piece in which every one of the league's other 28 head coaches was connected, in some way, to Fitch.

At age 36, Fitch was pried away from the University of Minnesota by the expansion Cleveland Cavaliers for his first NBA head coaching job in 1970. The team struggled for victories, but their colorful coach was never at a loss for words. "Remember, the name is Fitch, not Houdini," he once said. After losing his first 15 games, Fitch offered: "One thing's for sure: I'll be around when we start beating some of these teams."

Eventually, Fitch made good on that vow. He was named 1976 NBA Coach of the Year after guiding the Cavaliers to the Central Division title, their first-ever playoff berth and a first-round series win against Washington. Fitch won a second Coach of the Year Award in 1980, when in his second season as head coach of the Boston Celtics he steered the team to a championship. Fitch's first three years in Boston produced 61, 62 and 63 victories and a trio of division titles.

Fitch returned to the Finals with the Houston Rockets in 1986 but fell to the Celtics in six games. He later coached the New Jersey Nets and Los Angeles Clippers to varying levels of success. He helped the Clippers make a rare playoff trip. In 25 years as head coach—many with bad teams—Fitch reached the postseason 13 times.

One more victory would have given Fitch 1,000 for his career. He held the career record for coaching losses until Lenny Wilkens passed him in 2002–03.

COACHING RECORD			
	W	**L**	**Pct.**
Regular Season	944	1106	.460
Postseason	55	54	.505
NBA Championships	**1** (1981)		

LES HARRISON

Full Name: **Lester Harrison**
Date of Birth: **August 20, 1904 in Rochester, New York**
Died: **December 23, 1997**
Teams Coached: **1948–49 to 1954–55 Rochester Royals**

"I've got to get this team to Cincinnati."
—Rochester Royals owner/coach Les Harrison in 1956.

Moving the Royals from Rochester to Cincinnati was a risky move on Lester Harrison's part. It must have been difficult, too, since Harrison was a Rochester native and one-time East High School standout who founded the Royals as a semi-pro team in 1944.

Then again, bold moves were nothing new to Harrison. He was a driving force behind the merger of the National Basketball League and Basketball Association of America to form the National Basketball Association. He was an early proponent of the shot clock, and he helped break basketball's color barrier by signing the first black professional player, Long Island University's Dolly King, in 1946.

Oh yes. There was his coaching, too. Harrison, as both owner and coach, guided the Royals to a 99–43 record and two championships (1946 and '47) in three NBL seasons. The merger of leagues did not slow his success. His Royals garnered the 1951 NBA championship with a seven-game win against the New York Knicks. In 10 seasons, Harrison's record was 394–220 with five divisional titles.

His comment about moving the Royals to Cincinnati came following an exhibition game at Cincinnati Gardens in 1956. Before the start of the 1957–58 season, Harrison followed through on his plan and the Cincinnati Royals were born. Harrison sold the team after the next campaign, but he continued to influence the game.

In addition to his push for the 24-second shot clock, he organized the Kodak Classic Collegiate Tournament in 1963 and served as its director for three decades. The popular tournament later became known as the Rochester Basketball Classic.

Harrison coached six Hall of Fame players in his career—Al Cervi, Bob Davies, Alex Hannum, Red Holzman, Buddy Jeannette and Clyde Lovellette. He was enshrined in the Naismith Basketball Hall of Fame in 1980. Harrison is also honored in the International Jewish Sports Hall of Fame, the Rochester High School Athletics Hall of Fame and the Rochester Jewish Sports Hall of Fame.

COACHING RECORD			
	W	**L**	**Pct.**
Regular Season	295	181	.620
Postseason	19	19	.500
NBA Championships	**1** (1951)		

RED HOLZMAN

Full Name: **William "Red" Holzman**
Date of Birth: **August 10, 1920 in New York, New York**
Died: **November 13, 1998**
NBA Playing Career: **1948–49 to 1952–53 Rochester Royals, 1953–54 Milwaukee Hawks**
Teams Coached: **1953–54 to 1954–55 Milwaukee Hawks, 1955–56 to 1956–57 St. Louis Hawks, 1967–68 to 1976–77, 1978–79 to 1981–82 New York Knicks**

"Holzman does not beg players to do good deeds, nor does he set up elaborate codes of conduct. He expects everyone to act as a responsible adult and he treats players accordingly."
—Former Knicks star Bill Bradley on Red Holzman.

The name William "Red" Holzman is synonymous with New York basketball. The Big Apple native spent most of his waking hours on the city's courts and went on to play for Nat Holman at the City College of New York. Of course, the ultimate gift Holzman gave New York basketball fans came several years later, when he coached the New York Knicks to their memorable 1970 NBA championship.

Holzman experienced success early in his playing career. The concept of "team basketball" would stick with him and become his mantra as a coach. After a three-year tour of military duty, he joined the Rochester Royals and future Hall of Famers Les Harrison, Bob Davies and Al Cervi. They won the 1946 NBL championship in Holzman's rookie campaign. Holzman spent seven more seasons with the Royals, adding a 1951 NBA title to his resume, and served as player/coach for one year with the Milwaukee Hawks in 1953–54. He stayed with the team in a head coaching capacity when it moved to St. Louis in 1955, tutoring future Hall of Fame forward Bob Pettit, and later served for 10 years as an assistant with his hometown Knicks.

Holzman's big break was New York's, too. His hiring as the Knicks' head coach in 1967 signaled the start of a memorable run for the franchise. Holzman built a powerful club led by Willis Reed, Bill Bradley, Dave DeBusschere, "Clyde" Frazier and Dick Barnett. He was named Coach of the Year in 1970, when the Knicks outlasted the Lakers in seven games for the title.

"People come up to me and say thank-you for what happened," Holzman said in an NBA Entertainment interview in 1996, two years before his death. "That's unusual for people to do that, but they're still doing it, and it makes me feel good."

COACHING RECORD

	W	L	Pct.
Regular Season	696	604	.535
Postseason	58	48	.547
NBA Championships	**2** (1970, 1973)		

PHIL JACKSON

Full Name: **Philip D. Jackson**

Date of Birth: **September 17, 1945, Deer Lodge, Montana**

NBA Playing Career: **1967–68 to 1968–69, 1970–71 to 1977–78 New York Knicks, 1978–79 to 1979–80 New Jersey Nets**

Teams Coached: **1989–90 to 1997–98 Chicago Bulls, 1999–00 to 2002–03 L.A. Lakers**

"Sometimes you might not know exactly what he's talking about, but you still listen."—Lakers star Kobe Bryant on Phil Jackson.

Listening to Phil Jackson pays big dividends. They come in the form of NBA championship rings. Jackson coached the Chicago Bulls to six titles in the 1990s and the Los Angeles Lakers to three since 2000, matching Red Auerbach with nine in all.

Listening to Jackson, the "Zen Master," can also take some getting used to. The philosophical coach preaches balance in life, staying true to one's beliefs and living to a high standard through discipline. Pro athletes generally don't expect to be handed books to study on road trips, but the unexpected is the norm for Jackson.

"There's a statement that goes, 'Along with reading an open book, brings an open mind,'" Jackson once said. "Our audience, the lifestyle, the movement, all of those things change dramatically for these kids (who arrive in the NBA). And I think they need to have an open mind, and expand it, and continue their education."

Unselfish, team-first basketball was engrained into Jackson as a member of Red Holzman's New York Knicks and became the root of his coaching style. Jackson once quit his job after five years as coach of the CBA's Albany Patroons, deciding he might never get a chance on an NBA bench.

That chance came when the Bulls promoted him from assistant to head coach in 1989. The individual talents of Michael Jordan had made the Bulls a top box-office attraction, but Jackson helped nudge the focus toward stronger defense and an unselfish approach, with a boost from assistant coach Tex Winter's "triangle" offense. Jordan and Scottie Pippen developed a championship chemistry and the Bulls enjoyed two "three-peats" (1991–93 and 1996–98).

Jackson won three more titles in his first three years with the Lakers, running his personal streak to an NBA record 25 consecutive postseason series victories. He is the league's all-time leader in both regular-season and playoff winning percentage.

COACHING RECORD			
	W	**L**	**Pct.**
Regular Season	776	290	.728
Postseason	162	60	.730
NBA Championships	**9** (1991, 1992, 1993, 1996, 1997, 1998, 2000, 2001, 2002)		

K.C. JONES

Full Name: **K.C. Jones**

Date of Birth: **May 25, 1932 in Taylor, Texas**

NBA Playing Career: **1958–59 to 1966–67 Boston Celtics**

Teams Coached: **1973–74 Capital Bullets, 1974–75 to 1975–76 Washington Bullets, 1983–84 to 1987–88 Boston Celtics, 1990–91 to 1991–92 Seattle SuperSonics**

"He's the kind of person I'd like to be, but I don't have the time to work at it."
—Larry Bird on his former coach, K.C. Jones.

K.C. Jones would be the first to admit that his success as a head coach had everything to do with a talented group of players. Consider, however, the number of top-priced, talent-laden teams that fail to reach their potential. Those Boston Celtics of Larry Bird, Kevin McHale and Robert Parish needed a boss who understood how to handle high expectations, and few pulled the strings better than Jones.

K.C. was no stranger to superstars. A standout player himself, he teamed with Bill Russell in both college and the pros to win back-to-back NCAA championships and eight NBA titles. Jones' team-oriented and defensive-minded approach to playing the game made him a logical candidate to become a successful coach. That's just what he did.

Jones' first head coaching job was at Brandeis University from 1967–70. He served as an assistant for the 1971–72 Lakers team that won 69 games and the NBA championship, then took head coaching stints with the ABA's San Diego Conquistadors and the NBA's Washington Bullets. After two more tours as an assistant in Milwaukee and Boston, Jones was handed the keys to the Celtics' Cadillac before the 1983–84 season. "He's got our respect as a coach and a person," Bird said. Soon, Jones also had two more championship rings.

His first Celtics team won 62 games and outlasted the Lakers in a seven-game Finals. His second team won 63 games but failed to repeat. The 1985–86 squad was one of Boston's finest, rattling off a 67–15 record and another championship.

In all, Jones won 12 NBA titles as a player and coach. His record at the Celtics' helm was 308–102 over five seasons, with five Atlantic Division championships. Boston made him a team vice president following the 1987–88 season but he returned to coaching in several capacities thereafter, including head coaching stints with the Seattle SuperSonics and a professional women's team.

COACHING RECORD			
	W	**L**	**Pct.**
Regular Season	522	252	.674
Postseason	81	57	.587
NBA Championships	2 (1984, 1986)		

JOHN KUNDLA

Full Name: **John Kundla**

Date of Birth: **April 3, 1916, Star Junction, Pennsylvania**

Teams Coached: **1948–49 to 1958–59 Minneapolis Lakers**

"I've seen a lot of great teams, at least on paper, that won nothing. Sure Kundla had a great team. But he did great things with them."
—Red Auerbach on Minneapolis Lakers coach John Kundla.

John Kundla was not the kind of coach who kicked chairs, pounded tables, berated officials or made a spectacle of himself. He was not the kind of coach who craved the spotlight for himself in any way, shape or form. He willingly took a back seat to his players, and what great players they were—beginning with George Mikan, Vern Mikkelsen and Jim Pollard with the Minneapolis Lakers.

His coaching, however, was quite deserving of the Hall of Fame induction bestowed upon him in 1995. Kundla, the Lakers' first coach at the age of 31, steered the team to six championships: the 1948 National Basketball League title, the '49 Basketball Association of America crown and four NBA rings, including three in a row from 1952–54. Only Red Auerbach and Phil Jackson have since matched Kundla's three straight championships.

It was his understanding of players, combined with his sound game plans, which keyed Kundla's success. Considered one of the first "players' coaches," he adjusted his strategy to fit his personnel. With the unstoppable Mikan in the middle, Kundla designed offenses to exploit the pivot. Not even a widening of the lane designed to limit this dominance could slow the Laker juggernaut.

Kundla compiled a 466–319 record at the Lakers' helm and was 70–38 in playoff competition. The former University of Minnesota team captain who worked his way through the grade-school and high school coaching ranks also guided the United States to a World University Games gold medal.

In addition to Mikan, Mikkelsen and Pollard—the nucleus of his early Minneapolis teams—Kundla tutored Elgin Baylor, Clyde Lovellette and Slater Martin: six Hall of Famers in all. Following his NBA coaching career, he returned to his alma mater and coached the Golden Gophers for nine seasons. He and Mikkelson became the first coach/player tandem to enter the Hall of Fame in the same year.

COACHING RECORD			
	W	**L**	**Pct.**
Regular Season	423	302	.583
Postseason	60	35	.632
NBA Championships	**5** (1949, 1950, 1952, 1953, 1954)		

DICK MOTTA

Full Name: **John Richard Motta**

Date of Birth: **September 3, 1931, Midvale, Utah**

Teams Coached: **1968–69 to 1975–76 Chicago Bulls, 1976–77 to 1979–80 Washington Bullets, 1980–81 to 1986–87 Dallas Mavericks, 1989–90 to 1991–92 Sacramento Kings, 1994–95 to 1995–96 Dallas Mavericks, 1996–97 Denver Nuggets**

"Dick Motta was someone who... always was willing to make whatever changes he needed to, based on who he had."
—Sacramento coach Rick Adelman on Dick Motta.

Dick Motta once borrowed a circus tiger to use as a halftime motivational prop after two particularly pitiful quarters of basketball by his Dallas Mavericks. He was a believer in "the wounded tiger theory," which—in so many words—holds that a wounded tiger fights the hardest and is therefore the most difficult to subdue. Motta was fond of employing the theory whenever one of his teams encountered adversity.

As a coach, Motta was that kind of scrapper. His autobiography is entitled: "Stuff It: The Story of Dick Motta, Toughest Little Coach in the NBA." That "Little Coach" is the pride of the little town of Fish Haven in the little state of Idaho. He cut his coaching teeth in his home state at Grace High School, where he guided the Grizzlies to a state championship in 1959. He later directed Weber State University.

Once he reached the NBA, Motta was intent on proving he belonged. He did so as something of a wounded tiger himself, taking his lumps at several of his stops in a head coaching career that spanned 25 seasons. He also enjoyed plenty of success, finishing with 935 victories.

Motta jumped from the college ranks to the NBA when the Chicago Bulls hired him in 1968. He inherited a 29–53 team and, by his third season, began a run of four straight 50-win campaigns. Motta's most memorable season, however, came in his second year at the Washington Bullets' helm, when he copped the 1978 NBA championship with a team that posted a modest 44 regular-season wins.

Motta became the first head coach in Dallas Mavericks history in 1980 and served a second stint with the team in the mid-1990s after spending parts of three seasons with the Kings. Through it all, Motta preached the importance of preparation, saying "the most important part of the game takes place on the practice floor, not in the game."

COACHING RECORD			
	W	**L**	**Pct.**
Regular Season	935	1017	.479
Postseason	56	70	.444
NBA Championships	**1** (1978)		

DON NELSON

Full Name: **Donald Arvid Nelson**
Date of Birth: **May 15, 1940, Muskegon, Michigan**
NBA Playing Career: **1962–63 Chicago Zephyrs, 1963–64 to 1964–65 Los Angeles Lakers, 1965–66 to 1975–76 Boston Celtics**
Teams Coached: **1976–77 to 1986–87 Milwaukee Bucks, 1988–89 to 1994–95 Golden State Warriors, 1995–96 New York Knicks, 1997–98 to 2002–03 Dallas Mavericks**

"The best thing I like about Nellie is that he shoots straight. It's his presence. He's a legend."—Dennis Scott on Don Nelson.

When the top 10 coaches in NBA history were chosen in conjunction with the league's 50th anniversary celebration in 1996, only one had not directed a team to a championship. Don Nelson, who won five titles as a player with the 1960s and '70s Boston Celtics, is still looking for his first as a head coach. His inclusion on that list of basketball's championship coaches speaks volumes about his success on the sidelines.

Only Lenny Wilkens owns more career coaching victories than Nelson. Wilkens is also the only man with more combined games as a player and coach than Nelson, who has 40-plus years of experience when you count his service as general manager and one of the most respected executives in the game.

A native of Muskegon, Michigan, Nelson was a two-time All-American at Iowa and spent much of his NBA playing career coming off the bench. When the Celtics retired his number (19) in 1979, they called him "one of the NBA's greatest sixth men." As a player, Nelson was a keen student of the game. His lessons made him a natural coaching prospect, and the Milwaukee Bucks were the fortunate team that gave Nellie his first head coaching job in 1976. He produced a winning record in just his second season and went on to steer the Bucks to a string of seven consecutive divisional crowns.

Unfortunately for Nelson, the Celtics and Philadelphia 76ers had powerful teams during the same era, often leaving Milwaukee to play "third fiddle" in the East. Nelson's Bucks lost three times in the conference finals, never getting to an NBA championship series. Nelson guided Golden State for parts of seven seasons and spent one year with the Knicks before taking over in Dallas, where his moves lifted the Mavericks from one of the NBA's downtrodden franchises to a 2003 Western Conference finalist. Nelson and Pat Riley are the NBA's only three-time Coach of the Year Award winners.

COACHING RECORD			
	W	**L**	**Pct.**
Regular Season	1096	828	.570
Postseason	69	81	.460

JACK RAMSAY

Full Name: **Jack Ramsay**
Date of Birth: **February 21, 1925, Philadelphia, Pennsylvania**
Teams Coached: **1968–69 to 1971–72 Philadelphia 76ers, 1972–73 to 1975–76 Buffalo Braves, 1976–77 to 1985–86 Portland Trail Blazers, 1986–87 to 1988–89 Indiana Pacers**

"Great players aren't treated differently. They are treated with the knowledge that they are the team leaders."—Hall of Fame coach Jack Ramsay.

Dr. Jack Ramsay understood players, preparation and the subtle details of basketball better than almost every coach before or since. It's a combination that makes Ramsay an astute NBA radio/television analyst today, and it's what allowed him to win 1,164 games as a head coach at the high school, college and professional levels.

Ramsay was not the best player in the world, but few could match his mind. After graduating from St. Joseph's College, where he served as team captain, he earned his masters and doctorate degrees from the Ivy League University of Pennsylvania.

While continuing his education, Ramsay was also hitting the playbooks as a high school and college coach. In his first year at the helm of his alma mater, he guided St. Joseph's to a 23–6 record, its initial Big 5 championship and a berth in the National Invitation Tournament. The Hawks made the postseason 10 times in 11 years under Ramsay.

The Philadelphia 76ers named Ramsay general manager in 1966, but there was no keeping the good doctor off the sidelines. He put his 234–72 collegiate record to the test as head coach of the NBA's 76ers (1968–72), Buffalo Braves (1972–76), Portland Trail Blazers (1976–86) and Indiana Pacers (1986–87), racking up 826 victories—good for sixth place on the all-time list—against 732 defeats.

Ramsay became a legend for his work with the 1976–77 Blazers, who shocked everyone by winning the NBA championship. Before Ramsay's arrival, the franchise had never finished .500. Star center Bill Walton warned his new boss before the team gathered for training camp, "Coach, don't assume we know anything."

Ramsay fined Walton, Maurice Lucas and Herm Gilliam for being a few minutes late to the first team meeting, demanding respect from the start. By postseason time, the Blazers were rolling. They swept the Lakers in the conference finals and, after falling behind Philadelphia 2–0, Portland won the last four games of the Finals.

COACHING RECORD			
	W	**L**	**Pct.**
Regular Season	864	783	.525
Postseason	44	58	.431
NBA Championships	**1** (1977)		

PAT RILEY

Full Name: **Patrick James Riley**

Date of Birth: **March 20, 1945, Schenectady, New York**

NBA Playing Career: **1967–68 to 1969–70 San Diego Rockets, 1970–71 to 1975–76 Los Angeles Lakers, 1975–76 Phoenix Suns**

Teams Coached: **1981–82 to 1989–90 Los Angeles Lakers, 1991–92 to 1994–95 New York Knicks, 1995–96 to 2002–03 Miami Heat**

"My father was a coach. I've had 16 coaches in my life. I listened to them."
—Pat Riley.

The slicked-back hair, Armani suits and suave look have long earned Pat Riley more television air time than your average, run-of-the-mill basketball coach. Appearances can be deceiving, though. For all the outward polish, Riley is a product of old-fashioned hard work—a native of blue-collar Schenectady, New York who learned to pour his soul into his job and earned success at every stop in his coaching career.

Riley ranks among the top three coaches all-time in both regular-season and playoff victories. He is also among the leaders in regular-season and playoff winning percentage. His Lakers, Knicks and Heat teams won 50 or more games 14 times and he has won 60-plus games at least once with each of his three clubs. Of course, talented players were at the center of his success, and with talented players comes pressure to win. Few have handled the heat as well as Riley.

As a nine-year NBA player, the former Kentucky MVP won a title with the 1971–72 Lakers. When Jerry West hired him to coach his former team in 1984, it was with lofty expectations. Riley steered the "Showtime" Lakers of Kareem Abdul-Jabbar and Magic Johnson to the 1984–85 championship, then added two more crowns in the next three years. He was named NBA Coach of the Year in 1990.

Riley showed the ability to match his coaching style to his personnel upon taking the Knicks' reins in 1991–92. Trading the fastbreaking style that suited L.A. for a defensive, halfcourt pace that fit the talents of center Patrick Ewing and his New York teammates, Riley won 60 games and another Coach of the Year Award in 1992–93 and returned to the Finals the following year.

His third stop, Miami in 1995–96, saw Riley revamp the roster while continuing his streak of 16 playoff seasons in a row. He also won four straight division titles with the Heat and a third Coach of the Year Award in 1996–97, when Miami won 61 games.

COACHING RECORD			
	W	**L**	**Pct.**
Regular Season	1110	569	.661
Postseason	155	100	.608
NBA Championships	4 (1982, 1985, 1987, 1988)		

JERRY SLOAN

Full Name: **Gerald Eugene Sloan**
Date of Birth: **March 28, 1942, McLeansboro, Illinois**
NBA Playing Career: **1965–66 Baltimore Bullets, 1966–67 to 1975–76 Chicago Bulls**
Teams Coached: **1979–80 to 1981–82 Chicago Bulls, 1988–89 to 2002–03 Utah Jazz**

"Sloan just coaches the game. His teams are always prepared. They are always hard-working and effective. They always succeed. Jerry Sloan could be coach of any year."—Chicago Tribune NBA columnist Sam Smith.

In 18 seasons as an NBA head coach, including 15 straight with the Utah Jazz, Jerry Sloan has never won the Coach of the Year Award. One can hardly consider it a slight, however. Often, the Coach of the Year Award goes to someone who takes a team near the bottom of the standings and leads them to a dramatic turnaround the following season. Sloan's teams never struggle enough to require such a jump.

How about this for consistency? The worst of Sloan's Jazz teams finished six games over .500. He has guided Utah to 10 seasons of 50-plus wins, including three with 60 or more. Since Sloan arrived in 1988 with only three years of NBA head coaching experience (with Chicago from 1979–82), the Jazz have never missed the playoffs.

No one who saw Sloan battle as a player can be surprised by his success in the coaching ranks. The Evansville University product from rural Illinois would have led the NBA in charges drawn, floor burns and skinned knees—had such statistics been kept—during his 11 seasons. "Before I got to Chicago, I hated to play against him," Rick Adelman once said. "But when I got there, then you loved to play with him."

Sloan was a four-time member of the NBA All-Defensive Team and two-time All-Star who helped the Bulls earn a reputation as the hardest-working team in the league. Upon trading his hi-tops for a coach's whistle, Sloan naturally demanded that same commitment from his players.

Sloan's two-plus years at the Bulls' helm brought more losses than wins, but his second team did reach the second round of the playoffs. Sloan was much more prepared for his next head coaching job. With Karl Malone and John Stockton as pillars, he took the Jazz to back-to-back Finals appearances in 1997 and '98 with 64- and 62-win seasons, respectively.

COACHING RECORD

	W	L	Pct.
Regular Season	875	521	.627
Postseason	78	80	.494

LENNY WILKENS

Full Name: **Leonard Wilkens**

Date of Birth: **October 28, 1937, Brooklyn, New York**

NBA Playing Career: **1960–61 to 1967–68 St. Louis Hawks, 1968–69 to 1971–72 Seattle SuperSonics, 1972–73 to 1973–74 Cleveland Cavaliers, 1974–75 Portland Trail Blazers**

Teams Coached: **1969–70 to 1971–72 Seattle SuperSonics, 1974–75 to 1975–76 Portland Trail Blazers, 1977–78 to 1984–85 Seattle SuperSonics, 1986–87 to 1992–93 Cleveland Cavaliers, 1993–94 to 1999–2000 Atlanta Hawks, 2000–01 to 2002–03 Toronto Raptors**

"The obstacles and adversity that Lenny has had to overcome represent one of the greatest success stories in Americana."
—Hall of Famer Bill Walton on his first NBA coach, Lenny Wilkens.

Lenny Wilkens holds several distinctions among coaching greats. Most impressive, statistically, is his standing as the all-time league leader in victories. Wilkens "tops" the list in career losses, too, although most consider this a credit to his longevity. Wilkens is the only man in NBA history to serve for 30 years as a head coach.

When the league sought to identify its all-time greatest 50 players and top 10 coaches during its 50th anniversary season, it came as no surprise that Wilkens was the only man selected in both categories. If the NBA compiled a list of its all-time "class acts," Wilkens would be on that one, too.

Wilkens grew up in the rough Bedford-Stuyvesant area of Brooklyn, New York and overcame adversity as a youngster to star at Providence before enjoying a successful 15-year NBA playing career.

His coaching career began while Wilkens was still in uniform for both the Sonics and Blazers. After hanging up his sneakers in 1975, he coached Seattle to the Finals for the first time in 1978 and returned to win his only NBA championship in 1979 when the Sonics won a five-game series over Washington.

Wilkens guided Cleveland and Atlanta for seven years apiece in the 1980s and '90s, earning NBA Coach of the Year accolades in 1993–94, his first year with the Hawks. He posted three 50-win seasons apiece with the Sonics, Cavs and Hawks. Most recently, he spent three seasons coaching the Toronto Raptors. His teams have recorded winning records in 20 of his 30 campaigns.

Another distinction held by Wilkens: He has been inducted into the Hall of Fame twice—in 1989 as a player and in 1998 as a coach.

COACHING RECORD			
	W	**L**	**Pct.**
Regular Season	1292	1114	.537
Postseason	80	94	.460
NBA Championships	**1** (1979)		

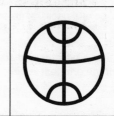

KEY
GAMES

DALLMAR SHOOTS WARRIORS TO FIRST TITLE

Philadelphia Warriors	**83**
Chicago Stags	**80**

April 22, 1947, Philadelphia Arena, Philadelphia, Pennsylvania

The Chicago Stags were supposed to be the better team. Joe Fulks was almost always the difference-maker for the Philadelphia Warriors. As it turned out, the Warriors' Howie Dallmar did not listen to conventional wisdom.

Dallmar, one of four players in the Basketball Association of America (the precursor of the NBA) to hand out more than 100 assists during the 1946–47 season, was not known as a shooter. He was also nursing callused feet entering Game 5 of the Finals, which Philly led 3–1. "No one expected him to play," Warriors coach Eddie Gottlieb said.

Dallmar spent much of Game 5 lobbying Gottlieb for playing time, and the coach finally gave in to his 6-foot-4 guard. Fulks was the scoring leader with 34 points, but it was a last-minute bucket by Dallmar that broke an 80-all tie and gave the Warriors the first championship.

COUSY, CELTICS OUTLAST NATS IN 4 OVERTIMES

Boston Celtics	**111**
Syracuse Nationals	**105 (4 OT)**

March 21, 1953, Boston Garden, Boston, Massachusetts

Before the 24-second shot clock, it was quite common for a team with a lead to stall. It sometimes happened as early as the first half. Games where both teams scored 100-plus points were hardly the norm. And although the Celtics and Nationals each topped the century mark in this memorable playoff affair, it too was a methodical battle.

Fouls slowed the play, as each team was afraid of letting the other build a significant lead. Open shots were difficult to find. When push came to shove, it turned out the ball-handling wizardry of Bob Cousy gave the Celtics the advantage.

Coach Red Auerbach ordered "Cooz" to dribble until he was fouled, and he made 30 of his NBA record 32 attempts from the free-throw line to finish with 50 points.

PETTIT, HAWKS TOPPLE CELTICS

St. Louis Hawks	**110**
Boston Celtics	**109**

April 12, 1958, Kiel Auditorium, St. Louis, Missouri

Familiarity often breeds rivalry, and that was the case between the early Boston Celtics and St. Louis Hawks. The teams squared off in pro basketball's championship series four times in five years beginning in 1957, when a potential tying shot by the Hawks' Bob Pettit in Game 7 bounced off the rim at the final buzzer.

The following season, Pettit made sure history did not repeat itself. Given the chance to close out the 1958 Finals at home in Game 6, Pettit overwhelmed Boston with a playoff record-tying 50-point game. The Hall of Fame forward scored 19 of his team's last 21 points in the fourth quarter of a tight contest.

Pettit's last two points came on a tip-in with 15 seconds remaining that provided a three-point lead and ensured St. Louis' lone championship.

WILT TOPS THE UNTHINKABLE CENTURY MARK

Philadelphia Warriors   169
New York Knicks   147

March 2, 1962, Hershey Arena, Hershey, Pennsylvania

Records are made to be broken—at least if you believe the popular sports adage. Wilt Chamberlain's might be the rare exception.

The Knicks' starting center, Phil Jordan, was sidelined by the flu, so the Warriors' strategy was obvious: Feed their unstoppable big man at every opportunity. No one knew just how frequently those opportunities would arise, or just how unstoppable Chamberlain would be in a half-filled Hershey Arena.

A 23-point opening quarter set the tone. Chamberlain had 41 points at halftime and 69 by the end of the third quarter. His previous NBA record of 78 points—just three months old—fell early in the final frame. His teammates fouled to give Wilt more chances, and with 46 seconds left he converted from short range for his 100th point.

Chamberlain finished the night 36-of-63 from the field and missed just four of 32 free-throw attempts.

CELTICS SURVIVE LAKERS IN GAME 7 OT

Boston Celtics	**110**
Los Angeles Lakers	**107 (7 OT)**

April 18, 1962, Boston Garden, Boston, Massachusetts

For years, many were convinced the Boston Garden held a very real "hex" that worked against the Celtics' visitors. One of the first bits of hard evidence came in the 1962 NBA Finals, when the Lakers were poised to upset the defending champs in the closing seconds of Game 7.

Earlier in the series, L.A. forward Elgin Baylor had set a Finals record with a 61-point game. His teammate, Frank Selvy, was poised to become the Game 7 hero with an open eight-footer at the end of regulation time. "I would trade all my points for that last basket," said the All-Star guard, whose baseline effort bounced off the rim.

The Celtics went on to win in overtime, claiming their fourth straight championship en route to an unprecedented eight in a row.

COUSY DRIBBLES OUT CLOCK FOR ONE MORE RING

Boston Celtics	112
Los Angeles Lakers	109

April 24, 1963, L.A. Sports Arena, Los Angeles, California

The Lakers had come so close to derailing the Celtics' dynasty in the 1962 NBA Finals. They felt their chances were even better in 1963 against a Boston team that some deemed to be too old to continue its dominance.

How wrong those "experts" were. Boston took a 3–1 series lead but squandered a chance to close out the series at home in Game 5. Heading to California for Game 6, fans couldn't help but anticipate a repeat of the previous season's seven-game classic.

The series never got that far. The Lakers trimmed a nine-point deficit to one entering the final minutes of Game 6, but 34-year-old Bob Cousy worked his ball-handling magic, forcing the Lakers to foul.

Cousy wound up dribbling out the clock in the final game of his career, retiring with five consecutive championships.

"HAVLICEK STOLE THE BALL!"

Boston Celtics	**110**
Philadelphia 76ers	**109**

April 15, 1965, Boston Garden, Boston, Massachusetts

The late Johnny Most endeared himself to Boston Celtics fans with his classic radio calls of most of the team's titles. He is best remembered not for a championship call, however, but for his exuberance at the end of Game 7 of the 1965 Eastern Conference Finals.

Boston led Philadelphia 110–109, but the 76ers had a chance to win as they prepared to inbound the ball from under the basket with five seconds remaining. Their hopes were dashed when John Havlicek stole guard Hal Greer's pass—intended for Chet Walker—and passed to Sam Jones, allowing the Celtics to run out the clock.

Or, as Most described it: "Greer is putting the ball into play. He gets it out deep. Havlicek steals it. Over to Sam Jones. Havlicek stole the ball! It's all over. Johnny Havlicek stole the ball!"

The Celtics went on to win their seventh straight NBA championship.

JERRY WEST AVERAGES 46.3 PPG IN SERIES

Los Angeles Lakers	**4**
Baltimore Bullets	**2**

Western Division Finals, 1965

Michael Jordan provided a few more memorable playoff moments than Jerry West. West's teammate, Elgin Baylor, had a higher-scoring postseason game, getting loose for 61 points in the 1962 Finals. For sustained dominance in a single series, though, no one can match West's work in the 1965 Western Finals.

Baylor blew out his knee in Game 1 against the Baltimore Bullets, leaving West to carry the load for the Lakers. The 6-foot-4 guard was up to the task. He tallied 49 points in that opening game, followed by a 52-point effort as L.A. took a 2–0 lead.

West's 44- and 48-point nights in Baltimore were not enough to keep the Bullets from pulling even with a pair of wins, but the Lakers took control from there. With 43 points in Game 5 and 42 in Game 6, L.A. advanced to the Finals, while West left a massive imprint in the record books.

No other player has hit 40 points in even four consecutive playoff games. West did it in six straight, setting a record with a 46.3-point average for the series.

ONE MORE TITLE FOR
PLAYER/COACH RUSSELL

Boston Celtics	**108**
Los Angeles Lakers	**106**

May 6, 1969, Great Western Forum, Inglewood, California

Southern California was ready to celebrate. The Lakers were hosting the Celtics for Game 7 of the NBA Finals, and this time L.A. was confident it could finally end Boston's dynasty. Thousands of balloons were held to the Forum ceiling by nets, waiting to be dropped in celebration. "We were better," said the Lakers' Jerry West.

If regular-season records were the gauge, West was correct. With star center Bill Russell serving as player/coach, Boston finished fourth in the East with a 48–34 record, its lowest win total in a dozen years, while the Lakers ran away with the West. For Russell and the Celtics, however, winning championships was second nature.

Don Nelson's late jumper bounced off the rim and into the hoop, providing Boston's 108–106 victory margin in Game 7. Russell walked off the court for the last time with a title—the Celtics' 11th in 13 years.

HOBBLED REED INSPIRES KNICKS TO A CHAMPIONSHIP

New York Knicks	**113**
Los Angeles Lakers	**99**

May 8, 1970, Madison Square Garden, New York, New York

Few who witnessed the series will ever forget the 1970 NBA Finals between the Lakers and Knicks. Game 3 saw the Lakers' Jerry West sink a 60-foot, game-tying prayer at the buzzer—one of the most memorable shots in NBA history—though New York went on to win the game in overtime.

The game Knicks fans remember most was the clincher. Star center Willis Reed had torn a muscle in his thigh in Game 5, an injury that forced him to watch Game 6 from the sideline as the Lakers evened the series.

No one was sure whether Reed would play in Game 7. He did not participate in warm-ups, but after a pain-killing injection in the locker room, he limped to the Madison Square Garden court, took the opening tip against Wilt Chamberlain and scored his team's first two baskets. Those were his only points of the game, but they sparked the Knicks to a 113–99 victory and their first championship.

LAKERS RUN WIN STREAK TO RECORD 33

Los Angeles Lakers	**134**
Atlanta Hawks	**90**

January 7, 1972, Alexander Memorial Coliseum, Atlanta, Georgia

Almost a month earlier, the Los Angeles Lakers had defeated the Atlanta Hawks 104–95 for their 21st consecutive win, breaking the previous NBA record of 20 set by the 1970–71 Milwaukee Bucks. Who would have guessed L.A.'s streak would be intact when the Lakers and Hawks met again?

This time, it was no contest. The Lakers pulled away for a 134–90 rout and their 33rd straight triumph. It was their most lopsided margin of the streak. "Our best game," offered Lakers coach Bill Sharman.

After the blowout, Hawks coach Richie Guerin said he could not wait to watch the Lakers' game against the Bucks in Milwaukee two days later. That's where the streak ended, as the Bucks won 120–104 on national television. L.A. went on to post a 69–13 mark—a record at the time—and beat New York in five games for the championship.

SUNS, CELTICS STAGE MEMORABLE MARATHON

Boston Celtics	**128**
Phoenix Suns	**126 (3 OT)**

June 6, 1976, Boston Garden, Boston, Massachusetts

It is often called the greatest game in the history of the NBA. Game 5 of the 1976 NBA Finals, Suns at Celtics. The winner would gain a 3–2 advantage in the series. It was a game neither team felt it could afford to lose, and that's how it was played for four quarters and three overtimes.

Boston's Paul Silas signaled for a timeout in the first OT that would have resulted in a technical foul, since the Celtics were out of timeouts, but referee Richie Powers decided to ignore the signal and play continued.

John Havlicek's 15-foot bank shot at the end of the second OT appeared to give Boston a one-point win, but 1 second was put back on the clock. Phoenix's Paul Westphal called a timeout he knew his team didn't have and the ensuing technical foul—while increasing Boston's lead to two—also gave the Suns the ball at midcourt. Gar Heard made the strategy pay off when his jumper at the horn forced a third OT.

Reserve Glenn McDonald scored six points in the third extra session as Boston prevailed, 128–126. The Celtics wrapped up the series two days later in Phoenix.

WALTON PUTS MONSTER NIGHT ON 76ERS

Portland Trail Blazers	**109**
Philadelphia 76ers	**107**

June 5, 1977, Memorial Coliseum, Portland, Oregon

Before the 1976–77 season, the Portland Trail Blazers had never earned so much as a winning season. They expected to be vastly improved under the direction of coach Jack Ramsay, but no one would have predicted a championship.

Portland finished second to the Lakers in the Pacific Division, but the Blazers' record was deceiving. When center Bill Walton was in the lineup, they were 44–21, compared to 5–12 when their big man sat out with injuries. Walton was healthy as Portland swept L.A. in the Western Conference finals, earning a Finals date with Philadelphia's 76ers.

Philly took the first two games before the Blazers won four straight for the title. Walton was dominant throughout, but the Game 6 clincher was his crowning achievement. He totaled 20 points, 23 rebounds, eight blocks and seven assists for the home crowd that night in leading a seven-year-old franchise to the pinnacle.

Said teammate Maurice Lucas of the Finals MVP: "Bill's my hero."

GERVIN EDGES THOMPSON FOR SCORING CROWN

New Orleans Jazz	**153**
San Antonio Spurs	**132**

April 9, 1978, Louisiana Superdome, New Orleans, Louisiana

George Gervin told his San Antonio teammates during the game to abandon their plans to ensure he won the scoring title. They didn't listen.

Earlier on that final day of the 1977–78 regular season, Denver's David Thompson had scored 73 points against the Detroit Pistons, the most by a guard in NBA history. It meant Gervin needed 58 at New Orleans that night to claim the scoring crown.

While Thompson scored 32 in the opening quarter of his earlier game, "The Iceman" came out cold. Gervin missed his first six shots, at which point he said, "Guys, let's just forget it." They ignored his request and kept feeding him the ball.

Gervin's points started piling up quickly. The 6-foot-7 guard had 53 by halftime and tallied 10 more in the third quarter before taking the final quarter off. His final average of 27.22 edged Thompson's 27.15 in the tightest scoring race in NBA history.

DR. J DEFIES LOGIC BEHIND THE GLASS

Philadelphia 76ers	**105**
Los Angeles Lakers	**102**

May 11, 1980, The Spectrum, Philadelphia, Pennsylvania

Former 76ers teammate Steve Mix calls it "The Move." It was the most breathtaking play in the career of Julius Erving, whose career was filled with breathtaking plays from which to choose.

Philadelphia trailed Los Angeles 2–1 in the NBA Finals and needed a win at home to pull even. The game was close in the fourth quarter when Erving beat defender Mark Landsberger to the baseline and took off toward the hoop.

What happened next made a lasting impression on everyone who saw it. Kareem Abdul-Jabbar, the Lakers' 7-foot tower, stepped into Dr. J's path intent on blocking the shot—or at least stopping it with a foul. Instead, Erving shifted his body in mid-air, soaring behind the backboard, and floated just long enough to stretch his right arm back toward the hoop to score on a once-in-a-lifetime reverse layup.

"My mouth just dropped open," the Lakers' Magic Johnson recalled. The 76ers won the game, 105–102, but lost the series in six.

ROOKIE POINT GUARD TAKES 'CENTER' STAGE

Los Angeles Lakers	**123**
Philadelphia 76ers	**107**

May 16, 1980, The Spectrum, Philadelphia, Pennsylvania

Magic Johnson was a 20-year-old rookie whose college classmates were still at Michigan State. All the Los Angeles Lakers wanted him to do was fill in for injured center Kareem Abdul-Jabbar in Game 6 of the NBA Finals. Johnson was a point guard!

"Never fear," he reportedly told his teammates on the flight to Philly. "E.J. is here." Actually, starting at center was Johnson's idea. He convinced coach Paul Westhead he could get the job done, and who could argue with his exuberance?

Johnson, at 6-foot-8, took the opening tap in place of the legendary Jabbar. Yes, he played center. But he also played all four other positions at various stages of the game. He scored 42 points, grabbed 15 rebounds and dished out seven assists as the Lakers wrapped up the NBA title with a 123–107 triumph.

Said 76ers star Julius Erving: "I don't even know if Kareem could have done the things Magic did tonight."

BIRD'S HEADS-UP MOVE: GREATEST PLAY EVER?

Boston Celtics	**98**
Houston Rockets	**95**

May 15, 1981, Boston Garden, Boston, Massachusetts

Growing up in French Lick, Indiana, Larry Bird launched so many shots, he seemingly knew exactly where the ball would end up the moment it left his hand. That uncanny anticipation paid big dividends during Game 1 of the 1981 NBA Finals.

The Houston Rockets were giving Bird's favored Boston Celtics all they could handle in the fourth quarter when Bird put up an 18-footer from the right side. He knew instantly the shot was off-target and raced to the hoop to chase the rebound.

On the run, Bird lept into the air and grabbed the carom in his right hand. As his momentum carried him over the baseline, he managed to switch the ball to his left hand, reach out and flip it into the hoop before landing out of bounds.

"I've never seen anything like it," said Celtics general manager Red Auerbach, who witnessed countless great plays over the decades. "It was one of the greatest plays of all time."

PISTONS, NUGGETS LIGHT UP THE SCOREBOARD

Detroit Pistons	**186**
Denver Nuggets	**184 (3 OT)**

December 13, 1983, McNichols Arena, Denver, Colorado

There was nothing to indicate history would take place when the Pistons visited the Nuggets on this night. Less than 10,000 fans were in attendance at McNichols Arena, and many headed home early. Denver was on its way to another sub-.500 season. Detroit was carving a path toward a second-place finish in the Central Division.

Along the way, a magical game took place. The teams launched shots and ran the floor at a thoroughbred pace, finishing four quarters with 145 points apiece. They remained tied after each of the first two overtimes before Detroit pulled out a 186–184 win in the highest-scoring game in NBA history.

Six scoring records were broken in the game. Kiki Vandeweghe scored 51 points and Alex English added 47 for the Nuggets. Isiah Thomas had 47 points and 17 assists for the Pistons, who also got 41 markers from John Long and 35 from Kelly Tripucka.

ABDUL-JABBAR BECOMES ALL-TIME NBA SCORING KING

Los Angeles Lakers	**129**
Utah Jazz	**115**

April 5, 1984, Thomas and Mack Center, Las Vegas, Nevada

Odds are everything in Las Vegas, and this was a longshot. What are the chances Kareem Abdul-Jabbar would break the NBA's career scoring record in a non-NBA city? That's precisely what happened in the Lakers' 129–115 victory over Utah in Las Vegas.

The Jazz had scheduled 11 games in America's gambling capital that season in an effort to attract new fans. If the site (UNLV's Thomas and Mack Center) was unusual, the story was not. Kareem broke Wilt Chamberlain's record with his patented sky-hook from mid-range, raising his career total to 31,420 points.

Fittingly, Magic Johnson fed the ball to Abdul-Jabbar for the record-setting basket. And as evidence to the unstoppable nature of Kareem's sky-hook, it was 7-foot-4 Utah center Mark Eaton who was defending on the play.

Abdul-Jabbar went on to compile 38,387 points in his 20-year NBA career.

KAREEM PLAYS YOUNG, SPARKS TITLE AT 38

Los Angeles Lakers	**4**
Boston Celtics	**2**

1985 NBA Finals

Kareem Abdul-Jabbar felt an apology was in order. The Lakers' 38-year-old center had played one of his worst games to open the 1985 NBA Finals, which the Celtics won by a surprisingly lopsided 148–114 score.

At a team meeting the following day, Abdul-Jabbar said he was "embarrassed" and promised his teammates a stronger effort. Then he delivered. Kareem dominated Game 2 with 30 points, 17 rebounds, eight assists and three steals as Los Angeles evened the series at one game apiece.

"Kareem was bad, knew he was bad, said he was bad," L.A. coach Pat Riley said of the series opener. "His commitment thereafter was astounding."

The series was tied 2–2 when Abdul-Jabbar erupted for 36 points in a 120–111 Game 5 win for the Lakers. After they closed out the series by winning Game 6 in Boston, Kareem became the oldest player in history to accept a Finals MVP Award.

JORDAN SCORES PLAYOFF RECORD 63 POINTS

Boston Celtics	**135**
Chicago Bulls	**131 (2 OT)**

April 20, 1986, Boston Garden, Boston, Massachusetts

There was no stopping Michael Jordan on this night. "I wasn't guarding him," Celtics guard Dennis Johnson said of the Chicago Bulls' second-year star. "No one was guarding him. No one can guard him." Johnson's teammate, Larry Bird, said it wasn't Jordan at all, but rather "God disguised as Michael Jordan."

Why all the fuss? Well, Jordan had broken his left foot three games into the season and was advised not to return until the 1986–87 campaign. Instead, he came back March 15 and helped Chicago reach the playoffs. Only a little more than a month later, in Game 2 of a first-round series, the high-flying guard put on a record-setting display against a Boston team that would go on to win the championship.

Jordan played all but five of the game's 58 minutes and scored an NBA playoff record 63 points—a mark that still stands. Jordan made 22 of 41 shots from the field and his two free throws with no time remaining forced the first OT.

SAMPSON'S BUZZER-BEATER ENDS LAKERS' RUN

Houston Rockets	**114**
Los Angeles Lakers	**112**

May 21, 1986, Great Western Forum, Inglewood, California

In retrospect, the Houston Rockets' "Twin Towers" frontcourt featuring 7-footers Ralph Sampson and Hakeem Olajuwon was not their best lineup. Sampson was an All-Star but did not turn out to be the dominant pro many thought he would be, and it was after he retired that Olajuwon led the Rockets to a pair of championships in the 1990s.

There was one memorable night, however, when Sampson was Houston's No. 1 hero. The Los Angeles Lakers had won 62 games—11 more than the Rockets—in 1985-86 and were expecting a chance to defend their NBA title. Instead, they found themselves in a 3–1 hole against Houston in the Western Conference Finals.

With the score tied and one second on the clock, the 7-foot-4 Sampson caught an inbound pass, turned and knocked down a jumper at the buzzer to send the Rockets to a clinching 114–112 win in Game 5. It earned Houston an unlikely Finals berth against eventual champion Boston.

"BIRD STEALS THE BALL!"

Boston Celtics	**108**
Detroit Pistons	**107**

May 26, 1987, Boston Garden, Boston, Massachusetts

All but the very young fans of the Boston Celtics remember where they were on May 26, 1987, when Larry Bird stole the ball and set up one of the most dramatic endings to a playoff game in the history of the NBA.

Detroit was growing into one of basketball's most rugged teams, and the Pistons appeared poised to steal a win in Boston in Game 5 of the Eastern Conference Finals. They led 107–106, had possession of the ball and needed only to run the last few seconds off the clock for a 3–2 lead and a chance to close out the series at home.

Out of the corner of his eye, Bird saw Detroit's Isiah Thomas make eye contact with Bill Laimbeer as he prepared to inbound the ball. Bird cut in front of the Pistons' center, intercepting the pass.

Before radio man Johnny Most could finish screaming—"Bird stole the ball! Bird stole the ball!"—Bird had dished to a cutting Dennis Johnson for the winning layup with one second left. The Celtics won the series in seven games.

MAGIC BORROWS PAGE FROM KAREEM'S BOOK

Los Angeles Lakers	**107**
Boston Celtics	**106**

June 9, 1987, Boston Garden, Boston, Massachusetts

The Lakers and Celtics had countless memorable moments, unforgettable games and fantastic plays in their long history of NBA Finals battles. One of the greatest shots in the series was also one of the most unlikely.

If Los Angeles was going to beat Boston with a hook shot in the 1980s, it certainly would be launched by center Kareem Abdul-Jabbar. Wouldn't it?

Actually, no, it was point guard Magic Johnson whose self-described "junior, junior sky-hook" won Game 4 of the 1987 Finals.

Trailing 106–105, Johnson caught an inbound pass on the left side and looked to shoot. With Kevin McHale in his face, he instead dribbled toward the middle. As Celtics 7-footer Robert Parish slid over to help, Magic tossed a running hook shot through the twine.

Boston's Larry Bird missed a shot at the buzzer, and the Lakers had a 107–106 victory and 3–1 series lead en route to the 1987 championship.

JORDAN, WILKINS PUT ON CLASSIC DUNK-FEST

Michael Jordan	**147**
Dominique Wilkins	**145**

February 6, 1988, Chicago Stadium, Chicago, Illinois

This was the Slam Dunk Contest by which all others are judged. And, if one can permit a little subjectivity, all others fall considerably short.

Michael Jordan and Dominique Wilkins were the two premier slam dunk artists of their era. No one could match their magic in the air. Wilkins had edged a rookie Jordan for his first dunk title three years earlier, but injuries to Jordan in 1986 and Wilkins in 1987 had delayed the rematch.

The setting in 1988 was Jordan's home court, Chicago Stadium. 'Nique's power and M.J.'s grace produced some of the best jams ever seen, as the two combined to score four perfect 50s out of six dunks in the final round.

Needing a 49 on his last attempt to successfully defend his 1987 crown, Jordan sprinted the length of the floor, took off from the free throw line, double-clutched in the air and threw down another gravity-defying 50.

BIRD, WILKINS GO BUCKET-FOR-BUCKET

Boston Celtics   **118**

Atlanta Hawks   **116**

May 22, 1988, Boston Garden, Boston, Massachusetts

Take it from a man who had a front-row seat: Larry Bird's fourth-quarter showdown with Dominique Wilkins in Game 7 of the 1988 Eastern Conference semifinals ranks among the greatest NBA spectacles of all time.

"It was like watching two great gunfighters, waiting for one of them to blink," said Kevin McHale, Bird's Boston Celtics teammate. "It was boom! Boom! Larry would make one and Dominique would make one. Larry would make one and Dominique would make one. It was unbelievable."

The score was tied at 86 with just over 10 minutes to play when Bird hit a jumper. Wilkins answered, and the two took over. Their torrid scoring pace saw Bird net 20 of his 34 points in the fourth quarter of a 118–116 Boston victory. Wilkins finished with 47 points and a new favorite memory.

"I couldn't miss. He couldn't miss," 'Nique said. "That's the greatest game I've ever played in or seen played."

PISTONS' THOMAS HOBBLES TO FINALS RECORD

Los Angeles Lakers	**103**
Detroit Pistons	**102**

June 19, 1988, Great Western Forum, Inglewood, California

It's not often that a performance in a losing effort becomes etched in the memory bank as a milestone moment. Isiah Thomas provided one such display in Game 6 of the 1988 NBA Finals.

Thomas was sparking his visiting Detroit Pistons to a third-quarter comeback against the Los Angeles Lakers when he landed on Michael Cooper's foot and had to be helped off the floor. His ankle was severely sprained. Other players might have called it a night.

Thomas came back 35 seconds later and, despite a limp, picked up right where he left off. He finished the third quarter with a Finals record 25 points on 11-of-13 shooting, lifting his team to a two-point lead.

The Lakers won the game, 103–102, despite Isiah's 43 points, eight assists and six steals. Although L.A. won the title two days later, it was Detroit's bruised, scratched and swollen Thomas who earned as much admiration as anyone.

JORDAN BREAKS CLEVELAND'S HEART WITH 'THE SHOT'

Chicago Bulls	**101**
Cleveland Cavaliers	**100**

May 7, 1989, The Coliseum, Richfield, Ohio

Cleveland has waited a long time for a winner. Just as John Elway and the Denver Broncos have broken the city's collective heart on the football field, Michael Jordan and the Chicago Bulls have done much of the damage on the hardwood.

Game 5 of a 1989 first-round playoff series was particularly painful for the Cavaliers. Unfortunately for their fans, it was also unforgettable.

Cleveland looked poised to avenge the previous year's playoff loss to the Bulls after stealing Game 4 of the best-of-five series with an overtime win in Chicago. The Cavs led the deciding game 100–99 on their home court, and the Bulls had just seconds to look for a final shot.

Jordan dribbled from the right side toward the middle, lept in the air—18 feet from the hoop—and drilled the winning jumper over the outstretched fingertips of Craig Ehlo. A fist pump completed the highlight-reel play and added to Cleveland's misery.

M.J. GOES UP AND UNDER
AGAINST THE LAKERS

Chicago Bulls	**107**
Los Angeles Lakers	**86**

June 5, 1991, Chicago Stadium, Chicago, Illinois

Calling one play the greatest of Michael Jordan's career is not unlike calling one raindrop wetter than another. However, those who witnessed Game 2 of the 1991 NBA Finals came away knowing they saw something special.

The Lakers had stolen the series opener in Chicago and the Bulls knew they needed a big performance before heading west. They got a spectacular one, particularly on Jordan's memorable drive to the bucket.

"His Airness" drove the lane past the Byron Scott with the ball in his right hand. As he took off for an intended dunk, Laker forward A.C. Green slid off his man to help. Not a problem for Jordan. He adjusted his body on the fly, switched the ball to his left hand while in mid-air and flipped a shot off the glass and into the hoop.

The play sparked the Bulls toward a 107–86 blowout, and they won the next three games as well to claim their first NBA championship.

MAGIC MAKES ALL-STAR COMEBACK, WINS MVP

West All-Stars	**153**
East All-Stars	**113**

February 9, 1992, Orlando Arena, Orlando, Florida

Fittingly, the 1992 NBA All-Star Game was played in the shadow of Walt Disney World. It certainly featured a "happily ever after" ending.

Three months earlier, Magic Johnson shocked the world—basketball and otherwise—when he announced he had contracted the HIV virus. Even though he stopped playing, he was voted a starter in the All-Star Game by his adoring fans.

With an OK from the NBA to participate, Johnson received a lengthy standing ovation from a sold-out Orlando Arena crowd and hugs from his fellow stars. He then proceeded to flash both his familiar smile and his considerable skills, leading the West to a one-sided victory with 25 points and nine assists, capping the night with a late 3-pointer.

When it came time to vote for the game's MVP, there was little doubt. Disney, after all, loves its Magic.

DREAM TEAM TAKES
BASKETBALL TO NEW LEVEL

United States	**117**
Croatia	**85**

August 8, 1992, Palau Sant Jordi, Barcelona, Spain

The date listed above was the culmination of a dominant run by the greatest collection of basketball talent ever assembled. From the time the Olympic Games were opened to professionals and the NBA's best players were teamed for the first time in a major international competition, basketball fans around the world looked on in awe.

Coach Chuck Daly compared the phenomenon to touring with Elvis Presley or the Beatles. Everywhere the "Dream Team" went, from its pre-Olympic exhibitions to the Games themselves, opposing players were right there with the fans chasing U.S. autographs.

And why not? The team featured 11 NBA All-Stars—Michael Jordan, Magic Johnson, Larry Bird, Charles Barkley, Karl Malone, John Stockton, Scottie Pippen, Chris Mullin, David Robinson, Patrick Ewing and Clyde Drexler—along with college star Christian Laettner.

The Americans defeated their eight Olympic opponents by an average of 44 points.

PAXSON'S TREY GIVES BULLS A 'THREE-PEAT'

Chicago Bulls	**99**
Phoenix Suns	**98**

June 20, 1993, America West Arena, Phoenix, Arizona

Michael Jordan was named Finals MVP after each of his six championships. However, it was a less likely hero who lifted Chicago to its first of two "three-peats" in the 1990s.

The setting was America West Arena in Game 6 of the 1993 Finals. The series had already featured some memorable games—a rare triple-overtime battle, a game in which Jordan and Phoenix's Charles Barkley scored 42 points apiece, and a 55-point eruption from Jordan in Game 4.

Game 6 was a dandy. The Bulls led 87–79 after three quarters, but a Phoenix rally put the Suns on top 98–94. Jordan made it a two-point game and was the logical choice to launch Chicago's last shot, but Horace Grant spotted an open John Paxson behind the 3-point arc.

"It felt good when it left," the veteran guard said. It was, with 3.9 seconds left. The Bulls had become the third team in history to capture three straight titles.

MILLER TIME: REGGIE ROLLS TO 25-POINT QUARTER

Indiana Pacers	**93**
New York Knicks	**86**

June 1, 1994, Madison Square Garden, New York, New York

Not even renowned movie producer and vocal Knicks fan Spike Lee could slow down Reggie Miller in this game.

Lee, a courtside ticket-holder, and Miller have engaged in some memorable verbal battles at Madison Square Garden through the years. In Game 5 of the 1994 Eastern Conference Finals, it was Miller's jump shot that did most of the talking.

The Pacers star drained a playoff record five 3-pointers in the fourth quarter, making the basket appear to be the size of an ocean. He wound up with 25 points in the final frame and 39 on the night as Indiana earned a 93–86 victory for a 3–2 lead in the series.

Lee's beloved Knicks got their revenge by winning the last two games to reach the Finals, where they lost to the Houston Rockets.

STOCKTON BECOMES ALL-TIME NBA ASSISTS KING

Utah Jazz	**129**
Denver Nuggets	**88**

February 1, 1995, Delta Center, Salt Lake City, Utah

Could there be any other way? When Utah Jazz point guard John Stockton passed Magic Johnson to become the NBA's career leader in assists, there was a familiar target on the receiving end of the pass.

Karl Malone caught the bounce pass and dropped in an 18-foot jump shot in Utah's victory over the Denver Nuggets. It was the 9,922nd assist of Stockton's career and it sent 19,911 Delta Center fans to their feet for an ovation that seemed to last forever.

"It does seem fitting," Stockton said of the record-setting play, noting that Malone was on the finishing end of a large percentage of his helpers.

Stockton went on to amass 15,806 assists in his 19-year career, all with the Jazz. It will be a long, long time before his record is eclipsed.

FIVE GAMES INTO COMEBACK, JORDAN NETS 55

Chicago Bulls	**113**
New York Knicks	**111**

March 28, 1995, Madison Square Garden, New York, New York

One number changed. He wore No. 45 on his jersey instead of his traditional No. 23. Another was quite familiar: 55, as in points. Five games into his first comeback, Michael Jordan reached that total for the 13th time in his career.

When Jordan had announced "I'm back" less than two weeks earlier in the 1994–95 season, most expected it would take him a while to readjust after 21 months off. The New York Knicks found out the hard way how wrong that was.

Jordan left a packed house at Madison Square Garden and a national TV audience breathless with an array of 3-pointers, double-pump layups and fadeaway jumpers in traffic.

For all the points, Jordan's best play of the night was a dramatic assist. He found teammate Bill Wennington for an uncontested slam dunk in the final seconds as the Bulls handed the Knicks a 113–111 setback.

BULLS BECOME FIRST TO REACH 70-WIN PLATEAU

Chicago Bulls	**86**
Milwaukee Bucks	**80**

April 16, 1996, Bradley Center, Milwaukee, Wisconsin

Chicago's six-point win up the road in Milwaukee will not go down as one of the greatest games ever played. Its significance, however, is difficult to dispute.

No team in NBA history had ever won a 70th game until the Bulls reached the milestone in this defensive battle at the Bradley Center. The 1971–72 Lakers had won 69.

Two weeks earlier, Chicago had set an NBA record by winning its 44th consecutive home game, a streak that spanned two seasons. Overall, the Bulls won 18 in a row during one stretch and 41 of 44 to start the campaign. Their final ledger of 72–10 remains a record.

Of course, Michael Jordan, Scottie Pippen & Co. would have considered it all for naught if a championship hadn't followed. They went on to defeat Seattle in six games for their fourth title in six years.

JORDAN'S LAST-SECOND SHOT SINKS JAZZ

Chicago Bulls	**87**
Utah Jazz	**86**

June 14, 1998, Delta Center, Salt Lake City, Utah

OK, so he pushed off on the play. There was no way an official was going to spoil what most figured was the last shot of Michael Jordan's brilliant career.

Battling through visible fatigue in Game 6 of the NBA Finals, Jordan had carried Chicago into position to clinch its sixth title of the 1990s with a 45-point night. Everyone at the Delta Center knew the ball would be in his hands in the final seconds as Utah tried to preserve a one-point lead.

Jazz defender Bryon Russell—with a little help from Jordan's hand on a fake—slipped to the floor as the game's greatest player pulled up and drained a 20-foot jumper with less than six seconds remaining.

Jordan won his sixth Finals MVP Award, seemingly putting the perfect exclamation point on his career. He "un-retired" for a second time in 2001, though, playing two seasons with the Washington Wizards.

TWIN TOWERS GIVE SPURS FIRST TITLE

San Antonio Spurs	**78**
New York Knicks	**77**

June 25, 1999, Madison Square Garden, New York, New York

Sometimes nice guys finish first. Some said the San Antonio Spurs were "too nice" to win an NBA championship. David Robinson needed a mean streak. Tim Duncan had to be more physical. There were any number of reasons people refused to believe the Spurs would reach the top.

None of those reasons held up.

Robinson had long been San Antonio's go-to big man. Once he was joined by Duncan, a rising star with limitless potential, the Spurs had the balance they needed to win it all.

"It's a journey that goes to show that hard word and persistence truly pays off," Robinson said after San Antonio polished off New York in five games to become the first former ABA team to win an NBA championship.

The Spurs' 15–2 run through the playoffs was the second-best in NBA history at the time. The 23-year-old Duncan was named Finals MVP, an honor he would garner again with the Spurs' second title in 2003.

LAKERS MAKE JACKSON KING OF THE 'THREE-PEAT'

Los Angeles Lakers	113
New Jersey Nets	107

June 12, 2002, The Meadowlands, East Rutherford, New Jersey

Pat Riley is the coach who first coined the phrase "three-peat." Phil Jackson is the coach who perfected it.

Before Jackson's Chicago Bulls won three straight titles from 1991–93, only two teams in NBA history had accomplished the feat. Jackson did it again with the Bulls from 1996–98, and his first three years with the Lakers produced another "three-peat" from 2000–02.

While Jackson was tying Red Auerbach with his nine championships as coach, it was Shaquille O'Neal and Kobe Bryant of the Lakers who were building their legacies as star players in a sweep of the Nets. O'Neal earned his third straight Finals MVP Award after setting a record for points (145) in a four-game Finals.

Once the Lakers survived a seven-game scare against Sacramento in the Western Conference Finals, they handled the rest of their job with relative ease. Jackson was given much of the credit. "I realize that if it wasn't for Phil, I wouldn't have any championships," Shaq said.

BRYANT MAKES 40-POINTERS LOOK ROUTINE

Los Angeles Lakers	106
Seattle SuperSonics	101

February 23, 2003, Staples Center, Los Angeles, California

Ho-hum. Another night, another 40-point game for Kobe Bryant.

When his team needed him most, the Los Angeles Lakers star made a valiant run at NBA history. His 41-point effort in the Lakers' 106–101 home triumph over Seattle was his ninth consecutive game with 40 or more points—a streak that only Wilt Chamberlain exceeded (with two runs of 14 and one of 10 in his career).

Michael Jordan also compiled a nine-game string of 40-point games in 1986–87. "To be mentioned in the same breath with those guys is an honor in itself," Bryant said.

With star center Shaquille O'Neal coming off an injury during the early part of the 2002–03 season, Bryant put the Lakers on his back. He scored 35 or more points in 13 straight games, also second to Chamberlain in NBA annals.

Bryant's streak ended with a 32-point effort—a number most players would gladly accept—in a victory against the Clippers.

THE STATS

CAREER REGULAR SEASON

CAREER REGULAR SEASON

Career Games Played

	PLAYER	GAMES PLAYED
1	Robert Parish	1611
2	Kareem Abdul-Jabbar	1560
3	John Stockton	1504
4	Karl Malone	1434
5	Kevin Willis	1342
6	Moses Malone	1329
7	Buck Williams	1307
8	Elvin Hayes	1303
9	Sam Perkins	1286
10	A.C. Green	1278
11	Charles Oakley	1275
12	Terry Porter	1274
13	John Havlicek	270
14	Otis Thorpe	1257
15	Mark Jackson	1254
	Paul Silas	1254
17	Reggie Miller	1243
18	Hakeem Olajuwon	1238
19	Dale Ellis	1209
20	Derek Harper	1199
	Eddie Johnson	1199
22	Alex English	1193
23	Terry Cummings	1183
	Patrick Ewing	1183
25	James Edwards	1168
26	Johnny Newman	1159
27	Tree Rollins	1156
28	Scottie Pippen	1155
29	Jerome Kersey	1153
30	Michael Cage	1140

Career Points Scored

	PLAYER	POINTS SCORED
1	Kareem Abdul-Jabbar	38387
2	Karl Malone	36374
3	Michael Jordan	32292
4	Wilt Chamberlain	31419
5	Moses Malone	27409
6	Elvin Hayes	27313
7	Hakeem Olajuwon	26946
8	Oscar Robertson	26710
9	Dominique Wilkins	26668
10	John Havlicek	26395
11	Alex English	25613
12	Jerry West	25192
13	Patrick Ewing	24815
14	Charles Barkley	23757
15	Reggie Miller	23505
16	Robert Parish	23334
17	Adrian Dantley	23177
18	Elgin Baylor	23149
19	Clyde Drexler	22195
20	Larry Bird	21791
21	Hal Greer	21586
22	Walt Bellamy	20941
23	Bob Pettit	20880
24	David Robinson	20790
25	George Gervin	20708
26	Mitch Richmond	20497
27	Shaquille O'Neal	20475
28	Tom Chambers	20049
29	John Stockton	19711
30	Bernard King	19655

Career Points Per Game (400 Games or 10000 Points)

	PLAYER	PPG
1	Michael Jordan	30.1
2	Wilt Chamberlain	30.1
3	Shaquille O'Neal	27.6
4	Elgin Baylor	27.4
5	Allen Iverson	27.0
6	Jerry West	27.0
7	Bob Pettit	26.4
8	George Gervin	26.2
9	Oscar Robertson	25.7
10	Karl Malone	25.4
11	Dominique Wilkins	24.8
12	Kareem Abdul-Jabbar	24.6
13	Larry Bird	24.3
14	Adrian Dantley	24.3
15	Pete Maravich	24.2
16	Rick Barry	23.2
17	George Mikan	23.1
18	Tim Duncan	22.9
19	Paul Arizin	22.8
20	Bernard King	22.5
21	Chris Webber	22.2
22	Charles Barkley	22.1
23	David Thompson	22.1
24	Bob McAdoo	22.1
25	Julius Erving	22.0
26	Geoff Petrie	21.8
27	Hakeem Olajuwon	21.8
28	Kobe Bryant	21.5
29	Alex English	21.5
30	Jerry Stackhouse	21.3

Field Goals Made

	PLAYER	FIELD GOALS
1	Kareem Abdul-Jabbar	15837
2	Karl Malone	13335
3	Wilt Chamberlain	12681
4	Michael Jordan	12192
5	Elvin Hayes	10976
6	Hakeem Olajuwon	10749
7	Alex English	10659
8	John Havlicek	10513
9	Dominique Wilkins	9963
10	Patrick Ewing	9702
11	Robert Parish	9614
12	Oscar Robertson	9508
13	Moses Malone	9435
14	Jerry West	9016
15	Elgin Baylor	8693
16	Larry Bird	8591
17	Hal Greer	8504
18	Charles Barkley	8435
19	Clyde Drexler	8335
20	Adrian Dantley	8169
21	Walter Davis	8118
22	Shaquille O'Neal	8116
23	Terry Cummings	8045
	George Gervin	8045
25	Walt Bellamy	7914
26	Bernard King	7830
27	Bob Lanier	7761
28	Eddie Johnson	7727
29	Reggie Miller	7667
30	Gary Payton	7513

CAREER REGULAR SEASON

Field Goal Percentage
(2000 Field Goals Made)

	PLAYER	PCT
1	Artis Gilmore	.599
2	Mark West	.580
3	Shaquille O'Neal	.577
4	Steve Johnson	.572
5	Darryl Dawkins	.572
6	James Donaldson	.571
7	Jeff Ruland	.564
8	Kareem Abdul-Jabbar	.559
9	Kevin McHale	.554
10	Bobby Jones	.550
11	Buck Williams	.549
12	Larry Nance	.546
13	Otis Thorpe	.546
14	Cedric Maxwell	.546
15	Charles Barkley	.541
16	Adrian Dantley	.540
17	Wilt Chamberlain	.540
18	Gene Banks	.539
19	Swen Nater	.537
20	Robert Parish	.537
21	Dale Davis	.536
22	Brad Daugherty	.532
23	Larry Smith	.531
24	Calvin Natt	.528
25	Bill Cartwright	.525
26	Alonzo Mourning	.525
27	Kiki Vandeweghe	.525
28	Clifford Ray	.524
29	Lewis Lloyd	.524
30	Maurice Cheeks	.523

3-Point Field Goals Made

	PLAYER	FIELD GOALS
1	Reggie Miller	2330
2	Dale Ellis	1719
3	Glen Rice	1554
4	Tim Hardaway	1542
5	Dan Majerle	1360
6	Nick Van Exel	1327
7	Mitch Richmond	1326
8	Terry Porter	1297
9	Mookie Blaylock	1283
10	Vernon Maxwell	1256
11	Dell Curry	1245
12	Hersey Hawkins	1226
13	John Starks	1222
14	Chuck Person	1220
15	Dennis Scott	1214
16	Allan Houston	1187
17	Ray Allen	1129
18	Dana Barros	1090
19	Derek Harper	1070
20	Steve Smith	1064
21	Nick Anderson	1055
22	Wesley Person	1054
23	Danny Ainge	1002
24	Joe Dumars	990
25	Clifford Robinson	989
26	Eddie Jones	982
27	Mark Price	976
	Walt Williams	976
29	Lindsey Hunter	965
	Scottie Pippen	965

3-Point Percentage
(250 3-Points Made)

	PLAYER	PCT
1	Steve Kerr	.454
2	Hubert Davis	.441
3	Michael Redd	.438
4	Drazen Petrovic	.437
5	Tim Legler	.431
6	B.J. Armstrong	.425
7	Steve Nash	.418
8	Wesley Person	.417
9	Pat Garrity	.413
10	Dana Barros	.411
11	Trent Tucker	.408
12	Dale Ellis	.403
13	Jeff Hornacek	.403
14	Brent Barry	.402
15	Eric Piatkowski	.402
16	Mark Price	.402
17	Ray Allen	.402
18	Dell Curry	.402
19	Glen Rice	.402
20	Michael Dickerson	.402
21	Allan Houston	.400
22	Craig Hodges	.400
23	Kenny Smith	.399
24	Reggie Miller	.398
25	Dennis Scott	.397
26	Hersey Hawkins	.394
27	Danny Ferry	.393
28	Jon Barry	.390
29	Bobby Phills	.390
30	Voshon Lenard	.389

Free Throws Made

	PLAYER	FREE THROWS
1	Karl Malone	9619
2	Moses Malone	8531
3	Oscar Robertson	7694
4	Michael Jordan	7327
5	Jerry West	7160
6	Adrian Dantley	6832
7	Kareem Abdul-Jabbar	6712
	Dolph Schayes	6712
9	Charles Barkley	6349
10	Bob Pettit	6182
11	Wilt Chamberlain	6057
12	David Robinson	6035
13	Dominique Wilkins	6031
14	Reggie Miller	5841
15	Elgin Baylor	5763
16	Hakeem Olajuwon	5423
17	Lenny Wilkens	5394
18	Patrick Ewing	5392
19	John Havlicek	5369
20	Elvin Hayes	5356
21	Walt Bellamy	5113
22	Chet Walker	5079
23	Tom Chambers	5066
24	Paul Arizin	5010
25	Magic Johnson	4960
26	John Stockton	4788
27	Bailey Howell	4740
28	World B. Free	4718
29	Clyde Drexler	4698
30	Tiny Archibald	4664

CAREER REGULAR SEASON

Free Throw Percentage
(1200 Free Throws Made)

	PLAYER	PCT
1	Mark Price	.904
2	Rick Barry	.900
3	Calvin Murphy	.892
4	Scott Skiles	.889
5	Reggie Miller	.886
6	Larry Bird	.886
7	Bill Sharman	.883
8	Ray Allen	.882
9	Jeff Hornacek	.877
10	Ricky Pierce	.875
11	Terrell Brandon	.873
12	Kiki Vandeweghe	.872
13	Jeff Malone	.871
14	Hersey Hawkins	.870
15	Mike Newlin	.870
16	Micheal Williams	.868
17	Chris Mullin	.865
18	John Long	.862
19	Allan Houston	.861
20	Derek Anderson	.860
21	Dana Barros	.858
22	Fred Brown	.858
23	Sam Cassell	.857
24	Larry Siegfried	.854
25	Mario Elie	.854
26	James Silas	.852
27	Walter Davis	.851
28	Mitch Richmond	.850
29	Jack Sikma	.849
30	Dolph Schayes	.849

Rebounds (total)

	PLAYER	REBOUNDS
1	Wilt Chamberlain	23924
2	Bill Russell	21620
3	Kareem Abdul-Jabbar	17440
4	Elvin Hayes	16279
5	Moses Malone	16212
6	Robert Parish	14715
7	Karl Malone	14601
8	Nate Thurmond	14464
9	Walt Bellamy	14241
10	Wes Unseld	13769
11	Hakeem Olajuwon	13748
12	Buck Williams	13017
13	Jerry Lucas	12942
14	Bob Pettit	12849
15	Charles Barkley	12546
16	Paul Silas	12357
17	Charles Oakley	12200
18	Dennis Rodman	11954
19	Kevin Willis	11719
20	Patrick Ewing	11607
21	Elgin Baylor	11463
22	Dolph Schayes	11256
23	Bill Bridges	11054
24	Jack Sikma	10816
25	David Robinson	10497
26	Dikembe Mutombo	10470
27	Dave Cowens	10444
28	Bill Laimbeer	10400
29	Otis Thorpe	10370
30	Red Kerr	10092

Rebounds (offensive)

	PLAYER	REBOUNDS
1	Moses Malone	6731
2	Robert Parish	4598
3	Buck Williams	4526
4	Dennis Rodman	4329
5	Charles Barkley	4260
6	Kevin Willis	4064
7	Hakeem Olajuwon	4034
8	Charles Oakley	3924
9	Karl Malone	3501
10	Otis Thorpe	3446
11	Larry Smith	3401
12	Horace Grant	3388
13	A.C. Green	3354
14	Michael Cage	3227
15	Terry Cummings	3183
16	Dikembe Mutombo	3169
17	David Robinson	3083
18	Shawn Kemp	3026
19	Kareem Abdul-Jabbar	2975
20	Dominique Wilkins	2950
21	Shaquille O'Neal	2947
22	Dale Davis	2913
23	Bill Laimbeer	2819
24	Alex English	2778
	Elvin Hayes	2778
26	Patrick Ewing	2752
27	Olden Polynice	2729
28	Vlade Divac	2727
29	Artis Gilmore	2639
30	Clyde Drexler	2615

Rebounds (defensive)

	PLAYER	REBOUNDS
1	Karl Malone	11100
2	Robert Parish	10117
3	Hakeem Olajuwon	9714
4	Moses Malone	9481
5	Kareem Abdul-Jabbar	9394
6	Patrick Ewing	8855
7	Buck Williams	8491
8	Charles Barkley	8286
9	Charles Oakley	8276
10	Jack Sikma	8274
11	Kevin Willis	7655
12	Dennis Rodman	7625
13	Bill Laimbeer	7581
14	David Robinson	7414
15	Dikembe Mutombo	7301
16	Larry Bird	7217
17	Elvin Hayes	6973
18	Otis Thorpe	6924
19	Artis Gilmore	6522
20	A.C. Green	6119
21	Vlade Divac	6104
22	Shaquille O'Neal	6065
23	Horace Grant	5822
24	Shawn Kemp	5808
25	Caldwell Jones	5621
26	Bob McAdoo	5502
27	Terry Cummings	5447
28	James Donaldson	5432
29	Michael Cage	5419
30	Maurice Lucas	5401

CAREER REGULAR SEASON

Assists

	PLAYER	ASSISTS
1	John Stockton	15806
2	Mark Jackson	10215
3	Magic Johnson	10141
4	Oscar Robertson	9887
5	Isiah Thomas	9061
6	Rod Strickland	7704
7	Gary Payton	7590
8	Maurice Cheeks	7392
9	Lenny Wilkens	7211
10	Terry Porter	7160
11	Tim Hardaway	7095
12	Bob Cousy	6955
13	Guy Rodgers	6917
14	Muggsy Bogues	6726
15	Kevin Johnson	6711
16	Derek Harper	6577
17	Tiny Archibald	6476
18	John Lucas	6454
19	Reggie Theus	6453
20	Norm Nixon	6386
21	Jerry West	6238
22	Clyde Drexler	6125
23	Jason Kidd	6120
24	John Havlicek	6114
25	Scottie Pippen	6085
26	Mookie Blaylock	5972
27	Avery Johnson	5735
28	Larry Bird	5695
29	Kareem Abdul-Jabbar	5660
30	Michael Jordan	5633

Steals

	PLAYER	STEALS
1	John Stockton	3265
2	Michael Jordan	2514
3	Maurice Cheeks	2310
4	Scottie Pippen	2286
5	Clyde Drexler	2207
6	Hakeem Olajuwon	2162
7	Gary Payton	2147
8	Alvin Robertson	2112
9	Mookie Blaylock	2075
10	Karl Malone	2035
11	Derek Harper	1957
12	Isiah Thomas	1861
13	Magic Johnson	1724
14	Ron Harper	1716
15	Fat Lever	1666
16	Charles Barkley	1648
17	Gus Williams	1638
18	Hersey Hawkins	1622
19	Mark Jackson	1591
20	Terry Porter	1583
21	Rod Strickland	1578
22	Doc Rivers	1563
23	Larry Bird	1556
24	Nate McMillan	1544
25	Jeff Hornacek	1536
26	Chris Mullin	1530
27	Julius Erving	1508
28	Dennis Johnson	1477
29	Micheal Ray Richardson	1463
30	Kendall Gill	1440

CAREER REGULAR SEASON

Blocks

	PLAYER	BLOCKS
1	Hakeem Olajuwon	3830
2	Kareem Abdul-Jabbar	3189
3	Mark Eaton	3064
4	David Robinson	2954
5	Patrick Ewing	2894
6	Dikembe Mutombo	2873
7	Tree Rollins	2542
8	Robert Parish	2361
9	Manute Bol	2086
10	George Johnson	2082
11	Larry Nance	2027
12	Shawn Bradley	1982
13	Shaquille O'Neal	1936
14	Alonzo Mourning	1883
15	Elvin Hayes	1771
16	Artis Gilmore	1747
17	Moses Malone	1733
18	Kevin McHale	1690
19	Herb Williams	1605
20	Benoit Benjamin	1581
21	Vlade Divac	1553
22	Elden Campbell	1545
23	Wayne Cooper	1535
24	Caldwell Jones	1517
25	Alton Lister	1473
26	Hot Rod Williams	1456
27	Mark West	1403
28	Terry Tyler	1342
29	Julius Erving	1293
30	Shawn Kemp	1279

Turnovers

	PLAYER	TURNOVERS
1	Karl Malone	4421
2	John Stockton	4244
3	Moses Malone	3804
4	Isiah Thomas	3682
5	Hakeem Olajuwon	3667
6	Patrick Ewing	3537
7	Magic Johnson	3506
8	Reggie Theus	3493
9	Charles Barkley	3376
10	Scottie Pippen	3228
11	Robert Parish	3183
12	Mark Jackson	3102
13	Clyde Drexler	2977
14	Michael Jordan	2924
15	Alex English	2821
16	Larry Bird	2816
17	Bernard King	2791
18	Charles Oakley	2784
	Buck Williams	2784
20	Otis Thorpe	2774
21	Shawn Kemp	2766
22	Rod Strickland	2761
23	Dominique Wilkins	2669
24	Terry Porter	2666
25	Jack Sikma	2586
26	Mitch Richmond	2579
27	Gary Payton	2563
28	Tom Chambers	2549
29	Walter Davis	2541
30	Kareem Abdul-Jabbar	2527

Fouls

	PLAYER	FOULS
1	Kareem Abdul-Jabbar	4657
2	Karl Malone	4462
3	Robert Parish	4443
4	Charles Oakley	4413
5	Hakeem Olajuwon	4383
6	Buck Williams	4267
7	Elvin Hayes	4193
8	Otis Thorpe	4146
9	Kevin Willis	4047
10	James Edwards	4042
11	Patrick Ewing	4034
12	John Stockton	3942
13	Jack Sikma	3879
14	Hal Greer	3855
15	Terry Cummings	3836
16	Shawn Kemp	3826
17	Tom Chambers	3742
18	Bill Laimbeer	3633
19	Walt Bellamy	3536
20	Caldwell Jones	3527
21	Rick Mahorn	3499
22	Bailey Howell	3498
23	Danny Schayes	3494
24	Sam Lacey	3473
25	Jerome Kersey	3455
26	Clifford Robinson	3454
27	Dolph Schayes	3432
28	Tree Rollins	3377
29	Bill Bridges	3375
30	Vlade Divac	3362

Disqualifications

	PLAYER	DISQUALS.
1	Vern Mikkelsen	127
2	Walter Dukes	121
3	Shawn Kemp	115
4	Chuck Share	105
5	Paul Arizin	101
6	Darryl Dawkins	100
7	James Edwards	96
8	Tom Gola	94
	Tom Sanders	94
10	Steve Johnson	93
	Tree Rollins	92
12	Dave Cowens	90
	Bailey Howell	90
	Dolph Schayes	90
15	Tom Meschery	89
16	Frank Ramsey	87
17	Robert Parish	86
18	John Drew	85
	Larry Foust	85
	Otis Thorpe	85
21	Alex Hannum	82
22	Hakeem Olajuwon	80
	Jack Sikma	80
24	Sam Lacey	78
25	Alton Lister	77
26	Mike Bantom	76
	Ray Felix	76
28	Tom Chambers	75
29	Mickey Johnson	74
	Rick Mahorn	74
	Norm Van Lier	74

CAREER REGULAR SEASON

Technicals (since 1991–92)

	PLAYER	TECHS.
1	Karl Malone	209
2	Gary Payton	205
3	Charles Barkley	200
4	Anthony Mason	194
5	Rasheed Wallace	179
6	Dennis Rodman	174
7	Reggie Miller	128
	Kevin Willis	128
9	Charles Oakley	115
10	Antoine Walker	111
11	Scottie Pippen	105
12	Chris Gatling	103
13	Nick Van Exel	102
14	Shawn Bradley	101
	Shawn Kemp	101
16	Dikembe Mutombo	100
17	Shaquille O'Neal	99
18	Alonzo Mourning	96
19	Vlade Divac	94
20	Clifford Robinson	92
21	Patrick Ewing	85
22	Vernon Maxwell	84
23	Jerry Stackhouse	82
24	Derrick Coleman	79
25	Kenny Anderson	77
	Allen Iverson	77
27	Dale Davis	76
28	Juwan Howard	75
	Larry Johnson	75
30	Tim Hardaway	74

THE STATS

CAREER
POSTSEASON

CAREER POSTSEASON

Games Played

	PLAYER	GAMES
1	Kareem Abdul-Jabbar	237
2	Scottie Pippen	208
3	Danny Ainge	193
4	Magic Johnson	190
5	Robert Parish	184
6	Byron Scott	183
7	John Stockton	182
8	Dennis Johnson	180
9	Michael Jordan	179
10	John Havlicek	172
	Karl Malone	172
12	Horace Grant	170
13	Kevin McHale	169
	Dennis Rodman	169
15	Michael Cooper	168
16	Sam Perkins	167
17	Robert Horry	165
	Bill Russell	165
19	Larry Bird	164
20	Paul Silas	163
21	Wilt Chamberlain	160
22	Sam Jones	154
23	A.C. Green	153
	Jerry West	153
25	Don Nelson	150
26	Clyde Drexler	145
	Hakeem Olajuwon	145
28	Charles Oakley	144
29	James Worthy	143
30	Derrick McKey	142

Points Scored

	PLAYER	PTS
1	Michael Jordan	5987
2	Kareem Abdul-Jabbar	5762
3	Karl Malone	4519
4	Jerry West	4457
5	Larry Bird	3897
6	Shaquille O'Neal	3821
7	John Havlicek	3776
8	Hakeem Olajuwon	3755
9	Magic Johnson	3701
10	Scottie Pippen	3642
11	Elgin Baylor	3623
12	Wilt Chamberlain	3607
13	Kevin McHale	3182
14	Dennis Johnson	3116
15	Julius Erving	3088
16	James Worthy	3022
17	Clyde Drexler	2963
18	Sam Jones	2909
19	Charles Barkley	2833
20	Robert Parish	2820
21	Patrick Ewing	2813
22	Bill Russell	2673
23	Reggie Miller	2618
24	Byron Scott	2451
25	John Stockton	2436
26	Isiah Thomas	2261
27	Bob Pettit	2240
28	David Robinson	2221
29	Elvin Hayes	2194
30	Kobe Bryant	2155

CAREER POSTSEASON

Points Per Game
(25 Games or 625 Points)

	PLAYER	PPG
1	Michael Jordan	33.4
2	Allen Iverson	30.6
3	Jerry West	29.1
4	Shaquille O'Neal	28.1
5	Elgin Baylor	27.0
6	George Gervin	27.0
7	Karl Malone	26.3
8	Hakeem Olajuwon	25.9
9	Paul Pierce	25.6
10	Dirk Nowitzki	25.5
11	Bob Pettit	25.5
12	Dominique Wilkins	25.4
13	Rick Barry	24.8
14	Bernard King	24.5
15	Alex English	24.4
16	Kareem Abdul-Jabbar	24.3
17	Paul Arizin	24.2
18	Ray Allen	24.2
19	Tim Duncan	24.2
20	George Mikan	24.0
21	Larry Bird	23.8
22	Charles Barkley	23.0
23	David Thompson	22.9
24	Bob Love	22.9
25	Elvin Hayes	22.9
26	Reggie Miller	22.8
27	Wilt Chamberlain	22.5
28	Kobe Bryant	22.2
29	Oscar Robertson	22.2
30	Moses Malone	22.1

Field Goals Made

	PLAYER	FIELD GOALS
1	Kareem Abdul-Jabbar	2356
2	Michael Jordan	2188
3	Karl Malone	1645
4	Jerry West	1622
5	Hakeem Olajuwon	1504
6	Shaquille O'Neal	1476
7	Larry Bird	1458
8	John Havlicek	1451
9	Wilt Chamberlain	1425
10	Elgin Baylor	1388
11	Scottie Pippen	1335
12	Magic Johnson	1291
13	James Worthy	1267
14	Kevin McHale	1204
15	Julius Erving	1187
16	Dennis Johnson	1167
17	Sam Jones	1149
18	Robert Parish	1132
19	Patrick Ewing	1104
20	Clyde Drexler	1076
21	Charles Barkley	1009
22	Bill Russell	1003
23	Byron Scott	934
24	Elvin Hayes	883
25	John Stockton	855
26	Reggie Miller	834
27	Isiah Thomas	825
28	Bob Dandridge	823
29	Tom Heinsohn	818
30	Horace Grant	786

CAREER POSTSEASON

Field Goal Percentage (150 Field Goals Made)

	PLAYER	PCT
1	James Donaldson	.627
2	Kurt Rambis	.574
3	Otis Thorpe	.569
4	Artis Gilmore	.568
5	Mark West	.566
6	Kevin McHale	.561
7	Bernard King	.559
8	Shaquille O'Neal	.558
9	Dale Davis	.548
10	Darryl Dawkins	.546
11	Cedric Maxwell	.545
12	James Worthy	.544
13	Larry Nance	.541
14	Randy Wittman	.540
15	Clifford Ray	.538
16	Bobby Jones	.535
17	Kareem Abdul-Jabbar	.533
18	Bob Lanier	.532
19	Horace Grant	.530
20	Hakeem Olajuwon	.528
21	Rodney McCray	.527
22	Doug Collins	.526
23	Bill Walton	.525
24	Adrian Dantley	.525
25	Anthony Mason	.524
26	Wilt Chamberlain	.522
27	Buck Williams	.520
28	Brad Daugherty	.519
29	Danny Schayes	.518
30	Antoine Carr	.514

3-point Shots Made

	PLAYER	3-POINTS
1	Reggie Miller	275
2	Scottie Pippen	200
3	Robert Horry	191
4	Dan Majerle	181
5	John Starks	176
6	Danny Ainge	172
7	Sam Perkins	152
8	Terry Porter	151
9	Michael Jordan	148
10	Clyde Drexler	141
11	Byron Scott	134
12	Steve Smith	130
13	Bryon Russell	126
14	Mookie Blaylock	125
15	Michael Cooper	124
16	Jeff Hornacek	122
17	Derek Fisher	121
18	Kenny Smith	117
19	John Stockton	111
	Nick Van Exel	111
21	Tim Hardaway	110
22	Gary Payton	105
23	Allen Iverson	103
24	Hersey Hawkins	99
	Toni Kukoc	99
26	Kobe Bryant	97
	Mark Jackson	97
28	Anfernee Hardaway	96
	Derek Harper	96
30	Dennis Scott	95

CAREER POSTSEASON

3-point Shots Ave
(35 3-Points Made)

	PLAYER	PCT
1	Bob Hansen	.500
2	Ray Allen	.463
3	B.J. Armstrong	.451
4	Kenny Smith	.448
5	Steve Nash	.444
6	Tim Thomas	.438
7	Derek Fisher	.434
8	Jeff Hornacek	.433
9	Keith Van Horn	.432
10	Tony Delk	.427
11	Rasheed Wallace	.421
12	Allan Houston	.420
13	Eddie Jones	.419
14	Trent Tucker	.417
15	Dirk Nowitzki	.415
16	Voshon Lenard	.412
17	Chris Mullin	.409
18	David Wesley	.407
19	Reggie Miller	.399
20	Danny Ainge	.397
21	Hersey Hawkins	.396
22	Byron Scott	.395
23	Michael Finley	.394
24	Damon Stoudamire	.393
25	Jon Barry	.393
26	Bruce Bowen	.393
27	Michael Cooper	.392
28	David Benoit	.392
29	Chuck Person	.391
30	Steve Smith	.389

Free Throws Made

	PLAYER	FREE THROWS
1	Michael Jordan	1463
2	Karl Malone	1223
3	Jerry West	1213
4	Magic Johnson	1068
5	Kareem Abdul-Jabbar	1050
6	Larry Bird	901
7	John Havlicek	874
8	Shaquille O'Neal	869
9	Elgin Baylor	847
10	Scottie Pippen	772
11	Kevin McHale	766
12	Wilt Chamberlain	757
13	Dennis Johnson	756
14	Charles Barkley	751
15	Hakeem Olajuwon	743
16	Dolph Schayes	723
17	Bob Pettit	708
18	Julius Erving	707
19	David Robinson	684
20	Reggie Miller	675
21	Clyde Drexler	670
22	Bill Russell	667
23	Bob Cousy	640
24	John Stockton	615
25	Sam Jones	611
26	Patrick Ewing	597
27	Kevin Johnson	594
28	Moses Malone	576
29	Oscar Robertson	560
30	Robert Parish	556

CAREER POSTSEASON

Free Throws Ave (100 Free Throws Made)

	PLAYER	PCT
1	Mark Price	.944
2	Calvin Murphy	.932
3	Bill Sharman	.911
4	Kiki Vandeweghe	.907
5	Hersey Hawkins	.907
6	Richard Hamilton	.906
7	Peja Stojakovic	.896
8	Dirk Nowitzki	.893
9	Larry Bird	.890
10	Vince Boryla	.889
11	Reggie Miller	.888
12	Steve Nash	.886
13	Jeff Hornacek	.886
14	Allan Houston	.884
15	Ray Allen	.884
16	Bobby Wanzer	.880
17	Rick Barry	.875
18	Cazzie Russell	.870
19	Rolando Blackman	.869
20	Ricky Pierce	.866
21	Al Cervi	.866
22	Steve Mix	.864
23	Eddie Johnson	.864
24	Allen Leavell	.863
25	Michael Finley	.863
26	Alex English	.862
	Jay Vincent	.862
28	Steve Smith	.860
29	Chris Mullin	.859
30	Kelly Tripucka	.856

Rebounds (total)

	PLAYER	REBOUNDS
1	Bill Russell	4104
2	Wilt Chamberlain	3913
3	Kareem Abdul-Jabbar	2481
4	Karl Malone	1877
5	Wes Unseld	1777
6	Robert Parish	1765
7	Shaquille O'Neal	1749
8	Elgin Baylor	1724
9	Larry Bird	1683
10	Dennis Rodman	1676
11	Hakeem Olajuwon	1621
12	Scottie Pippen	1583
13	Charles Barkley	1582
14	Paul Silas	1527
15	Magic Johnson	1465
16	Horace Grant	1457
17	Charles Oakley	1445
18	Patrick Ewing	1435
19	Bill Bridges	1305
20	Bob Pettit	1304
21	David Robinson	1301
22	Moses Malone	1295
23	Dave Cowens	1285
24	Kevin McHale	1253
25	Elvin Hayes	1244
26	John Havlicek	1186
27	Dave DeBusschere	1155
28	Michael Jordan	1152
29	Nate Thurmond	1101
30	Bill Laimbeer	1097

CAREER POSTSEASON

Rebounds (offense)

	PLAYER	REBOUNDS
1	Shaquille O'Neal	631
2	Dennis Rodman	626
3	Robert Parish	571
4	Horace Grant	549
5	Charles Oakley	519
6	Charles Barkley	510
	Moses Malone	510
8	Kareem Abdul-Jabbar	505
9	Hakeem Olajuwon	471
10	Scottie Pippen	466
11	Karl Malone	465
12	Kevin McHale	456
13	A.C. Green	390
14	David Robinson	367
15	Larry Bird	360
	Julius Erving	360
17	Clyde Drexler	359
18	Buck Williams	351
19	Magic Johnson	349
20	Dale Davis	346
21	Paul Silas	339
22	Patrick Ewing	337
23	Elvin Hayes	336
24	Shawn Kemp	314
25	Wes Unseld	306
26	Michael Jordan	305
27	Robert Horry	292
28	Vlade Divac	285
29	Jerome Kersey	283
30	Caldwell Jones	267

Rebounds (defense)

	PLAYER	REBOUNDS
1	Karl Malone	1412
2	Larry Bird	1323
3	Kareem Abdul-Jabbar	1273
4	Robert Parish	1194
5	Hakeem Olajuwon	1150
6	Shaquille O'Neal	1118
7	Scottie Pippen	1117
8	Magic Johnson	1116
9	Patrick Ewing	1098
10	Charles Barkley	1072
11	Dennis Rodman	1050
12	David Robinson	934
13	Charles Oakley	926
14	Horace Grant	908
15	Michael Jordan	847
16	Bill Laimbeer	840
17	Kevin McHale	797
18	Moses Malone	785
19	Elvin Hayes	768
20	Wes Unseld	742
21	Caldwell Jones	732
22	Robert Horry	731
23	Jack Sikma	719
24	Tim Duncan	710
25	A.C. Green	694
26	Sam Perkins	681
27	Dave Cowens	674
28	Dale Davis	643
	Clyde Drexler	643
30	Julius Erving	634

CAREER POSTSEASON

Assists

	PLAYER	ASSISTS
1	Magic Johnson	2346
2	John Stockton	1839
3	Larry Bird	1062
4	Scottie Pippen	1048
5	Michael Jordan	1022
6	Dennis Johnson	1006
7	Isiah Thomas	987
8	Jerry West	970
9	Bob Cousy	937
10	Kevin Johnson	935
11	Maurice Cheeks	922
12	Mark Jackson	899
13	Clyde Drexler	891
14	John Havlicek	825
15	Bill Russell	770
16	Oscar Robertson	769
17	Kareem Abdul-Jabbar	767
18	Michael Cooper	703
19	Wilt Chamberlain	673
20	Danny Ainge	656
21	Gary Payton	624
	Terry Porter	624
23	Walt Frazier	599
24	Julius Erving	594
25	Avery Johnson	562
	Jason Kidd	562
27	Elgin Baylor	541
28	Karl Malone	538
29	Jeff Hornacek	525
30	Derek Harper	513

Steals

	PLAYER	STEALS
1	Scottie Pippen	395
2	Michael Jordan	376
3	Magic Johnson	358
4	John Stockton	338
5	Larry Bird	296
6	Maurice Cheeks	295
7	Clyde Drexler	278
8	Dennis Johnson	247
9	Hakeem Olajuwon	245
10	Julius Erving	235
11	Karl Malone	234
	Isiah Thomas	234
13	Robert Horry	226
	Byron Scott	226
15	Michael Cooper	203
16	Charles Barkley	193
17	Kareem Abdul-Jabbar	189
18	Charles Oakley	178
19	James Worthy	177
20	Gus Williams	174
21	Danny Ainge	172
22	Horace Grant	171
23	Jeff Hornacek	170
24	Jerome Kersey	168
25	Dan Majerle	164
	Gary Payton	164
27	David Robinson	151
28	Derek Harper	148
29	Robert Parish	145
30	Ron Harper	141

CAREER POSTSEASON

Blocks

	PLAYER	BLOCKS
1	Kareem Abdul-Jabbar	476
2	Hakeem Olajuwon	472
3	Shaquille O'Neal	313
4	David Robinson	312
5	Robert Parish	309
6	Patrick Ewing	303
7	Kevin McHale	281
8	Julius Erving	239
9	Dikembe Mutombo	224
10	Caldwell Jones	223
11	Elvin Hayes	222
12	Tim Duncan	221
13	Mark Eaton	210
14	Scottie Pippen	185
15	Horace Grant	173
16	Darryl Dawkins	165
	Robert Horry	165
18	Greg Ostertag	163
19	Vlade Divac	160
20	John Salley	159
21	Michael Jordan	158
22	Bobby Jones	156
23	Alonzo Mourning	155
24	Moses Malone	151
	Bob McAdoo	151
26	Larry Bird	145
27	Larry Nance	144
28	Alton Lister	142
29	Shawn Kemp	137
30	Tree Rollins	134

Turnovers

	PLAYER	TURNOVERS
1	Magic Johnson	696
2	Scottie Pippen	602
3	Michael Jordan	546
4	John Stockton	517
5	Larry Bird	506
6	Karl Malone	503
7	Dennis Johnson	480
8	Kareem Abdul-Jabbar	447
9	Hakeem Olajuwon	424
10	Shaquille O'Neal	420
11	Clyde Drexler	397
12	Julius Erving	396
13	Isiah Thomas	369
14	Robert Parish	365
15	Kevin Johnson	354
16	Charles Barkley	353
17	Patrick Ewing	345
18	Kevin McHale	326
19	Maurice Cheeks	318
20	Charles Oakley	308
21	James Worthy	298
22	Mark Jackson	290
23	David Robinson	280
24	Shawn Kemp	275
25	Byron Scott	266
26	Kobe Bryant	258
	Dennis Rodman	258
28	Danny Ainge	257
	Andrew Toney	257
30	Vlade Divac	246

Fouls

	PLAYER	FOULS
1	Kareem Abdul-Jabbar	797
2	Scottie Pippen	686
3	Dennis Rodman	630
4	Robert Parish	617
5	Karl Malone	597
6	Dennis Johnson	575
7	Kevin McHale	571
8	Hakeem Olajuwon	562
9	Bill Russell	546
10	Michael Jordan	541
11	John Stockton	539
12	Robert Horry	538
13	Danny Ainge	533
14	John Havlicek	527
15	Magic Johnson	524
16	Patrick Ewing	522
17	Horace Grant	515
18	Tom Sanders	508
19	Charles Oakley	503
20	Clyde Drexler	486
21	Michael Cooper	474
22	Paul Silas	469
23	Larry Bird	466
24	Shaquille O'Neal	462
25	Jerry West	451
26	Clifford Robinson	447
27	Byron Scott	445
28	Sam Perkins	441
29	Darryl Dawkins	438
30	Derrick McKey	436

Disqualifications

	PLAYER	DISQUALS.
1	Tom Sanders	26
2	Vern Mikkelsen	24
3	Bailey Howell	21
4	Chuck Share	17
	Jack Sikma	17
6	Darryl Dawkins	16
	Robert Parish	16
8	Dave Cowens	15
9	Vlade Divac	14
	Walter Dukes	14
	Tom Heinsohn	14
	Frank Ramsey	14
	Charlie Scott	14
14	Hal Greer	13
	Alex Hannum	13
	Bill Laimbeer	13
	Rudy LaRusso	13
	Rik Smits	13
19	Al Attles	12
	Antoine Carr	12
	Bob Dandridge	12
	Cliff Hagan	12
	Jim Krebs	12
	Dennis Rodman	12
25	Larry Costello	11
	Dugie Martin	11
	Scottie Pippen	11
28	Bill Bridges	10
	Jerome Kersey	10
	Alton Lister	10
	George Mikan	10
	Tree Rollins	10
	Dolph Schayes	10
	Lonnie Shelton	10
	Buck Williams	10

CAREER POSTSEASON

Technicals

	PLAYER	TECHS.
1	Dennis Rodman	48
2	Karl Malone	31
3	Sam Cassell	23
4	Scottie Pippen	22
	Rasheed Wallace	22
6	Vlade Divac	21
7	Charles Oakley	20
8	Shaquille O'Neal	18
	Gary Payton	18
10	Patrick Ewing	17
	Vernon Maxwell	17
12	Charles Barkley	16
	Allen Iverson	16
14	Rick Fox	15
	Robert Horry	15
	Anthony Mason	15
17	Chris Childs	14
18	Michael Jordan	12
	John Starks	12
	Chris Webber	12
21	Clyde Drexler	11
	Derek Harper	11
	Hakeem Olajuwon	11
24	Dale Davis	10
	Reggie Miller	10
	Antoine Walker	10
27	Antonio Davis	9
	Larry Johnson	9
	Greg Ostertag	9
	Clifford Robinson	9
	Kurt Thomas	9

THE STATS

SINGLE SEASON – REGULAR

SINGLE SEASON — REGULAR

Minutes played

	PLAYER/SEASON	MINUTES
1	Wilt Chamberlain (1961–62)	3882
2	Wilt Chamberlain (1967–68)	3836
3	Wilt Chamberlain (1962–63)	3806
4	Wilt Chamberlain (1960–61)	3773
5	Wilt Chamberlain (1965–66)	3737
6	John Havlicek (1971–72)	3698
7	Elvin Hayes (1968–69)	3695
8	Wilt Chamberlain (1963–64)	3689
9	Wilt Chamberlain (1966–67)	3682
10	Tiny Archibald (1972–73)	3681
11	John Havlicek (1970–71)	3678
12	Wilt Chamberlain (1968–69)	3669
13	Elvin Hayes (1969–70)	3665
14	Truck Robinson (1977–78)	3638
15	Elvin Hayes (1970–71)	3633
16	Wilt Chamberlain (1970–71)	3630
17	Jerry Lucas (1967–68)	3619
18	Elvin Hayes (1973–74)	3602
19	Kareem Abdul-Jabbar (1971–72)	3583
20	Oscar Robertson (1963–64)	3559
21	Jerry Lucas (1966–67)	3558
22	Kareem Abdul-Jabbar (1973–74)	3548
23	Wilt Chamberlain (1972–73)	3542
24	Bob McAdoo (1974–75)	3539
25	Kareem Abdul-Jabbar (1969–70)	3534
26	Latrell Sprewell (1993–94)	3533
27	Oscar Robertson (1962–63)	3521
28	Jerry Lucas (1965–66)	3517
29	Oscar Robertson (1961–62)	3503
30	Bill Russell (1962–63)	3500

Points Scored

	PLAYER/SEASON	POINTS
1	Wilt Chamberlain (1961–62)	4029
2	Wilt Chamberlain (1962–63)	3586
3	Michael Jordan (1986–87)	3041
4	Wilt Chamberlain (1960–61)	3033
5	Wilt Chamberlain (1963–64)	2948
6	Michael Jordan (1987–88)	2868
7	Bob McAdoo (1974–75)	2831
8	Kareem Abdul-Jabbar (1971–72)	2822
9	Rick Barry (1966–67)	2775
10	Michael Jordan (1989–90)	2753
11	Elgin Baylor (1962–63)	2719
	Tiny Archibald (1972–73)	2719
13	Wilt Chamberlain (1959–60)	2707
14	Wilt Chamberlain (1965–66)	2649
15	Michael Jordan (1988–89)	2633
16	Kareem Abdul-Jabbar (1970–71)	2596
17	George Gervin (1979–80)	2585
18	Michael Jordan (1990–91)	2580
19	George Gervin (1981–82)	2551
20	Michael Jordan (1992–93)	2541
21	Karl Malone (1989–90)	2540
22	Elgin Baylor (1960–61)	2538
23	Wilt Chamberlain (1964–65)	2534
24	Moses Malone (1981–82)	2520
25	Walt Bellamy (1961–62)	2495
26	Michael Jordan (1995–96)	2491
27	Oscar Robertson (1963–64)	2480
28	Jerry West (1965–66)	2476
29	Kobe Bryant (2002–03)	2461
30	Adrian Dantley (1981–82)	2457

SINGLE SEASON — REGULAR

Points Per Game
(70 Games or 1400 Points)

	PLAYER/SEASON	PPG
1	Wilt Chamberlain (1961–62)	50.4
2	Wilt Chamberlain (1962–63)	44.8
3	Wilt Chamberlain (1960–61)	38.4
4	Elgin Baylor (1961–62)	38.3
5	Wilt Chamberlain (1959–60)	37.6
6	Michael Jordan (1986–87)	37.1
7	Wilt Chamberlain (1963–64)	36.9
8	Rick Barry (1966–67)	35.6
9	Michael Jordan (1987–88)	35.0
10	Kareem Abdul-Jabbar (1971–72)	34.8
11	Elgin Baylor (1960–61)	34.8
12	Wilt Chamberlain (1964–65)	34.7
13	Bob McAdoo (1974–75)	34.5
14	Elgin Baylor (1962–63)	34.0
	Tiny Archibald (1972–73)	34.0
16	Michael Jordan (1989–90)	33.6
17	Wilt Chamberlain (1965–66)	33.5
18	George Gervin (1979–80)	33.1
19	Bernard King (1984–85)	32.9
20	Michael Jordan (1992–93)	32.6
21	Michael Jordan (1988–89)	32.5
22	George Gervin (1981–82)	32.3
23	Tracy McGrady (2002–03)	32.1
24	Kareem Abdul–Jabbar (1970–71)	31.7
25	Walt Bellamy (1961–62)	31.6
26	Michael Jordan (1990–91)	31.5
27	Oscar Robertson (1963–64)	31.4
28	Allen Iverson (2001–02)	31.4
29	Jerry West (1965–66)	31.3
30	Oscar Robertson (1965–66)	31.3

Field Goals Made

	PLAYER/SEASON	FIELD GOALS
1	Wilt Chamberlain (1961–62)	1597
2	Wilt Chamberlain (1962–63)	1463
3	Wilt Chamberlain (1960–61)	1251
4	Wilt Chamberlain (1963–64)	1204
5	Kareem Abdul-Jabbar (1971–72)	1159
6	Michael Jordan (1986–87)	1098
7	Bob McAdoo (1974–75)	1095
8	Wilt Chamberlain (1965–66)	1074
9	Michael Jordan (1987–88)	1069
10	Wilt Chamberlain (1959–60)	1065
11	Wilt Chamberlain (1964–65)	1063
	Kareem Abdul-Jabbar (1970–71)	1063
13	Michael Jordan (1989–90)	1034
14	Elgin Baylor (1962–63)	1029
15	Tiny Archibald (1972–73)	1028
	Rick Barry (1974–75)	1028
17	George Gervin (1979–80)	1024
18	Rick Barry (1966–67)	1011
19	George Gervin (1981–82)	993
20	Michael Jordan (1992–93)	992
21	Michael Jordan (1990–91)	990
22	Kareem Abdul-Jabbar (1972–73)	982
23	Walt Bellamy (1961–62)	973
24	Michael Jordan (1988–89)	966
25	Alex English (1986–87)	965
26	Alex English (1982–83)	959
27	Shaquille O'Neal (1999–00)	956
28	Shaquille O'Neal (1993–94)	953
29	Alex English (1985–86)	951
30	Elvin Hayes (1970–71)	948
	Kareem Abdul-Jabbar (1973–74)	948

SINGLE SEASON — REGULAR

Field Goal Percentage
(300 Field Goals Made)

	PLAYER/SEASON	PCT
1	Wilt Chamberlain (1972–73)	.727
2	Wilt Chamberlain (1966–67)	.683
3	Artis Gilmore (1980–81)	.670
4	Artis Gilmore (1981–82)	.652
5	Wilt Chamberlain (1971–72)	.649
6	James Donaldson (1984–85)	.637
7	Chris Gatling (1994–95)	.633
8	Steve Johnson (1985–86)	.632
9	Artis Gilmore (1983–84)	.631
10	Artis Gilmore (1982–83)	.626
11	Mark West (1989–90)	.625
12	Steve Johnson (1982–83)	.624
13	Artis Gilmore (1984–85)	.623
14	Artis Gilmore (1985–86)	.618
15	Steve Johnson (1981–82)	.613
16	Cedric Maxwell (1979–80)	.609
17	Darryl Dawkins (1980–81)	.607
18	Kevin McHale (1986–87)	.604
19	Gheorghe Muresan (1996–97)	.604
20	Buck Williams (1991–92)	.604
21	Kareem Abdul-Jabbar (1979–80)	.604
22	Kevin McHale (1987–88)	.604
23	Buck Williams (1990–91)	.602
24	Otis Thorpe (1984–85)	.600
	Tyrone Hill (1996–97)	.600
26	Charles Barkley (1989–90)	.600
27	Darryl Dawkins (1982–83)	.599
28	Kareem Abdul-Jabbar (1984–85)	.599
29	Shaquille O'Neal (1993–94)	.599
30	Robert Parish (1990–91)	.598

3-point
Shots Made

	PLAYER/SEASON	3-POINTS
1	Dennis Scott (1995–96)	267
2	George McCloud (1995–96)	257
3	Mookie Blaylock (1995–96)	231
4	Reggie Miller (1996–97)	229
	Ray Allen (2001–02)	229
6	Mitch Richmond (1995–96)	225
7	Antoine Walker (2001–02)	222
8	Mookie Blaylock (1996–97)	221
	Antoine Walker (2000–01)	221
10	John Starks (1994–95)	217
11	Paul Pierce (2001–02)	210
12	Glen Rice (1996–97)	207
13	Mitch Richmond (1996–97)	204
14	Tim Hardaway (1996–97)	203
15	Ray Allen (2000–01)	202
16	Ray Allen (2002–03)	201
17	Mookie Blaylock (1994–95)	199
	Dan Majerle (1994–95)	199
19	Dana Barros (1994–95)	197
20	Reggie Miller (1994–95)	195
21	Dan Majerle (1993–94)	192
	Dale Ellis (1996–97)	192
	Wesley Person (1997–98)	192
24	Allan Houston (1995–96)	191
25	Chuck Person (1995–96)	190
26	Tim Hardaway (2000–01)	189
27	Antoine Walker (2002–03)	188
28	Glen Rice (1994–95)	185
29	Nick Van Exel (1994–95)	183
	Voshon Lenard (1996–97)	183

SINGLE SEASON — REGULAR

3-point Shooting Percentage
(55 3-Points Made)

Free Throws
Made

	PLAYER/SEASON	PCT		PLAYER/SEASON	FREE THROWS
1	Steve Kerr (1994–95)	.524	1	Jerry West (1965–66)	840
2	Tim Legler (1995–96)	.522	2	Wilt Chamberlain (1961–62)	835
3	Steve Kerr (1995–96)	.515	3	Michael Jordan (1986–87)	833
4	Detlef Schrempf (1994–95)	.514	4	Adrian Dantley (1983–84)	813
5	Steve Kerr (1989–90)	.507	5	Oscar Robertson (1963–64)	800
6	Craig Hodges (1987–88)	.491	6	Rick Barry (1966–67)	753
7	Hubert Davis (1999–00)	.491	7	Oscar Robertson (1965–66)	742
8	Mark Price (1987–88)	.486	8	Moses Malone (1984–85)	737
9	Craig Hodges (1989–90)	.481	9	Oscar Robertson (1966–67)	736
10	Jeff Hornacek (1999–00)	.478	10	Michael Jordan (1987–88)	723
11	Dale Ellis (1988–89)	.478	11	Charles Barkley (1987–88)	714
12	Brent Barry (2000–01)	.476	12	Jerry West (1961–62)	712
13	Dell Curry (1998–99)	.476	13	Karl Malone (1988–89)	703
14	Hubert Davis (1995–96)	.476	14	Oscar Robertson (1961–62)	700
15	B.J. Armstrong (1995–96)	.473	15	Karl Malone (1989–90)	696
16	Steve Smith (2001–02)	.472	16	Bob Pettit (1961–62)	695
17	Glen Rice (1996–97)	.470	17	David Robinson (1993–94)	693
18	Jon Barry (2001–02)	.469	18	Bob Pettit (1962–63)	685
19	Eric Piatkowski (2001–02)	.466	19	Karl Malone (1990–91)	684
20	Jeff Hornacek (1995–96)	.466	20	Dolph Schayes (1960–61)	680
21	Chris Mullin (1998–99)	.465	21	Tiny Archibald (1971–72)	677
22	Steve Kerr (1996–97)	.464	22	Elgin Baylor (1960–61)	676
23	Dana Barros (1994–95)	.464	23	Michael Jordan (1988–89)	674
24	Dale Ellis (1997–98)	.464	24	Karl Malone (1991–92)	673
25	John Stockton (2000–01)	.462	25	Bob Pettit (1958–59)	667
26	Brent Price (1995–96)	.462	26	Jerry Stackhouse (2000–01)	666
27	Jim Les (1990–91)	.461	27	Oscar Robertson (1964–65)	665
28	Shammond Williams (2000–01)	.459	28	Tiny Archibald (1972–73)	663
29	Hubert Davis (2000–01)	.456	29	Elgin Baylor (1962–63)	661
30	Wally Szczerbiak (2001–02)	.455	30	Wilt Chamberlain (1962–63)	660

SINGLE SEASON — REGULAR

Free Throw Percentage
(125 Free Throw Made)

	PLAYER/SEASON	PCT
1	Calvin Murphy (1980–81)	.958
2	Mahmoud Abdul-Rauf (1993–94)	.956
3	Jeff Hornacek (1999–00)	.950
4	Mark Price (1992–93)	.948
5	Mark Price (1991–92)	.947
6	Rick Barry (1978–79)	.947
7	Ernie DiGregorio (1976–77)	.945
8	Chris Mullin (1997–98)	.939
9	Mahmoud Abdul-Rauf (1992–93)	.935
10	Ricky Sobers (1980–81)	.935
11	Rick Barry (1979–80)	.935
12	Spud Webb (1994–95)	.934
13	Bill Sharman (1958–59)	.932
14	Larry Bird (1989–90)	.930
15	Mahmoud Abdul-Rauf (1995–96)	.930
16	Calvin Murphy (1978–79)	.928
17	Reggie Miller (2000–01)	.928
18	Larry Bird (1991–92)	.926
19	Rick Barry (1977–78)	.924
20	Rick Barry (1975–76)	.923
21	Jack Sikma (1987–88)	.922
22	Bill Sharman (1960–61)	.921
23	Calvin Murphy (1982–83)	.920
24	Allan Houston (2002–03)	.919
25	Reggie Miller (1999–00)	.919
26	Reggie Miller (1990–91)	.918
27	Calvin Murphy (1977–78)	.918
28	Eddie Johnson (1989–90)	.917
29	Jeff Malone (1990–91)	.917
30	Ricky Pierce (1991–92)	.916

Rebounds
(total)

	PLAYER/SEASON	REBOUNDS
1	Wilt Chamberlain (1960–61)	2149
2	Wilt Chamberlain (1961–62)	2052
3	Wilt Chamberlain (1966–67)	1957
4	Wilt Chamberlain (1967–68)	1952
5	Wilt Chamberlain (1962–63)	1946
6	Wilt Chamberlain (1965–66)	1943
7	Wilt Chamberlain (1959–60)	1941
8	Bill Russell (1963–64)	1930
9	Bill Russell (1964–65)	1878
10	Bill Russell (1960–61)	1868
11	Bill Russell (1962–63)	1843
12	Bill Russell (1961–62)	1790
13	Wilt Chamberlain (1963–64)	1787
14	Bill Russell (1965–66)	1779
15	Bill Russell (1959–60)	1778
16	Wilt Chamberlain (1968–69)	1712
17	Bill Russell (1966–67)	1700
18	Wilt Chamberlain (1964–65)	1673
19	Jerry Lucas (1965–66)	1668
20	Bill Russell (1958–59)	1612
21	Wilt Chamberlain (1971–72)	1572
22	Bill Russell (1957–58)	1564
23	Jerry Lucas (1967–68)	1560
24	Jerry Lucas (1966–67)	1547
25	Bob Pettit (1960–61)	1540
26	Dennis Rodman (1991–92)	1530
27	Wilt Chamberlain (1972–73)	1526
28	Walt Bellamy (1961–62)	1500
29	Wilt Chamberlain (1970–71)	1493
30	Wes Unseld (1968–69)	1491

Rebounds (offense)

	PLAYER/SEASON	REBOUNDS
1	Moses Malone (1978–79)	587
2	Moses Malone (1979–80)	573
3	Moses Malone (1981–82)	558
4	Dennis Rodman (1991–92)	523
5	Moses Malone (1980–81)	474
6	Dennis Rodman (1993–94)	453
7	Moses Malone (1982–83)	445
8	Jayson Williams (1997–98)	443
9	Hakeem Olajuwon (1984–85)	440
10	Moses Malone (1976–77)	437
11	Larry Smith (1980–81)	433
12	Dennis Rodman (1997–98)	421
13	Kevin Willis (1991–92)	418
14	Larry Smith (1984–85)	405
15	Charles Barkley (1988–89)	403
16	Elton Brand (2001–02)	396
17	Charles Barkley (1986–87)	390
18	Moses Malone (1988–89)	386
19	Moses Malone (1984–85)	385
	Charles Barkley (1987–88)	385
21	Larry Smith (1985–86)	384
	Shaquille O'Neal (1993–94)	384
23	Moses Malone (1977–78)	380
24	Moses Malone (1987–88)	372
25	Michael Cage (1987–88)	371
26	Dennis Rodman (1992–93)	367
27	Larry Smith (1986–87)	366
28	Paul Silas (1975–76)	365
	Buck Williams (1982–83)	365
30	Moses Malone (1989–90)	364

Rebounds (defense)

	PLAYER/SEASON	REBOUNDS
1	Kareem Abdul-Jabbar (1975–76)	1111
2	Elvin Hayes (1973–74)	1109
3	Dennis Rodman (1991–92)	1007
4	Dave Cowens (1973–74)	993
5	Truck Robinson (1977–78)	990
6	Sam Lacey (1974–75)	921
7	Dennis Rodman (1993–94)	914
8	Dave Cowens (1975–76)	911
9	Kareem Abdul-Jabbar (1973–74)	891
10	Swen Nater (1979–80)	864
11	Kevin Garnett (2002–03)	858
12	Moses Malone (1978–79)	857
13	Dikembe Mutombo (1999–00)	853
14	Hakeem Olajuwon (1989–90)	850
15	Bob McAdoo (1974–75)	848
16	Kevin Willis (1991–92)	840
17	Bob McAdoo (1973–74)	836
18	Ben Wallace (2002–03)	833
19	Dave Cowens (1977–78)	830
20	Kareem Abdul-Jabbar (1976–77)	824
21	Kareem Abdul-Jabbar (1978–79)	818
22	Jack Sikma (1981–82)	815
23	Sam Lacey (1975–76)	806
24	Bob Lanier (1973–74)	805
25	Patrick Ewing (1992–93)	789
26	Hakeem Olajuwon (1992–93)	785
27	Tim Duncan (2002–03)	784
28	Elvin Hayes (1974–75)	783
29	Jack Sikma (1978–79)	781
30	Shaquille O'Neal (1992–93)	780
	Dennis Rodman (1997–98)	780

SINGLE SEASON — REGULAR

Assists

	PLAYER/SEASON	ASSISTS
1	John Stockton (1990–91)	1164
2	John Stockton (1989–90)	1134
3	John Stockton (1987–88)	1128
4	John Stockton (1991–92)	1126
5	Isiah Thomas (1984–85)	1123
6	John Stockton (1988–89)	1118
7	Kevin Porter (1978–79)	1099
8	John Stockton (1993–94)	1031
9	John Stockton (1994–95)	1011
10	Kevin Johnson (1988–89)	991
11	Magic Johnson (1990–91)	989
12	Magic Johnson (1988–89)	988
13	John Stockton (1992–93)	987
14	Magic Johnson (1986–87)	977
15	Magic Johnson (1984–85)	968
16	Mark Jackson (1996–97)	935
17	John Stockton (1995–96)	916
18	Norm Nixon (1983–84)	914
	Isiah Thomas (1983–84)	914
20	Tiny Archibald (1972–73)	910
21	Guy Rodgers (1966–67)	908
22	Magic Johnson (1985–86)	907
	Magic Johnson (1989–90)	907
24	Oscar Robertson (1961–62)	899
25	Andre Miller (2001–02)	882
26	Magic Johnson (1983–84)	875
27	Oscar Robertson (1963–64)	868
	Mark Jackson (1987–88)	868
29	Muggsy Bogues (1989–90)	867
30	Oscar Robertson (1964–65)	861

Steals

	PLAYER/SEASON	STEALS
1	Alvin Robertson (1985–86)	301
2	Don Buse (1976–77)	281
3	Micheal Ray Richardson (1979–80)	265
4	John Stockton (1988–89)	263
5	Slick Watts (1975–76)	261
6	Alvin Robertson (1986–87)	260
7	Michael Jordan (1987–88)	259
8	Alvin Robertson (1990–91)	246
9	John Stockton (1991–92)	244
10	Micheal Ray Richardson (1984–85)	243
	Alvin Robertson (1987–88)	243
12	John Stockton (1987–88)	242
13	Michael Jordan (1986–87)	236
14	Michael Jordan (1988–89)	234
	John Stockton (1990–91)	234
16	Micheal Williams (1991–92)	233
17	Micheal Ray Richardson (1980–81)	232
	Scottie Pippen (1994–95)	232
19	Gary Payton (1995–96)	231
20	Johnny Moore (1984–85)	229
21	Rick Barry (1974–75)	228
22	Michael Jordan (1989–90)	227
23	Ron Lee (1977–78)	225
	Allen Iverson (2002–03)	225
25	Eddie Jordan (1979–80)	223
	Fat Lever (1987–88)	223
	Michael Jordan (1990–91)	223
28	Michael Jordan (1992–93)	221
29	Rickey Green (1982–83)	220
30	Larry Steele (1973–74)	217

SINGLE SEASON — REGULAR

Blocks

	PLAYER/SEASON	BLOCKS
1	Mark Eaton (1984–85)	456
2	Manute Bol (1985–86)	397
3	Elmore Smith (1973–74)	393
4	Hakeem Olajuwon (1989–90)	376
5	Mark Eaton (1985–86)	369
6	Mark Eaton (1983–84)	351
7	Manute Bol (1988–89)	345
8	Tree Rollins (1982–83)	343
9	Hakeem Olajuwon (1992–93)	342
10	Kareem Abdul-Jabbar (1975–76)	338
11	Dikembe Mutombo (1993–94)	336
12	Dikembe Mutombo (1995–96)	332
13	Patrick Ewing (1989–90)	327
14	Mark Eaton (1986–87)	321
	Dikembe Mutombo (1994–95)	321
16	David Robinson (1990–91)	320
17	David Robinson (1989–90)	319
18	Kareem Abdul-Jabbar (1978–79)	316
19	Mark Eaton (1988–89)	315
20	David Robinson (1991–92)	305
21	Mark Eaton (1987–88)	304
	Hakeem Olajuwon (1991–92)	304
23	Manute Bol (1986–87)	302
24	Hakeem Olajuwon (1993–94)	297
25	Alonzo Mourning (1999–00)	294
26	Shawn Bradley (1995–96)	288
27	Dikembe Mutombo (1992–93)	287
28	Shaquille O'Neal (1992–93)	286
29	Kareem Abdul–Jabbar (1973–74)	283
30	Hakeem Olajuwon (1988–89)	282

Turnovers

	PLAYER/SEASON	TURNOVERS
1	Artis Gilmore (1977–78)	366
2	Kevin Porter (1977–78)	360
3	Micheal Ray Richardson (1979–80)	359
4	Ricky Sobers (1977–78)	352
5	Charles Barkley (1985–86)	350
6	Reggie Theus (1979–80)	348
7	Bob McAdoo (1977–78)	346
	George McGinnis (1978–79)	346
9	Ron Harper (1986–87)	345
10	Isiah Thomas (1986–87)	343
11	Jeff Ruland (1983–84)	342
12	Kevin Porter (1978–79)	337
	Allen Iverson (1996–97)	337
14	Ray Williams (1982–83)	335
15	Jim Jackson (1993–94)	334
16	Jason Kidd (1995–96)	328
17	Reggie Theus (1985–86)	327
18	Moses Malone (1978–79)	326
	Isiah Thomas (1982–83)	326
	Ralph Sampson (1984–85)	326
	Jerry Stackhouse (2000–01)	326
22	Karl Malone (1987–88)	325
23	Phil Ford (1978–79)	323
	Bernard King (1978–79)	323
25	Eric Money (1977–78)	322
	Charles Barkley (1986–87)	322
	Kevin Johnson (1988–89)	322
	Isiah Thomas (1989–90)	322
	Latrell Sprewell (1996–97)	322
30	Reggie Theus (1982–83)	321

SINGLE SEASON — REGULAR

Fouls

	PLAYER/SEASON	FOULS
1	Darryl Dawkins (1983–84)	386
2	Darryl Dawkins (1982–83)	379
3	Steve Johnson (1981–82)	372
4	Shawn Kemp (1999–00)	371
5	Bill Robinzine (1978–79)	367
6	Bill Bridges (1967–68)	366
7	Lonnie Shelton (1976–77)	363
	James Edwards (1978–79)	363
9	Kevin Kunnert (1976–77)	361
10	Dan Roundfield (1978–79)	358
	Rick Mahorn (1983–84)	358
12	Charlie Scott (1975–76)	356
13	Darnell Hillman (1976–77)	353
14	Dave Cowens (1970–71)	350
	Lonnie Shelton (1977–78)	350
16	Rick Mahorn (1981–82)	349
17	James Edwards (1981–82)	347
18	Bailey Howell (1964–65)	345
19	Zelmo Beaty (1965–66)	344
	Joe Strawder (1966–67)	344
	John Tresvant (1967–68)	344
	Don Adams (1970–71)	344
	Hakeem Olajuwon (1984–85)	344
	Kurt Thomas (2002–03)	344
25	Willis Reed (1967–68)	343
	Norm Van Lier (1970–71)	343
27	Ben Poquette (1980–81)	342
28	Tom Chambers (1981–82)	341
	Kurt Thomas (2001–02)	341
30	Steve Johnson (1986–87)	340

Disqualifications

	PLAYER/SEASON	DISQUALS.
1	Monk Meineke (1952–53)	26
2	Steve Johnson (1981–82)	25
3	Darryl Dawkins (1982–83)	23
4	Walter Dukes (1958–59)	22
	Darryl Dawkins (1983–84)	22
6	Joe Meriweather (1976–77)	21
7	Joe Fulks (1952–53)	20
	Vern Mikkelsen (1957–58)	20
	Walter Dukes (1959–60)	20
	Walter Dukes (1961–62)	20
	George Johnson (1977–78)	20
12	Cal Christensen (1950–51)	19
	Tom Sanders (1965–66)	19
	Joe Strawder (1966–67)	19
	Bill Robinzine (1975–76)	19
	John Drew (1978–79)	19
	Tree Rollins (1978–79)	19
18	Paul Arizin (1950–51)	18
	Don Boven (1951–52)	18
	Joe Graboski (1952–53)	18
	Alex Hannum (1952–53)	18
	Bob Lavoy (1952–53)	18
	Vern Mikkelsen (1956–57)	18
	Paul Arizin (1961–62)	18
	Joe Strawder (1967–68)	18
	John Tresvant (1967–68)	18
	Norm Van Lier (1969–70)	18
	John Brown (1977–78)	18
	Ben Poquette (1980–81)	18
	Alton Lister (1982–83)	18
	Shawn Bradley (1994–95)	18

SINGLE SEASON — REGULAR

Technicals (since 1992–93)

	PLAYER/SEASON	TECHS.
1	Rasheed Wallace (2000–01)	40
2	Rasheed Wallace (1999–00)	38
3	Dennis Rodman (1993–94)	33
4	Charles Barkley (1992–93)	32
	Charles Barkley (1994–95)	32
6	Charles Barkley (1995–96)	29
	Dennis Rodman (1995–96)	29
8	Karl Malone (1997–98)	27
	Rasheed Wallace (2001–02)	27
10	Charles Barkley (1993–94)	26
	Gary Payton (1993–94)	26
	Gary Payton (1995–96)	26
	Charles Barkley (1997–98)	26
14	Anthony Mason (1996–97)	25
	Dennis Rodman (1996–97)	25
16	Gary Payton (1994–95)	23
	Steve Francis (2000–01)	23
	Antoine Walker (2002–03)	23
19	Charles Barkley (1991–92)	22
	Anthony Mason (1993–94)	22
	Dennis Rodman (1994–95)	22
	Anthony Mason (1995–96)	22
	Charles Barkley (1996–97)	22
24	Karl Malone (1992–93)	21
	Anthony Mason (1992–93)	21
	Karl Malone (1995–96)	21
	Rasheed Wallace (1995–96)	21
	Gary Payton (1998–99)	21
	Karl Malone (2000–01)	21
	Steve Francis (2002–03)	21

THE STATS

SINGLE SEASON – POST

SINGLE SEASON — POST

Minutes played

	PLAYER/SEASON	MINUTES
1	Dan Majerle (1993)	1071
2	Patrick Ewing (1994)	1032
3	Charles Barkley (1993)	1026
4	Tim Duncan (2003)	1021
5	Allen Iverson (2001)	1016
6	Larry Bird (1987)	1015
7	Shaquille O'Neal (2000)	1000
8	Charles Oakley (1994)	992
9	Hakeem Olajuwon (1994)	989
10	Dikembe Mutombo (2001)	981
11	Magic Johnson (1988)	965
12	Dennis Johnson (1987)	964
	Jalen Rose (2000)	964
14	Larry Bird (1984)	961
15	Moses Malone (1981)	955
16	Hakeem Olajuwon (1995)	929
17	Michael Jordan (1992)	920
18	Kevin Johnson (1993)	914
19	Isiah Thomas (1988)	911
	Gary Payton (1996)	911
21	Marvin Webster (1978)	904
22	Scottie Pippen (1992)	899
23	Byron Scott (1988)	897
24	James Worthy (1988)	896
25	Reggie Miller (2000)	892
	Aaron McKie (2001)	892
27	Vernon Maxwell (1994)	880
28	Michael Jordan (1998)	872
29	Terry Porter (1992)	870
30	Bill Russell (1968)	869
	Robert Parish (1984)	869
	Horace Grant (1995)	869

Points Scored

	PLAYER/SEASON	POINTS
1	Michael Jordan (1992)	759
2	Hakeem Olajuwon (1995)	725
3	Allen Iverson (2001)	723
4	Shaquille O'Neal (2000)	707
5	Michael Jordan (1998)	680
6	Michael Jordan (1993)	666
7	Hakeem Olajuwon (1994)	664
8	Charles Barkley (1993)	638
9	Larry Bird (1984)	632
10	Larry Bird (1987)	622
11	Tim Duncan (2003)	593
12	Michael Jordan (1989)	591
13	Michael Jordan (1997)	590
14	Michael Jordan (1990)	587
15	Jerry West (1970)	562
	Moses Malone (1981)	562
17	Jerry West (1969)	556
18	Clyde Drexler (1992)	553
19	Michael Jordan (1996)	552
20	Patrick Ewing (1994)	547
21	Shaquille O'Neal (2002)	541
22	Shaquille O'Neal (1995)	539
23	Hakeem Olajuwon (1986)	537
24	Michael Jordan (1991)	529
25	Reggie Miller (2000)	527
26	Karl Malone (1998)	526
27	Rick Barry (1967)	521
28	Larry Bird (1985)	520
29	Karl Malone (1997)	519
30	Julius Erving (1977)	518

SINGLE SEASON — POST

Points Per Game
(8 Games or 200 Points)

	PLAYER/SEASON	PPG
1	Jerry West (1965)	40.6
2	Elgin Baylor (1962)	38.6
3	Elgin Baylor (1961)	38.1
4	Bob McAdoo (1975)	37.4
5	Michael Jordan (1990)	36.7
6	Michael Jordan (1988)	36.3
7	Kareem Abdul–Jabbar (1970)	35.2
8	Michael Jordan (1993)	35.1
9	Wilt Chamberlain (1962)	35.0
10	Michael Jordan (1989)	34.8
11	Bernard King (1984)	34.8
12	Rick Barry (1967)	34.7
13	Wilt Chamberlain (1964)	34.7
14	Kareem Abdul-Jabbar (1977)	34.6
15	Michael Jordan (1992)	34.5
16	Jerry West (1966)	34.2
17	Elgin Baylor (1960)	33.4
18	Wilt Chamberlain (1960)	33.2
19	Hakeem Olajuwon (1995)	33.0
20	Allen Iverson (2001)	32.9
21	Elgin Baylor (1963)	32.6
22	Michael Jordan (1998)	32.4
23	Kareem Abdul-Jabbar (1974)	32.2
24	Adrian Dantley (1984)	32.2
25	Kobe Bryant (2003)	32.1
26	Kareem Abdul-Jabbar (1980)	31.9
27	Bob Pettit (1963)	31.8
28	Oscar Robertson (1963)	31.8
29	Tracy McGrady (2003)	31.7
30	Allen Iverson (2003)	31.7

Field Goals
Made

	PLAYER/SEASON	FIELD GOALS
1	Hakeem Olajuwon (1995)	306
2	Michael Jordan (1992)	290
3	Shaquille O'Neal (2000)	286
4	Hakeem Olajuwon (1994)	267
5	Allen Iverson (2001)	257
6	Michael Jordan (1993)	251
7	Michael Jordan (1998)	243
8	Charles Barkley (1993)	230
9	Larry Bird (1984)	229
10	Michael Jordan (1997)	227
11	Kareem Abdul-Jabbar (1974)	224
12	Michael Jordan (1990)	219
13	Tim Duncan (2003)	218
14	Larry Bird (1987)	216
15	Patrick Ewing (1994)	210
16	Moses Malone (1981)	207
17	Kareem Abdul-Jabbar (1984)	206
18	Hakeem Olajuwon (1986)	205
19	Julius Erving (1977)	204
	James Worthy (1988)	204
21	Shaquille O'Neal (2002)	203
22	John Havlicek (1974)	199
	Michael Jordan (1989)	199
24	Kareem Abdul-Jabbar (1980)	198
	Clyde Drexler (1992)	198
	Karl Malone (1998)	198
27	Rick Barry (1967)	197
	Michael Jordan (1991)	197
29	Jerry West (1969)	196
	Jerry West (1970)	196
	Larry Bird (1985)	196

SINGLE SEASON — POST

Field Goal Percentage
(300 Field Goals Made)

	PLAYER/SEASON	PCT
1	James Donaldson (1986)	.750
2	Vlade Divac (1990)	.727
3	Antoine Carr (1987)	.696
4	David Robinson (1991)	.686
5	James Donaldson (1988)	.654
6	Kurt Rambis (1984)	.652
7	Dale Davis (1998)	.651
8	Horace Grant (1996)	.649
9	Wes Matthews (1986)	.648
10	Alton Lister (1986)	.641
11	Mark West (1989)	.640
12	Otis Thorpe (1993)	.635
13	Cedric Maxwell (1980)	.634
14	Bob Lanier (1977)	.630
15	Brian Winters (1976)	.629
16	Dikembe Mutombo (1997)	.628
17	Danny Schayes (1988)	.625
18	James Worthy (1985)	.622
19	Alex English (1978)	.615
20	Hakeem Olajuwon (1987)	.615
21	Shaquille O'Neal (1998)	.612
22	Kevin McHale (1990)	.609
23	Mychal Thompson (1981)	.608
	Anthony Mason (1995)	.608
25	Clifford Ray (1976)	.608
26	Kareem Abdul-Jabbar (1977)	.607
27	John Mengelt (1976)	.607
28	Shaquille O'Neal (1996)	.606
29	Avery Johnson (1998)	.604
30	Ed Pinckney (1992)	.603

3-Point
Field Goals Made

	PLAYER/SEASON	3-POINTS
1	Reggie Miller (2000)	58
2	Ray Allen (2001)	57
3	Dennis Scott (1995)	56
4	Dan Majerle (1993)	54
	Reggie Miller (1995)	54
6	Allen Iverson (2001)	48
7	John Starks (1994)	47
	Michael Finley (2003)	47
9	Kenny Smith (1995)	46
10	Vernon Maxwell (1994)	45
11	Robert Horry (1995)	44
	Nick Van Exel (2003)	44
13	Matt Maloney (1997)	43
14	Tim Hardaway (1997)	42
	Antoine Walker (2002)	42
16	Nick Anderson (1995)	41
	Gary Payton (1996)	41
18	Terry Porter (1990)	40
	Anfernee Hardaway (1995)	40
20	Scottie Pippen (1997)	39
21	Clyde Drexler (1997)	38
	Reggie Miller (1998)	38
	Stephen Jackson (2003)	38
24	Terry Porter (1992)	37
	Keith Van Horn (2002)	37
	Steve Nash (2003)	37
27	Voshon Lenard (1997)	36
	Bryon Russell (1997)	36
29	Craig Hodges (1989)	35
	Reggie Miller (1994)	35
	Derek Fisher (2001)	35
	Bruce Bowen (2003)	35

SINGLE SEASON — POST

3-Point Field Goal Percentage
(10 3-Points Made)

	PLAYER/SEASON	PCT
1	Brad Davis (1986)	.667
2	John Paxson (1993)	.625
3	Derek Fisher (2003)	.617
4	Vinny Del Negro (1996)	.593
5	Dana Barros (1992)	.588
6	Jeff Hornacek (1996)	.586
7	Derek Harper (1995)	.574
8	George McCloud (1998)	.571
	Dirk Nowitzki (2002)	.571
	Tim Thomas (2003)	.571
11	Detlef Schrempf (1995)	.556
12	Detlef Schrempf (1997)	.552
13	Chuck Person (1991)	.548
14	Steve Smith (2000)	.547
15	Hersey Hawkins (1991)	.538
16	Matt Bullard (1993)	.536
17	Chuck Person (1996)	.532
18	Bob Hansen (1988)	.528
19	Byron Scott (1991)	.526
	Reggie Miller (1993)	.526
	Hubert Davis (1996)	.526
	Eddie Jones (1996)	.526
	Joe Dumars (1999)	.526
24	Sam Cassell (2003)	.524
25	Derek Fisher (2001)	.515
26	B.J. Armstrong (1993)	.512
27	Kenny Smith (1993)	.500
	Jeff Turner (1995)	.500
	David Benoit (1996)	.500
	Allan Houston (1997)	.500
	Steve Smith (1998)	.500
	Allan Houston (2000)	.500
	Pat Garrity (2001)	.500

Free Throws
Made

	PLAYER/SEASON	FREE THROWS
1	Michael Jordan (1989)	183
2	Michael Jordan (1998)	181
3	Larry Bird (1987)	176
4	Jerry West (1970)	170
5	Karl Malone (1992)	169
6	Charles Barkley (1993)	168
7	Larry Bird (1984)	167
8	Jerry West (1969)	164
9	Michael Jordan (1992)	162
10	Allen Iverson (2001)	161
11	Magic Johnson (1991)	157
	Tim Duncan (2003)	157
13	Michael Jordan (1996)	153
14	Shaquille O'Neal (1995)	149
15	Moses Malone (1981)	148
16	Karl Malone (1997)	144
17	Adrian Dantley (1988)	140
18	Terry Porter (1990)	139
19	Clyde Drexler (1992)	138
20	Jerry West (1965)	137
21	Michael Jordan (1993)	136
22	Shaquille O'Neal (2000)	135
	Shaquille O'Neal (2002)	135
24	George Mikan (1950)	134
25	Oscar Robertson (1963)	133
	Michael Jordan (1990)	133
27	Jerry West (1968)	132
	Magic Johnson (1988)	132
29	Elgin Baylor (1962)	130
	Karl Malone (1998)	130

SINGLE SEASON — POST

Free Throw Percentage
(20 Free Throws Made)

	PLAYER/SEASON	PCT
1	Kiki Vandeweghe (1986)	1.000
	Mark Price (1990)	1.000
	Allan Houston (2001)	1.000
	John Stockton (2003)	1.000
5	Jack Sikma (1987)	.980
6	Steve Nash (2002)	.971
7	Mark Price (1995)	.970
8	Moses Malone (1984)	.969
9	Peja Stojakovic (2001)	.968
10	Calvin Murphy (1981)	.967
	Ron Anderson (1990)	.967
	Steve Smith (2002)	.967
13	Bill Sharman (1959)	.966
14	Glen Rice (1999)	.966
15	Kiki Vandeweghe (1984)	.964
	Howard Eisley (1997)	.964
17	Mike Gminski (1986)	.963
	Sidney Moncrief (1988)	.963
19	Dan Majerle (1992)	.962
20	Willis Reed (1967)	.960
	Ray Williams (1985)	.960
	Mark Price (1988)	.960
	John Battle (1991)	.960
24	Bobby Wanzer (1952)	.959
25	Bob Cousy (1955)	.958
	Mitch Richmond (1991)	.958
	Mark Price (1993)	.958
	Eddie Johnson (1997)	.958
29	Al Cervi (1952)	.957
	Jim Krebs (1959)	.957

Rebounds
(total)

	PLAYER/SEASON	REBOUNDS
1	Wilt Chamberlain (1969)	444
2	Wilt Chamberlain (1967)	437
3	Bill Russell (1968)	434
4	Bill Russell (1966)	428
5	Wilt Chamberlain (1970)	399
6	Wilt Chamberlain (1973)	383
7	Bill Russell (1962)	370
8	Bill Russell (1969)	369
	Tim Duncan (2003)	369
10	Shaquille O'Neal (2000)	355
11	Nate Thurmond (1967)	346
12	Wes Unseld (1971)	339
13	Bill Russell (1960)	336
14	Bill Russell (1963)	326
	Charles Barkley (1993)	326
16	Wilt Chamberlain (1968)	321
17	Wilt Chamberlain (1962)	319
18	Dikembe Mutombo (2001)	316
19	Wilt Chamberlain (1972)	315
20	Bill Russell (1959)	305
	Moses Malone (1981)	305
22	Wilt Chamberlain (1964)	302
	Bill Russell (1965)	302
24	Bill Russell (1961)	299
	Wilt Chamberlain (1965)	299
26	Dave Cowens (1976)	296
27	Patrick Ewing (1994)	293
28	Charles Oakley (1994)	292
29	Marvin Webster (1978)	289
30	Bill Walton (1977)	288

SINGLE SEASON — POST

Rebounds (offensive)

	PLAYER/SEASON	REBOUNDS
1	Moses Malone (1981)	125
2	Shaquille O'Neal (2000)	119
3	Charles Oakley (1994)	116
4	Dikembe Mutombo (2001)	113
5	Elvin Hayes (1978)	103
6	Hakeem Olajuwon (1986)	101
7	Dennis Rodman (1998)	99
8	Dennis Rodman (1996)	98
9	Tim Duncan (2003)	96
10	Marvin Webster (1978)	95
	Shaquille O'Neal (1995)	95
12	Elvin Hayes (1979)	94
13	Charles Barkley (1993)	93
14	Shaquille O'Neal (2001)	91
15	Wes Unseld (1979)	90
16	Roy Tarpley (1988)	88
	Patrick Ewing (1994)	88
18	Dave Cowens (1976)	87
19	Ben Wallace (2003)	86
20	Moses Malone (1977)	84
21	Dale Davis (2000)	83
22	Shawn Kemp (1993)	80
23	Paul Silas (1976)	78
24	Robert Parish (1984)	76
	Horace Grant (1992)	76
26	Kevin McHale (1985)	74
	Horace Grant (1995)	74
28	Paul Silas (1978)	73
	Horace Grant (1990)	73
30	Wes Unseld (1978)	72

Rebounds (defensive)

	PLAYER/SEASON	REBOUNDS
1	Tim Duncan (2003)	273
2	Shaquille O'Neal (2000)	236
3	Charles Barkley (1993)	233
4	Bill Walton (1977)	232
5	Wes Unseld (1975)	211
6	Dave Cowens (1976)	209
7	Patrick Ewing (1994)	205
8	Dikembe Mutombo (2001)	203
9	Hakeem Olajuwon (1994)	199
10	Marvin Webster (1978)	194
11	Ben Wallace (2003)	191
12	Larry Bird (1984)	190
	Larry Bird (1987)	190
14	Larry Bird (1981)	189
15	Kareem Abdul-Jabbar (1974)	186
16	Hakeem Olajuwon (1995)	183
17	Dirk Nowitzki (2003)	181
18	Dave Cowens (1974)	180
	Moses Malone (1981)	180
	Dale Davis (2000)	180
21	Bill Laimbeer (1988)	178
22	Elvin Hayes (1978)	176
	Charles Oakley (1994)	176
24	Elvin Hayes (1979)	172
	Robert Parish (1984)	172
	Shaquille O'Neal (2002)	172
27	Bill Laimbeer (1990)	170
	Karl Malone (1998)	170
29	Paul Silas (1976)	168
	Karl Malone (1997)	168

SINGLE SEASON — POST

Assists

	PLAYER/SEASON	ASSISTS
1	Magic Johnson (1988)	303
2	Magic Johnson (1985)	289
3	Magic Johnson (1984)	284
4	Magic Johnson (1991)	240
5	Magic Johnson (1987)	219
6	John Stockton (1992)	217
7	Magic Johnson (1986)	211
8	Dennis Johnson (1987)	205
9	Isiah Thomas (1988)	201
10	John Stockton (1996)	195
11	Magic Johnson (1983)	192
12	John Stockton (1997)	191
13	Kevin Johnson (1993)	182
	Jason Kidd (2002)	182
15	Mark Jackson (2000)	178
16	Maurice Cheeks (1982)	172
17	Kevin Johnson (1990)	170
18	Larry Bird (1987)	165
	Magic Johnson (1989)	165
20	John Stockton (1988)	163
	Isiah Thomas (1990)	163
	Jason Kidd (2003)	163
23	Anfernee Hardaway (1995)	162
24	Johnny Moore (1983)	161
25	John Stockton (1994)	157
26	Walt Frazier (1970)	156
27	Terry Porter (1990)	155
	John Stockton (1998)	155
29	Dennis Johnson (1985)	154
30	Jerry West (1970)	151
	Magic Johnson (1980)	151

Steals

	PLAYER/SEASON	STEALS
1	Isiah Thomas (1988)	66
2	Larry Bird (1984)	54
3	Clyde Drexler (1990)	53
4	Allen Iverson (2001)	52
5	Rick Barry (1975)	50
	Robert Reid (1981)	50
7	Magic Johnson (1980)	49
8	Maurice Cheeks (1982)	48
9	Lionel Hollins (1977)	47
	Scottie Pippen (1996)	47
11	Gus Williams (1978)	45
	Maurice Cheeks (1980)	45
	Michael Jordan (1990)	45
	Scottie Pippen (1998)	45
15	Michael Jordan (1992)	44
16	Isiah Thomas (1990)	43
17	Magic Johnson (1984)	42
	Michael Jordan (1989)	42
	Scottie Pippen (1991)	42
	Derek Harper (1994)	42
	Ben Wallace (2003)	42
22	Julius Erving (1977)	41
	Byron Scott (1985)	41
	Danny Ainge (1986)	41
	Jerome Kersey (1992)	41
	Scottie Pippen (1992)	41
	Scottie Pippen (1993)	41
29	Maurice Cheeks (1981)	40
	Magic Johnson (1982)	40
	Hakeem Olajuwon (1986)	40
	Michael Jordan (1991)	40
	Nate McMillan (1993)	40
	Hakeem Olajuwon (1994)	40
	Anfernee Hardaway (1995)	40

SINGLE SEASON — POST

Blocks

	PLAYER/SEASON	BLOCKS
1	Hakeem Olajuwon (1994)	92
2	Tim Duncan (2003)	79
3	Patrick Ewing (1994)	76
4	Dikembe Mutombo (2001)	72
5	Hakeem Olajuwon (1986)	69
	Dikembe Mutombo (1994)	69
7	Bill Walton (1977)	64
8	Hakeem Olajuwon (1995)	62
9	Oliver Miller (1993)	59
	Hakeem Olajuwon (1993)	59
11	Marvin Webster (1978)	58
	Kareem Abdul-Jabbar (1980)	58
13	Kareem Abdul-Jabbar (1983)	55
	Shaquille O'Neal (2000)	55
15	Elvin Hayes (1978)	52
	Elvin Hayes (1979)	52
	Ben Wallace (2003)	52
18	Robert Parish (1982)	48
	Shaquille O'Neal (2002)	48
20	Greg Ostertag (1997)	47
21	Kevin McHale (1985)	46
	Larry Nance (1992)	46
	Alonzo Mourning (1997)	46
24	Kareem Abdul-Jabbar (1982)	45
	Kareem Abdul-Jabbar (1984)	45
	Tim Duncan (1999)	45
27	Kevin McHale (1986)	43
	Hakeem Olajuwon (1987)	43
	Raef LaFrentz (2003)	43
30	Darryl Dawkins (1980)	42

Turnovers

	PLAYER/SEASON	TURNOVERS
1	Larry Bird (1984)	87
2	Isiah Thomas (1988)	85
3	Kevin Johnson (1993)	84
4	Magic Johnson (1988)	83
	Patrick Ewing (1994)	83
	Hakeem Olajuwon (1994)	83
7	Michael Jordan (1992)	81
8	Shawn Kemp (1996)	80
9	Magic Johnson (1984)	79
	Jason Kidd (2003)	79
11	Magic Johnson (1991)	77
12	Magic Johnson (1985)	76
	Tim Duncan (2003)	76
14	Anfernee Hardaway (1995)	73
	Shaquille O'Neal (1995)	73
16	Dennis Johnson (1985)	72
	Isiah Thomas (1990)	72
18	Ralph Sampson (1986)	71
	Larry Bird (1987)	71
	Scottie Pippen (1993)	71
21	Scottie Pippen (1992)	70
	Alonzo Mourning (1997)	70
23	Hakeem Olajuwon (1995)	69
24	Michael Jordan (1989)	68
	Stephen Jackson (2003)	68
26	Julius Erving (1982)	67
	Andrew Toney (1982)	67
	Clyde Drexler (1990)	67
	Detlef Schrempf (1996)	67
	Jason Kidd (2002)	67

SINGLE SEASON — POST

Fouls

	PLAYER/SEASON	FOULS
1	Jack Sikma (1978)	101
2	Robert Parish (1984)	100
3	Charlie Scott (1976)	97
4	Hakeem Olajuwon (1995)	95
5	Darryl Dawkins (1982)	94
	Patrick Ewing (1994)	94
7	Charles Smith (1994)	92
	Kenyon Martin (2003)	92
9	Kobe Bryant (2000)	89
10	John Salley (1988)	88
	Dennis Rodman (1998)	88
	Robert Horry (2000)	88
13	Hakeem Olajuwon (1986)	87
	Dennis Rodman (1988)	87
	Jerome Kersey (1990)	87
	Charles Oakley (1994)	87
17	Elvin Hayes (1978)	86
	Andrew Toney (1982)	86
	John Starks (1994)	86
	Otis Thorpe (1994)	86
	Kenyon Martin (2002)	86
	Raef LaFrentz (2003)	86
23	Dave Cowens (1974)	85
	Dave Cowens (1976)	85
	Jerome Kersey (1992)	85
26	Bailey Howell (1968)	84
	Bailey Howell (1969)	84
	Bob Gross (1977)	84
	Clifford Robinson (1992)	84
	Shaquille O'Neal (1995)	84
	Shawn Kemp (1996)	84
	Rik Smits (2000)	84

Disqualifications

	PLAYER/SEASON	DISQUALS.
1	Charlie Scott (1976)	11
2	Jack Sikma (1978)	7
3	Bailey Howell (1968)	6
	Robert Parish (1984)	6
	Vlade Divac (2002)	6
6	George Mikan (1953)	5
	Chuck Share (1953)	5
	Arnie Risen (1957)	5
	Walter Dukes (1962)	5
	Jim Loscutoff (1962)	5
	Al Attles (1964)	5
	Tom Sanders (1964)	5
	Tom Meschery (1967)	5
	Bob Gross (1977)	5
	Antonio Davis (1998)	5
	Aaron Williams (2002)	5
17	Nathaniel Clifton (1951)	4
	Ernie Vandeweghe (1951)	4
	Nathaniel Clifton (1952)	4
	Dugie Martin (1952)	4
	Vern Mikkelsen (1952)	4
	Monk Meineke (1953)	4
	Bob Donham (1954)	4
	Vern Mikkelsen (1955)	4
	Chuck Share (1956)	4
	Jack McMahon (1957)	4
	Vern Mikkelsen (1957)	4
	Chuck Share (1958)	4
	Lou Tsioropoulos (1958)	4
	Al Bianchi (1959)	4
	Frank Ramsey (1959)	4
	Lenny Wilkens (1961)	4
	Al Attles (1962)	4

Tom Heinsohn (1962)	4	
Jim Krebs (1962)	4	
Tom Sanders (1962)	4	
Cliff Hagan (1963)	4	
Jim Krebs (1963)	4	
Tom Sanders (1963)	4	
Rudy LaRusso (1965)	4	
Tom Sanders (1965)	4	
Tom Sanders (1968)	4	
Hal Greer (1971)	4	
Dave Cowens (1976)	4	
Caldwell Jones (1977)	4	
Lonnie Shelton (1979)	4	
Darryl Dawkins (1982)	4	
Darryl Dawkins (1984)	4	
Robert Parish (1987)	4	
Luc Longley (1996)	4	
Dennis Rodman (1998)	4	
Dale Davis (2000)	4	

Technicals (since 1991–92)

	PLAYER/SEASON	TECHS.
1	Dennis Rodman (1997)	18
2	Dennis Rodman (1996)	12
3	Vernon Maxwell (1994)	11
4	Rasheed Wallace (1999)	8
	Rick Fox (2000)	8
	Rasheed Wallace (2000)	8
	Allen Iverson (2001)	8
	Vlade Divac (2002)	8
9	Dennis Rodman (1995)	7
	Sam Cassell (2001)	7
11	Patrick Ewing (1994)	6
	Anthony Mason (1994)	6
	Gary Payton (1996)	6

	Chris Webber (2002)	6
15	Larry Johnson (1993)	5
	Derek Harper (1994)	5
	Karl Malone (1996)	5
	Clyde Drexler (1997)	5
	Karl Malone (1997)	5
	Charles Oakley (1997)	5
	Hakeem Olajuwon (1997)	5
	Chris Childs (1999)	5
	Karl Malone (2000)	5
	Chris Childs (2001)	5
	Shaquille O'Neal (2001)	5
	Antoine Walker (2002)	5
	Kenyon Martin (2003)	5
	Antoine Walker (2003)	5
29	Xavier McDaniel (1992)	4
	Clifford Robinson (1992)	4
	Charles Barkley (1993)	4
	Patrick Ewing (1993)	4
	Kevin Johnson (1993)	4
	Charles Oakley (1993)	4
	Charles Barkley (1994)	4
	Sam Cassell (1994)	4
	Charles Oakley (1994)	4
	Scottie Pippen (1994)	4
	Dennis Rodman (1994)	4
	Frank Brickowski (1996)	4
	Detlef Schrempf (1996)	4
	Charles Barkley (1997)	4
	P.J. Brown (1997)	4
	Michael Jordan (1997)	4
	Kevin Willis (1997)	4
	Dennis Rodman (1998)	4
	Rik Smits (1999)	4
	Kurt Thomas (1999)	4

SINGLE SEASON — POST

Reggie Miller (2000)	4
Shaquille O'Neal (2000)	4
Doug Christie (2002)	4
Paul Pierce (2002)	4
Sam Cassell (2003)	4
Allen Iverson (2003)	4
Ervin Johnson (2003)	4

THE STATS

FINAL
STANDINGS

FINAL STANDINGS

1946–47 NBA Final Standings

EASTERN DIVISION	W	L	PCT
Washington Capitols	49	11	.817
Philadelphia Warriors	35	25	.583
New York Knicks	33	27	.550
Providence Steamrollers	28	32	.467
Boston Celtics	22	38	.367
Toronto Huskies	22	38	.367

WESTERN DIVISION	W	L	PCT
Chicago Stags	39	22	.639
St. Louis Bombers	38	23	.623
Cleveland Rebels	30	30	.500
Detroit Falcons	20	40	.333
Pittsburgh Ironmen	15	45	.250

1947–48 NBA Final Standings

EASTERN DIVISION	W	L	PCT
Philadelphia Warriors	27	21	.563
New York Knicks	26	22	.542
Boston Celtics	20	28	.417
Providence Steamrollers	6	42	.125

WESTERN DIVISION	W	L	PCT
St. Louis Bombers	29	19	.604
Baltimore Bullets	28	20	.583
Chicago Stags	28	20	.583
Washington Capitols	28	20	.583

1948–49 NBA Final Standings

EASTERN DIVISION	W	L	PCT
Washington Capitols	38	22	.633
New York Knicks	32	28	.533
Baltimore Bullets	29	31	.483
Philadelphia Warriors	28	32	.467
Boston Celtics	25	35	.417
Providence Steamrollers	12	48	.200

WESTERN DIVISION	W	L	PCT
Rochester Royals	45	15	.750
Minneapolis Lakers	44	16	.733
Chicago Stags	38	22	.633
St. Louis Bombers	29	31	.483
Fort Wayne Pistons	22	38	.367
Indianapolis Jets	18	42	.300

1949–50 NBA Final Standings

EASTERN DIVISION	W	L	PCT
Syracuse Nationals	51	13	.797
New York Knicks	40	28	.588
Washington Capitols	32	36	.471
Philadelphia Warriors	26	42	.382
Baltimore Bullets	25	43	.368
Boston Celtics	22	46	.324

WESTERN DIVISION	W	L	PCT
Indianapolis Olympians	39	25	.609
Anderson Packers	37	27	.578
Tri–Cities Blackhawks	29	35	.453
Sheboygan Redskins	22	40	.355
Waterloo Hawks	19	43	.306
Denver Nuggets	11	51	.177

CENTRAL DIVISION	W	L	PCT
Minneapolis Lakers	51	17	.750
Rochester Royals	51	17	.750
Chicago Stags	40	28	.588
Fort Wayne Pistons	40	28	.588
St. Louis Bombers	26	42	.382

FINAL STANDINGS

1950–51 NBA Final Standings

EASTERN DIVISION	W	L	PCT
Philadelphia Warriors	40	26	.606
Boston Celtics	39	30	.565
New York Knicks	36	30	.545
Syracuse Nationals	32	34	.485
Baltimore Bullets	24	42	.364
Washington Capitols	10	25	.286

WESTERN DIVISION	W	L	PCT
Minneapolis Lakers	44	24	.647
Rochester Royals	41	27	.603
Fort Wayne Pistons	32	36	.471
Indianapolis Olympians	31	37	.456
Tri–Cities Blackhawks	25	43	.368

1951–52 NBA Final Standings

EASTERN DIVISION	W	L	PCT
Syracuse Nationals	40	26	.606
Boston Celtics	39	27	.591
New York Knicks	37	29	.561
Philadelphia Warriors	33	33	.500
Baltimore Bullets	20	46	.303

WESTERN DIVISION	W	L	PCT
Rochester Royals	41	25	.621
Minneapolis Lakers	40	26	.606
Indianapolis Olympians	34	32	.515
Fort Wayne Pistons	29	37	.439
Milwaukee Hawks	17	49	.258

1952–53 NBA Final Standings

EASTERN DIVISION	W	L	PCT
New York Knicks	47	23	.671
Syracuse Nationals	47	24	.662
Boston Celtics	46	25	.648
Baltimore Bullets	16	54	.229
Philadelphia Warriors	12	57	.174

WESTERN DIVISION	W	L	PCT
Minneapolis Lakers	48	22	.686
Rochester Royals	44	26	.629
Fort Wayne Pistons	36	33	.522
Indianapolis Olympians	28	43	.394
Milwaukee Hawks	27	44	.380

1953–54 NBA Final Standings

EASTERN DIVISION	W	L	PCT
New York Knicks	44	28	.611
Boston Celtics	42	30	.583
Syracuse Nationals	42	30	.583
Philadelphia Warriors	29	43	.403
Baltimore Bullets	16	56	.222

WESTERN DIVISION	W	L	PCT
Minneapolis Lakers	46	26	.639
Rochester Royals	44	28	.611
Fort Wayne Pistons	40	32	.556
Milwaukee Hawks	21	51	.292

FINAL STANDINGS

1954–55 NBA Final Standings

EASTERN DIVISION	W	L	PCT
Syracuse Nationals	43	29	.597
New York Knicks	38	34	.528
Boston Celtics	36	36	.500
Baltimore Bullets	0	0	–
Philadelphia Warriors	33	39	.458

WESTERN DIVISION	W	L	PCT
Fort Wayne Pistons	43	29	.597
Minneapolis Lakers	40	32	.556
Rochester Royals	29	43	.403
Milwaukee Hawks	26	46	.361

1955–56 NBA Final Standings

EASTERN DIVISION	W	L	PCT
Philadelphia Warriors	45	27	.625
Boston Celtics	39	33	.542
New York Knicks	35	37	.486
Syracuse Nationals	35	37	.486

WESTERN DIVISION	W	L	PCT
Fort Wayne Pistons	37	35	.514
Minneapolis Lakers	33	39	.458
St. Louis Hawks	33	39	.458
Rochester Royals	31	41	.431

1956–57 NBA Final Standings

EASTERN DIVISION	W	L	PCT
Boston Celtics	44	28	.611
Syracuse Nationals	38	34	.528
Philadelphia Warriors	37	35	.514
New York Knicks	36	36	.500

WESTERN DIVISION	W	L	PCT
Fort Wayne Pistons	34	38	.472
Minneapolis Lakers	34	38	.472
St. Louis Hawks	34	38	.472
Rochester Royals	31	41	.431

1957–58 NBA Final Standings

EASTERN DIVISION	W	L	PCT
Boston Celtics	49	23	.681
Syracuse Nationals	41	31	.569
Philadelphia Warriors	37	35	.514
New York Knicks	35	37	.486

WESTERN DIVISION	W	L	PCT
St. Louis Hawks	41	31	.569
Cincinnati Royals	33	39	.458
Detroit Pistons	33	39	.458
Minneapolis Lakers	19	53	.264

FINAL STANDINGS

1958–59 NBA Final Standings

EASTERN DIVISION	W	L	PCT
Boston Celtics	52	20	.722
New York Knicks	40	32	.556
Syracuse Nationals	35	37	.486
Philadelphia Warriors	32	40	.444

WESTERN DIVISION	W	L	PCT
St. Louis Hawks	49	23	.681
Minneapolis Lakers	33	39	.458
Detroit Pistons	28	44	.389
Cincinnati Royals	19	53	.264

1960–61 NBA Final Standings

EASTERN DIVISION	W	L	PCT
Boston Celtics	57	22	.722
Philadelphia Warriors	46	33	.582
Syracuse Nationals	38	41	.481
New York Knicks	21	58	.266

WESTERN DIVISION	W	L	PCT
St. Louis Hawks	51	28	.646
Los Angeles Lakers	36	43	.456
Detroit Pistons	34	45	.430
Cincinnati Royals	33	46	.418

1959–60 NBA Final Standings

EASTERN DIVISION	W	L	PCT
Boston Celtics	59	16	.787
Philadelphia Warriors	49	26	.653
Syracuse Nationals	45	30	.600
New York Knicks	27	48	.360

WESTERN DIVISION	W	L	PCT
St. Louis Hawks	46	29	.613
Detroit Pistons	30	45	.400
Minneapolis Lakers	25	50	.333
Cincinnati Royals	19	56	.253

1961–62 NBA Final Standings

EASTERN DIVISION	W	L	PCT
Boston Celtics	60	20	.750
Philadelphia Warriors	49	31	.613
Syracuse Nationals	41	39	.513
New York Knicks	29	51	.363

WESTERN DIVISION	W	L	PCT
Los Angeles Lakers	54	26	.675
Cincinnati Royals	43	37	.538
Detroit Pistons	37	43	.463
St. Louis Hawks	29	51	.363
Chicago Packers	18	62	.225

FINAL STANDINGS

1962–63 NBA Final Standings

EASTERN DIVISION	W	L	PCT
Boston Celtics	58	22	.725
Syracuse Nationals	48	32	.600
Cincinnati Royals	42	38	.525
New York Knicks	21	59	.263

WESTERN DIVISION	W	L	PCT
Los Angeles Lakers	53	27	.663
St. Louis Hawks	48	32	.600
Detroit Pistons	34	46	.425
San Francisco Warriors	31	49	.388
Chicago Zephyrs	25	55	.313

1964–65 NBA Final Standings

EASTERN DIVISION	W	L	PCT
Boston Celtics	62	18	.775
Cincinnati Royals	48	32	.600
Philadelphia 76ers	40	40	.500
New York Knicks	31	49	.388

WESTERN DIVISION	W	L	PCT
Los Angeles Lakers	49	31	.613
St. Louis Hawks	45	35	.563
Baltimore Bullets	37	43	.463
Detroit Pistons	31	49	.388
San Francisco Warriors	17	63	.213

1963–64 NBA Final Standings

EASTERN DIVISION	W	L	PCT
Boston Celtics	59	21	.738
Cincinnati Royals	55	25	.688
Philadelphia 76ers	34	46	.425
New York Knicks	22	58	.275

WESTERN DIVISION	W	L	PCT
San Francisco Warriors	48	32	.600
St. Louis Hawks	46	34	.575
Los Angeles Lakers	42	38	.525
Baltimore Bullets	31	49	.388
Detroit Pistons	23	57	.288

1965–66 NBA Final Standings

EASTERN DIVISION	W	L	PCT
Philadelphia 76ers	55	25	.688
Boston Celtics	54	26	.675
Cincinnati Royals	45	35	.563
New York Knicks	30	50	.375

WESTERN DIVISION	W	L	PCT
Los Angeles Lakers	45	35	.563
Baltimore Bullets	38	42	.475
St. Louis Hawks	36	44	.450
San Francisco Warriors	35	45	.438
Detroit Pistons	22	58	.275

FINAL STANDINGS

1966–67 NBA Final Standings

EASTERN DIVISION	W	L	PCT
Philadelphia 76ers	68	13	.840
Boston Celtics	60	21	.741
Cincinnati Royals	39	42	.481
New York Knicks	36	45	.444
Baltimore Bullets	20	61	.247

WESTERN DIVISION	W	L	PCT
San Francisco Warriors	44	37	.543
St. Louis Hawks	39	42	.481
Los Angeles Lakers	36	45	.444
Chicago Bulls	33	48	.407
Detroit Pistons	30	51	.370

1967–68 NBA Final Standings

EASTERN DIVISION	W	L	PCT
Philadelphia 76ers	62	20	.756
Boston Celtics	54	28	.659
New York Knicks	43	39	.524
Detroit Pistons	40	42	.488
Cincinnati Royals	39	43	.476
Baltimore Bullets	36	46	.439

WESTERN DIVISION	W	L	PCT
St. Louis Hawks	56	26	.683
Los Angeles Lakers	52	30	.634
San Francisco Warriors	43	39	.524
Chicago Bulls	29	53	.354
Seattle SuperSonics	23	59	.280
San Diego Rockets	15	67	.183

1968–69 NBA Final Standings

EASTERN DIVISION	W	L	PCT
Baltimore Bullets	57	25	.695
Philadelphia 76ers	55	27	.671
New York Knicks	54	28	.659
Boston Celtics	48	34	.585
Cincinnati Royals	41	41	.500
Detroit Pistons	32	50	.390
Milwaukee Bucks	27	55	.329

WESTERN DIVISION	W	L	PCT
Los Angeles Lakers	55	27	.671
Atlanta Hawks	48	34	.585
San Francisco Warriors	41	41	.500
San Diego Rockets	37	45	.451
Chicago Bulls	33	49	.402
Seattle SuperSonics	30	52	.366
Phoenix Suns	16	66	.195

1969–70 NBA Final Standings

EASTERN DIVISION	W	L	PCT
New York Knicks	60	22	.732
Milwaukee Bucks	56	26	.683
Baltimore Bullets	50	32	.610
Philadelphia 76ers	42	40	.512
Cincinnati Royals	36	46	.439
Boston Celtics	34	48	.415
Detroit Pistons	31	51	.378

WESTERN DIVISION	W	L	PCT
Atlanta Hawks	48	34	.585
Los Angeles Lakers	46	36	.561
Chicago Bulls	39	43	.476
Phoenix Suns	39	43	.476
Seattle SuperSonics	36	46	.439
San Francisco Warriors	30	52	.366
San Diego Rockets	27	55	.329

FINAL STANDINGS

1970–71 NBA Final Standings

EASTERN CONFERENCE

ATLANTIC DIVISION	W	L	PCT
New York Knicks	52	30	.634
Philadelphia 76ers	47	35	.573
Boston Celtics	44	38	.537
Buffalo Braves	22	60	.268

CENTRAL DIVISION	W	L	PCT
Baltimore Bullets	42	40	.512
Atlanta Hawks	36	46	.439
Cincinnati Royals	33	49	.402
Cleveland Cavaliers	15	67	.183

WESTERN CONFERENCE

MIDWEST DIVISION	W	L	PCT
Milwaukee Bucks	66	16	.805
Chicago Bulls	51	31	.622
Phoenix Suns	48	34	.585
Detroit Pistons	45	37	.549

PACIFIC DIVISION	W	L	PCT
Los Angeles Lakers	48	34	.585
San Francisco Warriors	41	41	.500
San Diego Rockets	40	42	.488
Seattle SuperSonics	38	44	.463
Portland Trail Blazers	29	53	.354

1971–72 NBA Final Standings

EASTERN CONFERENCE

ATLANTIC DIVISION	W	L	PCT
Boston Celtics	56	26	.683
New York Knicks	48	34	.585
Philadelphia 76ers	30	52	.366
Buffalo Braves	22	60	.268

CENTRAL DIVISION	W	L	PCT
Baltimore Bullets	38	44	.463
Atlanta Hawks	36	46	.439
Cincinnati Royals	30	52	.366
Cleveland Cavaliers	23	59	.280

WESTERN CONFERENCE

MIDWEST DIVISION	W	L	PCT
Milwaukee Bucks	63	19	.768
Chicago Bulls	57	25	.695
Phoenix Suns	49	33	.598
Detroit Pistons	26	56	.317

PACIFIC DIVISION	W	L	PCT
Los Angeles Lakers	69	13	.841
Golden State Warriors	51	31	.622
Seattle SuperSonics	47	35	.573
Houston Rockets	34	48	.415
Portland Trail Blazers	18	64	.220

FINAL STANDINGS

1972–73 NBA Final Standings

EASTERN CONFERENCE

ATLANTIC DIVISION	W	L	PCT
Boston Celtics	68	14	.829
New York Knicks	57	25	.695
Buffalo Braves	21	61	.256
Philadelphia 76ers	9	73	.110

CENTRAL DIVISION	W	L	PCT
Baltimore Bullets	52	30	.634
Atlanta Hawks	46	36	.561
Houston Rockets	33	49	.402
Cleveland Cavaliers	32	50	.390

WESTERN CONFERENCE

MIDWEST DIVISION	W	L	PCT
Milwaukee Bucks	60	22	.732
Chicago Bulls	51	31	.622
Detroit Pistons	40	42	.488
Kansas City–Omaha Kings	36	46	.439

PACIFIC DIVISION	W	L	PCT
Los Angeles Lakers	60	22	.732
Golden State Warriors	47	35	.573
Phoenix Suns	38	44	.463
Seattle SuperSonics	26	56	.317
Portland Trail Blazers	21	61	.256

1973–74 NBA Final Standings

EASTERN CONFERENCE

ATLANTIC DIVISION	W	L	PCT
Boston Celtics	56	26	.683
New York Knicks	49	33	.598
Buffalo Braves	42	40	.512
Philadelphia 76ers	25	57	.305

CENTRAL DIVISION	W	L	PCT
Capital Bullets	47	35	.573
Atlanta Hawks	35	47	.427
Houston Rockets	32	50	.390
Cleveland Cavaliers	29	53	.354

WESTERN CONFERENCE

MIDWEST DIVISION	W	L	PCT
Milwaukee Bucks	59	23	.720
Chicago Bulls	54	28	.659
Detroit Pistons	52	30	.634
Kansas City–Omaha Kings	33	49	.402

PACIFIC DIVISION	W	L	PCT
Los Angeles Lakers	47	35	.573
Golden State Warriors	44	38	.537
Seattle SuperSonics	36	46	.439
Phoenix Suns	30	52	.366
Portland Trail Blazers	27	55	.329

FINAL STANDINGS

1974–75 NBA Final Standings

EASTERN CONFERENCE

ATLANTIC DIVISION	W	L	PCT
Boston Celtics	60	22	.732
Buffalo Braves	49	33	.598
New York Knicks	40	42	.488
Philadelphia 76ers	34	48	.415

CENTRAL DIVISION	W	L	PCT
Washington Bullets	60	22	.732
Houston Rockets	41	41	.500
Cleveland Cavaliers	40	42	.488
Atlanta Hawks	31	51	.378
New Orleans Jazz	23	59	.280

WESTERN CONFERENCE

MIDWEST DIVISION	W	L	PCT
Chicago Bulls	47	35	.573
Kansas City–Omaha Kings	44	38	.537
Detroit Pistons	40	42	.488
Milwaukee Bucks	38	44	.463

PACIFIC DIVISION	W	L	PCT
Golden State Warriors	48	34	.585
Seattle SuperSonics	43	39	.524
Portland Trail Blazers	38	44	.463
Phoenix Suns	32	50	.390
Los Angeles Lakers	30	52	.366

1975–76 NBA Final Standings

EASTERN CONFERENCE

ATLANTIC DIVISION	W	L	PCT
Boston Celtics	54	28	.659
Buffalo Braves	46	36	.561
Philadelphia 76ers	46	36	.561
New York Knicks	38	44	.463

CENTRAL DIVISION	W	L	PCT
Cleveland Cavaliers	49	33	.598
Washington Bullets	48	34	.585
Houston Rockets	40	42	.488
New Orleans Jazz	38	44	.463
Atlanta Hawks	29	53	.354

WESTERN CONFERENCE

MIDWEST DIVISION	W	L	PCT
Milwaukee Bucks	38	44	.463
Detroit Pistons	36	46	.439
Kansas City Kings	31	51	.378
Chicago Bulls	24	58	.293

PACIFIC DIVISION	W	L	PCT
Golden State Warriors	59	23	.720
Seattle SuperSonics	43	39	.524
Phoenix Suns	42	40	.512
Los Angeles Lakers	40	42	.488
Portland Trail Blazers	37	45	.451

FINAL STANDINGS

1976–77 NBA Final Standings

EASTERN CONFERENCE

ATLANTIC DIVISION	W	L	PCT
Philadelphia 76ers	50	32	.610
Boston Celtics	44	38	.537
New York Knicks	40	42	.488
Buffalo Braves	30	52	.366
New York Nets	22	60	.268

CENTRAL DIVISION	W	L	PCT
Houston Rockets	49	33	.598
Washington Bullets	48	34	.585
San Antonio Spurs	44	38	.537
Cleveland Cavaliers	43	39	.524
New Orleans Jazz	35	47	.427
Atlanta Hawks	31	51	.378

WESTERN CONFERENCE

MIDWEST DIVISION	W	L	PCT
Denver Nuggets	50	32	.610
Chicago Bulls	44	38	.537
Detroit Pistons	44	38	.537
Kansas City Kings	40	42	.488
Indiana Pacers	36	46	.439
Milwaukee Bucks	30	52	.366

PACIFIC DIVISION	W	L	PCT
Los Angeles Lakers	53	29	.646
Portland Trail Blazers	49	33	.598
Golden State Warriors	46	36	.561
Seattle SuperSonics	40	42	.488
Phoenix Suns	34	48	.415

1977–78 NBA Final Standings

EASTERN CONFERENCE

ATLANTIC DIVISION	W	L	PCT
Philadelphia 76ers	55	27	.671
New York Knicks	43	39	.524
Boston Celtics	32	50	.390
Buffalo Braves	27	55	.329
New Jersey Nets	24	58	.293

CENTRAL DIVISION	W	L	PCT
San Antonio Spurs	52	30	.634
Washington Bullets	44	38	.537
Cleveland Cavaliers	43	39	.524
Atlanta Hawks	41	41	.500
New Orleans Jazz	39	43	.476
Houston Rockets	28	54	.341

WESTERN CONFERENCE

MIDWEST DIVISION	W	L	PCT
Denver Nuggets	48	34	.585
Milwaukee Bucks	44	38	.537
Chicago Bulls	40	42	.488
Detroit Pistons	38	44	.463
Indiana Pacers	31	51	.378
Kansas City Kings	31	51	.378

PACIFIC DIVISION	W	L	PCT
Portland Trail Blazers	58	24	.707
Phoenix Suns	49	33	.598
Seattle SuperSonics	47	35	.573
Los Angeles Lakers	45	37	.549
Golden State Warriors	43	39	.524

FINAL STANDINGS

1978–79 NBA Final Standings

EASTERN CONFERENCE

ATLANTIC DIVISION	W	L	PCT
Washington Bullets	54	28	.659
Philadelphia 76ers	47	35	.573
New Jersey Nets	37	45	.451
New York Knicks	31	51	.378
Boston Celtics	29	53	.354

CENTRAL DIVISION	W	L	PCT
San Antonio Spurs	48	34	.585
Houston Rockets	47	35	.573
Atlanta Hawks	46	36	.561
Cleveland Cavaliers	30	52	.366
Detroit Pistons	30	52	.366
New Orleans Jazz	26	56	.317

WESTERN CONFERENCE

MIDWEST DIVISION	W	L	PCT
Kansas City Kings	48	34	.585
Denver Nuggets	47	35	.573
Indiana Pacers	38	44	.463
Milwaukee Bucks	38	44	.463
Chicago Bulls	31	51	.378

PACIFIC DIVISION	W	L	PCT
Seattle SuperSonics	52	30	.634
Phoenix Suns	50	32	.610
Los Angeles Lakers	47	35	.573
Portland Trail Blazers	45	37	.549
San Diego Clippers	43	39	.524
Golden State Warriors	38	44	.463

1979–80 NBA Final Standings

EASTERN CONFERENCE

ATLANTIC DIVISION	W	L	PCT
Boston Celtics	61	21	.744
Philadelphia 76ers	59	23	.720
New York Knicks	39	43	.476
Washington Bullets	39	43	.476
New Jersey Nets	34	48	.415

CENTRAL DIVISION	W	L	PCT
Atlanta Hawks	50	32	.610
Houston Rockets	41	41	.500
San Antonio Spurs	41	41	.500
Cleveland Cavaliers	37	45	.451
Indiana Pacers	37	45	.451
Detroit Pistons	16	66	.195

WESTERN CONFERENCE

MIDWEST DIVISION	W	L	PCT
Milwaukee Bucks	49	33	.598
Kansas City Kings	47	35	.573
Chicago Bulls	30	52	.366
Denver Nuggets	30	52	.366
Utah Jazz	24	58	.293

PACIFIC DIVISION	W	L	PCT
Los Angeles Lakers	60	22	.732
Seattle SuperSonics	56	26	.683
Phoenix Suns	55	27	.671
Portland Trail Blazers	38	44	.463
San Diego Clippers	35	47	.427
Golden State Warriors	24	58	.293

FINAL STANDINGS

1980–81 NBA Final Standings

EASTERN CONFERENCE

ATLANTIC DIVISION	W	L	PCT
Boston Celtics	62	20	.756
Philadelphia 76ers	62	20	.756
New York Knicks	50	32	.610
Washington Bullets	39	43	.476
New Jersey Nets	24	58	.293

CENTRAL DIVISION	W	L	PCT
Milwaukee Bucks	60	22	.732
Chicago Bulls	45	37	.549
Indiana Pacers	44	38	.537
Atlanta Hawks	31	51	.378
Cleveland Cavaliers	28	54	.341
Detroit Pistons	21	61	.256

WESTERN CONFERENCE

MIDWEST DIVISION	W	L	PCT
San Antonio Spurs	52	30	.634
Houston Rockets	40	42	.488
Kansas City Kings	40	42	.488
Denver Nuggets	37	45	.451
Utah Jazz	28	54	.341
Dallas Mavericks	15	67	.183

PACIFIC DIVISION	W	L	PCT
Phoenix Suns	57	25	.695
Los Angeles Lakers	54	28	.659
Portland Trail Blazers	45	37	.549
Golden State Warriors	39	43	.476
San Diego Clippers	36	46	.439
Seattle SuperSonics	34	48	.415

1981–82 NBA Final Standings

EASTERN CONFERENCE

ATLANTIC DIVISION	W	L	PCT
Boston Celtics	63	19	.768
Philadelphia 76ers	58	24	.707
New Jersey Nets	44	38	.537
Washington Bullets	43	39	.524
New York Knicks	33	49	.402

CENTRAL DIVISION	W	L	PCT
Milwaukee Bucks	55	27	.671
Atlanta Hawks	42	40	.512
Detroit Pistons	39	43	.476
Indiana Pacers	35	47	.427
Chicago Bulls	34	48	.415
Cleveland Cavaliers	15	67	.183

WESTERN CONFERENCE

MIDWEST DIVISION	W	L	PCT
San Antonio Spurs	48	34	.585
Denver Nuggets	46	36	.561
Houston Rockets	46	36	.561
Kansas City Kings	30	52	.366
Dallas Mavericks	28	54	.341
Utah Jazz	25	57	.305

PACIFIC DIVISION	W	L	PCT
Los Angeles Lakers	57	25	.695
Seattle SuperSonics	52	30	.634
Phoenix Suns	46	36	.561
Golden State Warriors	45	37	.549
Portland Trail Blazers	42	40	.512
San Diego Clippers	17	65	.207

FINAL STANDINGS

1982–83 NBA Final Standings

EASTERN CONFERENCE

ATLANTIC DIVISION	W	L	PCT
Philadelphia 76ers	65	17	.793
Boston Celtics	56	26	.683
New Jersey Nets	49	33	.598
New York Knicks	44	38	.537
Washington Bullets	42	40	.512

CENTRAL DIVISION	W	L	PCT
Milwaukee Bucks	51	31	.622
Atlanta Hawks	43	39	.524
Detroit Pistons	37	45	.451
Chicago Bulls	28	54	.341
Cleveland Cavaliers	23	59	.280
Indiana Pacers	20	62	.244

WESTERN CONFERENCE

MIDWEST DIVISION	W	L	PCT
San Antonio Spurs	53	29	.646
Denver Nuggets	45	37	.549
Kansas City Kings	45	37	.549
Dallas Mavericks	38	44	.463
Utah Jazz	30	52	.366
Houston Rockets	14	68	.171

PACIFIC DIVISION	W	L	PCT
Los Angeles Lakers	58	24	.707
Phoenix Suns	53	29	.646
Seattle SuperSonics	48	34	.585
Portland Trail Blazers	46	36	.561
Golden State Warriors	30	52	.366
San Diego Clippers	25	57	.305

1983–84 NBA Final Standings

EASTERN CONFERENCE

ATLANTIC DIVISION	W	L	PCT
Boston Celtics	62	20	.756
Philadelphia 76ers	52	30	.634
New York Knicks	47	35	.573
New Jersey Nets	45	37	.549
Washington Bullets	35	47	.427

CENTRAL DIVISION	W	L	PCT
Milwaukee Bucks	50	32	.610
Detroit Pistons	49	33	.598
Atlanta Hawks	40	42	.488
Cleveland Cavaliers	28	54	.341
Chicago Bulls	27	55	.329
Indiana Pacers	26	56	.317

WESTERN CONFERENCE

MIDWEST DIVISION	W	L	PCT
Utah Jazz	45	37	.549
Dallas Mavericks	43	39	.524
Denver Nuggets	38	44	.463
Kansas City Kings	38	44	.463
San Antonio Spurs	37	45	.451
Houston Rockets	29	53	.354

PACIFIC DIVISION	W	L	PCT
Los Angeles Lakers	54	28	.659
Portland Trail Blazers	48	34	.585
Seattle SuperSonics	42	40	.512
Phoenix Suns	41	41	.500
Golden State Warriors	37	45	.451
San Diego Clippers	30	52	.366

FINAL STANDINGS

1984–85 NBA Final Standings

EASTERN CONFERENCE

ATLANTIC DIVISION	W	L	PCT
Boston Celtics	63	19	.768
Philadelphia 76ers	58	24	.707
New Jersey Nets	42	40	.512
Washington Bullets	40	42	.488
New York Knicks	24	58	.293

CENTRAL DIVISION	W	L	PCT
Milwaukee Bucks	59	23	.720
Detroit Pistons	46	36	.561
Chicago Bulls	38	44	.463
Cleveland Cavaliers	36	46	.439
Atlanta Hawks	34	48	.415
Indiana Pacers	22	60	.268

WESTERN CONFERENCE

MIDWEST DIVISION	W	L	PCT
Denver Nuggets	52	30	.634
Houston Rockets	48	34	.585
Dallas Mavericks	44	38	.537
San Antonio Spurs	41	41	.500
Utah Jazz	41	41	.500
Kansas City Kings	31	51	.378

PACIFIC DIVISION	W	L	PCT
Los Angeles Lakers	62	20	.756
Portland Trail Blazers	42	40	.512
Phoenix Suns	36	46	.439
Los Angeles Clippers	31	51	.378
Seattle SuperSonics	31	51	.378
Golden State Warriors	22	60	.268

1985–86 NBA Final Standings

EASTERN CONFERENCE

ATLANTIC DIVISION	W	L	PCT
Boston Celtics	67	15	.817
Philadelphia 76ers	54	28	.659
New Jersey Nets	39	43	.476
Washington Bullets	39	43	.476
New York Knicks	23	59	.280

CENTRAL DIVISION	W	L	PCT
Milwaukee Bucks	57	25	.695
Atlanta Hawks	50	32	.610
Detroit Pistons	46	36	.561
Chicago Bulls	30	52	.366
Cleveland Cavaliers	29	53	.354
Indiana Pacers	26	56	.317

WESTERN CONFERENCE

MIDWEST DIVISION	W	L	PCT
Houston Rockets	51	31	.622
Denver Nuggets	47	35	.573
Dallas Mavericks	44	38	.537
Utah Jazz	42	40	.512
Sacramento Kings	37	45	.451
San Antonio Spurs	35	47	.427

PACIFIC DIVISION	W	L	PCT
Los Angeles Lakers	62	20	.756
Portland Trail Blazers	40	42	.488
Los Angeles Clippers	32	50	.390
Phoenix Suns	32	50	.390
Seattle SuperSonics	31	51	.378
Golden State Warriors	30	52	.366

FINAL STANDINGS

1986–87 NBA Final Standings

EASTERN CONFERENCE

ATLANTIC DIVISION	W	L	PCT
Boston Celtics	59	23	.720
Philadelphia 76ers	45	37	.549
Washington Bullets	42	40	.512
New Jersey Nets	24	58	.293
New York Knicks	24	58	.293

CENTRAL DIVISION	W	L	PCT
Atlanta Hawks	57	25	.695
Detroit Pistons	52	30	.634
Milwaukee Bucks	50	32	.610
Indiana Pacers	41	41	.500
Chicago Bulls	40	42	.488
Cleveland Cavaliers	31	51	.378

WESTERN CONFERENCE

MIDWEST DIVISION	W	L	PCT
Dallas Mavericks	55	27	.671
Utah Jazz	44	38	.537
Houston Rockets	42	40	.512
Denver Nuggets	37	45	.451
Sacramento Kings	29	53	.354
San Antonio Spurs	28	54	.341

PACIFIC DIVISION	W	L	PCT
Los Angeles Lakers	65	17	.793
Portland Trail Blazers	49	33	.598
Golden State Warriors	42	40	.512
Seattle SuperSonics	39	43	.476
Phoenix Suns	36	46	.439
Los Angeles Clippers	12	70	.146

1987–88 NBA Final Standings

EASTERN CONFERENCE

ATLANTIC DIVISION	W	L	PCT
Boston Celtics	57	25	.695
New York Knicks	38	44	.463
Washington Bullets	38	44	.463
Philadelphia 76ers	36	46	.439
New Jersey Nets	19	63	.232

CENTRAL DIVISION	W	L	PCT
Detroit Pistons	54	28	.659
Atlanta Hawks	50	32	.610
Chicago Bulls	50	32	.610
Cleveland Cavaliers	42	40	.512
Milwaukee Bucks	42	40	.512
Indiana Pacers	38	44	.463

WESTERN CONFERENCE

MIDWEST DIVISION	W	L	PCT
Denver Nuggets	54	28	.659
Dallas Mavericks	53	29	.646
Utah Jazz	47	35	.573
Houston Rockets	46	36	.561
San Antonio Spurs	31	51	.378
Sacramento Kings	24	58	.293

PACIFIC DIVISION	W	L	PCT
Los Angeles Lakers	62	20	.756
Portland Trail Blazers	53	29	.646
Seattle SuperSonics	44	38	.537
Phoenix Suns	28	54	.341
Golden State Warriors	20	62	.244
Los Angeles Clippers	17	65	.207

FINAL STANDINGS

1988–89 NBA Final Standings

EASTERN CONFERENCE

ATLANTIC DIVISION	W	L	PCT
New York Knicks	52	30	.634
Philadelphia 76ers	46	36	.561
Boston Celtics	42	40	.512
Washington Bullets	40	42	.488
New Jersey Nets	26	56	.317
Charlotte Hornets	20	62	.244

CENTRAL DIVISION	W	L	PCT
Detroit Pistons	63	19	.768
Cleveland Cavaliers	57	25	.695
Atlanta Hawks	52	30	.634
Milwaukee Bucks	49	33	.598
Chicago Bulls	47	35	.573
Indiana Pacers	28	54	.341

WESTERN CONFERENCE

MIDWEST DIVISION	W	L	PCT
Utah Jazz	51	31	.622
Houston Rockets	45	37	.549
Denver Nuggets	44	38	.537
Dallas Mavericks	38	44	.463
San Antonio Spurs	21	61	.256
Miami Heat	15	67	.183

PACIFIC DIVISION	W	L	PCT
Los Angeles Lakers	57	25	.695
Phoenix Suns	55	27	.671
Seattle SuperSonics	47	35	.573
Golden State Warriors	43	39	.524
Portland Trail Blazers	39	43	.476
Sacramento Kings	27	55	.329
Los Angeles Clippers	21	61	.256

1989–90 NBA Final Standings

EASTERN CONFERENCE

ATLANTIC DIVISION	W	L	PCT
Philadelphia 76ers	53	29	.646
Boston Celtics	52	30	.634
New York Knicks	45	37	.549
Washington Bullets	31	51	.378
Miami Heat	18	64	.220
New Jersey Nets	17	65	.207

CENTRAL DIVISION	W	L	PCT
Detroit Pistons	59	23	.720
Chicago Bulls	55	27	.671
Milwaukee Bucks	44	38	.537
Cleveland Cavaliers	42	40	.512
Indiana Pacers	42	40	.512
Atlanta Hawks	41	41	.500
Orlando Magic	18	64	.220

WESTERN CONFERENCE

MIDWEST DIVISION	W	L	PCT
San Antonio Spurs	56	26	.683
Utah Jazz	55	27	.671
Dallas Mavericks	47	35	.573
Denver Nuggets	43	39	.524
Houston Rockets	41	41	.500
Minnesota Timberwolves	22	60	.268
Charlotte Hornets	19	63	.232

PACIFIC DIVISION	W	L	PCT
Los Angeles Lakers	63	19	.768
Portland Trail Blazers	59	23	.720
Phoenix Suns	54	28	.659
Seattle SuperSonics	41	41	.500
Golden State Warriors	37	45	.451
Los Angeles Clippers	30	52	.366
Sacramento Kings	23	59	.280

FINAL STANDINGS

1990–91 NBA Final Standings

EASTERN CONFERENCE

ATLANTIC DIVISION	W	L	PCT
Boston Celtics	56	26	.683
Philadelphia 76ers	44	38	.537
New York Knicks	39	43	.476
Washington Bullets	30	52	.366
New Jersey Nets	26	56	.317
Miami Heat	24	58	.293

CENTRAL DIVISION	W	L	PCT
Chicago Bulls	61	21	.744
Detroit Pistons	50	32	.610
Milwaukee Bucks	48	34	.585
Atlanta Hawks	43	39	.524
Indiana Pacers	41	41	.500
Cleveland Cavaliers	33	49	.402
Charlotte Hornets	26	56	.317

WESTERN CONFERENCE

MIDWEST DIVISION	W	L	PCT
San Antonio Spurs	55	27	.671
Utah Jazz	54	28	.659
Houston Rockets	52	30	.634
Orlando Magic	31	51	.378
Minnesota Timberwolves	29	53	.354
Dallas Mavericks	28	54	.341
Denver Nuggets	20	62	.244

PACIFIC DIVISION	W	L	PCT
Portland Trail Blazers	63	19	.768
Los Angeles Lakers	58	24	.707
Phoenix Suns	55	27	.671
Golden State Warriors	44	38	.537
Seattle SuperSonics	41	41	.500
Los Angeles Clippers	31	51	.378
Sacramento Kings	25	57	.305

1991–92 NBA Final Standings

EASTERN CONFERENCE

ATLANTIC DIVISION	W	L	PCT
Boston Celtics	51	31	.622
New York Knicks	51	31	.622
New Jersey Nets	40	42	.488
Miami Heat	38	44	.463
Philadelphia 76ers	35	47	.427
Washington Bullets	25	57	.305
Orlando Magic	21	61	.256

CENTRAL DIVISION	W	L	PCT
Chicago Bulls	67	15	.817
Cleveland Cavaliers	57	25	.695
Detroit Pistons	48	34	.585
Indiana Pacers	40	42	.488
Atlanta Hawks	38	44	.463
Milwaukee Bucks	31	51	.378
Charlotte Hornets	31	51	.378

WESTERN CONFERENCE

MIDWEST DIVISION	W	L	PCT
Utah Jazz	55	27	.671
San Antonio Spurs	47	35	.573
Houston Rockets	42	40	.512
Denver Nuggets	24	58	.293
Dallas Mavericks	22	60	.268
Minnesota Timberwolves	15	67	.183

PACIFIC DIVISION	W	L	PCT
Portland Trail Blazers	57	25	.695
Golden State Warriors	55	27	.671
Phoenix Suns	53	29	.646
Seattle SuperSonics	47	35	.573
Los Angeles Clippers	45	37	.549
Los Angeles Lakers	43	39	.524
Sacramento Kings	29	53	.354

FINAL STANDINGS

1992–93 NBA Final Standings

EASTERN CONFERENCE

ATLANTIC DIVISION	W	L	PCT
New York Knicks	60	22	.732
Boston Celtics	48	34	.585
New Jersey Nets	43	39	.524
Orlando Magic	41	41	.500
Miami Heat	36	46	.439
Philadelphia 76ers	26	56	.317
Washington Bullets	22	60	.268

CENTRAL DIVISION	W	L	PCT
Chicago Bulls	57	25	.695
Cleveland Cavaliers	54	28	.659
Charlotte Hornets	44	38	.537
Atlanta Hawks	43	39	.524
Indiana Pacers	41	41	.500
Detroit Pistons	40	42	.488
Milwaukee Bucks	28	54	.341

WESTERN CONFERENCE

MIDWEST DIVISION	W	L	PCT
Houston Rockets	55	27	.671
San Antonio Spurs	49	33	.598
Utah Jazz	47	35	.573
Denver Nuggets	36	46	.439
Minnesota Timberwolves	19	63	.232
Dallas Mavericks	11	71	.134

Pacific Division	W	L	Pct
Phoenix Suns	62	20	.756
Seattle SuperSonics	55	27	.671
Portland Trail Blazers	51	31	.622
Los Angeles Clippers	41	41	.500
Los Angeles Lakers	39	43	.476
Golden State Warriors	34	48	.415
Sacramento Kings	25	57	.305

1993–94 NBA Final Standings

EASTERN CONFERENCE

ATLANTIC DIVISION	W	L	PCT
New York Knicks	57	25	.695
Orlando Magic	50	32	.610
New Jersey Nets	45	37	.549
Miami Heat	42	40	.512
Boston Celtics	32	50	.390
Philadelphia 76ers	25	57	.305
Washington Bullets	24	58	.293

CENTRAL DIVISION	W	L	PCT
Atlanta Hawks	57	25	.695
Chicago Bulls	55	27	.671
Indiana Pacers	47	35	.573
Cleveland Cavaliers	47	35	.573
Charlotte Hornets	41	41	.500
Milwaukee Bucks	20	62	.244
Detroit Pistons	20	62	.244

WESTERN CONFERENCE

MIDWEST DIVISION	W	L	PCT
Houston Rockets	58	24	.707
San Antonio Spurs	55	27	.671
Utah Jazz	53	29	.646
Denver Nuggets	42	40	.512
Minnesota Timberwolves	20	62	.244
Dallas Mavericks	13	69	.159

PACIFIC DIVISION	W	L	PCT
Seattle SuperSonics	63	19	.768
Phoenix Suns	56	26	.683
Golden State Warriors	50	32	.610
Portland Trail Blazers	47	35	.573
Los Angeles Lakers	33	49	.402
Sacramento Kings	28	54	.341
Los Angeles Clippers	27	55	.329

FINAL STANDINGS

1994–95 NBA Final Standings

EASTERN CONFERENCE

ATLANTIC DIVISION	W	L	PCT
Orlando Magic	57	25	.695
New York Knicks	55	27	.671
Boston Celtics	35	47	.427
Miami Heat	32	50	.390
New Jersey Nets	30	52	.366
Philadelphia 76ers	24	58	.293
Washington Bullets	21	61	.256

CENTRAL DIVISION	W	L	PCT
Indiana Pacers	52	30	.634
Charlotte Hornets	50	32	.610
Chicago Bulls	47	35	.573
Cleveland Cavaliers	43	39	.524
Atlanta Hawks	42	40	.512
Milwaukee Bucks	34	48	.415
Detroit Pistons	28	54	.341

WESTERN CONFERENCE

MIDWEST DIVISION	W	L	PCT
San Antonio Spurs	62	20	.756
Utah Jazz	60	22	.732
Houston Rockets	47	35	.573
Denver Nuggets	41	41	.500
Dallas Mavericks	36	46	.439
Minnesota Timberwolves	21	61	.256

PACIFIC DIVISION	W	L	PCT
Phoenix Suns	59	23	.720
Seattle SuperSonics	57	25	.695
Los Angeles Lakers	48	34	.585
Portland Trail Blazers	44	38	.537
Sacramento Kings	39	43	.476
Golden State Warriors	26	56	.317
Los Angeles Clippers	17	65	.207

1995–96 NBA Final Standings

EASTERN CONFERENCE

ATLANTIC DIVISION	W	L	PCT
Orlando Magic	60	22	.732
New York Knicks	47	35	.573
Miami Heat	42	40	.512
Washington Bullets	39	43	.476
Boston Celtics	33	49	.402
New Jersey Nets	30	52	.366
Philadelphia 76ers	18	64	.220

CENTRAL DIVISION	W	L	PCT
Chicago Bulls	72	10	.878
Indiana Pacers	52	30	.634
Cleveland Cavaliers	47	35	.573
Atlanta Hawks	46	36	.561
Detroit Pistons	46	36	.561
Charlotte Hornets	41	41	.500
Milwaukee Bucks	25	57	.305
Toronto Raptors	21	61	.256

WESTERN CONFERENCE

MIDWEST DIVISION	W	L	PCT
San Antonio Spurs	59	23	.720
Utah Jazz	55	27	.671
Houston Rockets	48	34	.585
Denver Nuggets	35	47	.427
Minnesota Timberwolves	26	56	.317
Dallas Mavericks	26	56	.317
Vancouver Grizzlies	15	67	.183

PACIFIC DIVISION	W	L	PCT
Seattle SuperSonics	64	18	.780
Los Angeles Lakers	53	29	.646
Portland Trail Blazers	44	38	.537
Phoenix Suns	41	41	.500
Sacramento Kings	39	43	.476
Golden State Warriors	36	46	.439
Los Angeles Clippers	29	53	.354

FINAL STANDINGS

1996–97 NBA Final Standings

EASTERN CONFERENCE

ATLANTIC DIVISION	W	L	PCT
Miami Heat	61	21	.744
New York Knicks	57	25	.695
Orlando Magic	45	37	.549
Washington Bullets	44	38	.537
New Jersey Nets	26	56	.317
Philadelphia 76ers	22	60	.268
Boston Celtics	15	67	.183

CENTRAL DIVISION	W	L	PCT
Chicago Bulls	69	13	.841
Atlanta Hawks	56	26	.683
Detroit Pistons	54	28	.659
Charlotte Hornets	54	28	.659
Cleveland Cavaliers	42	40	.512
Indiana Pacers	39	43	.476
Milwaukee Bucks	33	49	.402
Toronto Raptors	30	52	.366

WESTERN CONFERENCE

MIDWEST DIVISION	W	L	PCT
Utah Jazz	64	18	.780
Houston Rockets	57	25	.695
Minnesota Timberwolves	40	42	.488
Dallas Mavericks	24	58	.293
Denver Nuggets	21	61	.256
San Antonio Spurs	20	62	.244
Vancouver Grizzlies	14	68	.171

PACIFIC DIVISION	W	L	PCT
Seattle SuperSonics	57	25	.695
Los Angeles Lakers	56	26	.683
Portland Trail Blazers	49	33	.598
Phoenix Suns	40	42	.488
Los Angeles Clippers	36	46	.439
Sacramento Kings	34	48	.415
Golden State Warriors	30	52	.366

1997–98 NBA Final Standings

EASTERN CONFERENCE

ATLANTIC DIVISION	W	L	PCT
Miami Heat	55	27	.671
New York Knicks	43	39	.524
New Jersey Nets	43	39	.524
Washington Wizards	42	40	.512
Orlando Magic	41	41	.500
Boston Celtics	36	46	.439
Philadelphia 76ers	31	51	.378

CENTRAL DIVISION	W	L	PCT
Chicago Bulls	62	20	.756
Indiana Pacers	58	24	.707
Charlotte Hornets	51	31	.622
Atlanta Hawks	50	32	.610
Cleveland Cavaliers	47	35	.573
Detroit Pistons	37	45	.451
Milwaukee Bucks	36	46	.439
Toronto Raptors	16	66	.195

WESTERN CONFERENCE

MIDWEST DIVISION	W	L	PCT
Utah Jazz	62	20	.756
San Antonio Spurs	56	26	.683
Minnesota Timberwolves	45	37	.549
Houston Rockets	41	41	.500
Dallas Mavericks	20	62	.244
Vancouver Grizzlies	19	63	.232
Denver Nuggets	11	71	.134

PACIFIC DIVISION	W	L	PCT
Seattle SuperSonics	61	21	.744
Los Angeles Lakers	61	21	.744
Phoenix Suns	56	26	.683
Portland Trail Blazers	46	36	.561
Sacramento Kings	27	55	.329
Golden State Warriors	19	63	.232
Los Angeles Clippers	17	65	.207

FINAL STANDINGS

1998–99 NBA Final Standings

EASTERN CONFERENCE

ATLANTIC DIVISION	W	L	PCT
Miami Heat	33	17	.660
Orlando Magic	33	17	.660
Philadelphia 76ers	28	22	.560
New York Knicks	27	23	.540
Boston Celtics	19	31	.380
Washington Wizards	18	32	.360
New Jersey Nets	16	34	.320

CENTRAL DIVISION	W	L	PCT
Indiana Pacers	33	17	.660
Atlanta Hawks	31	19	.620
Detroit Pistons	29	21	.580
Milwaukee Bucks	28	22	.560
Charlotte Hornets	26	24	.520
Toronto Raptors	23	27	.460
Cleveland Cavaliers	22	28	.440
Chicago Bulls	13	37	.260

WESTERN CONFERENCE

MIDWEST DIVISION	W	L	PCT
San Antonio Spurs	37	13	.740
Utah Jazz	37	13	.740
Houston Rockets	31	19	.620
Minnesota Timberwolves	25	25	.500
Dallas Mavericks	19	31	.380
Denver Nuggets	14	36	.280
Vancouver Grizzlies	8	42	.160

PACIFIC DIVISION	W	L	PCT
Portland Trail Blazers	35	15	.700
Los Angeles Lakers	31	19	.620
Sacramento Kings	27	23	.540
Phoenix Suns	27	23	.540
Seattle SuperSonics	25	25	.500
Golden State Warriors	21	29	.420
Los Angeles Clippers	9	41	.180

1999–00 NBA Final Standings

EASTERN CONFERENCE

ATLANTIC DIVISION	W	L	PCT
Miami Heat	52	30	.634
New York Knicks	50	32	.610
Philadelphia 76ers	49	33	.598
Orlando Magic	41	41	.500
Boston Celtics	35	47	.427
New Jersey Nets	31	51	.378
Washington Wizards	29	53	.354

CENTRAL DIVISION	W	L	PCT
Indiana Pacers	56	26	.683
Charlotte Hornets	49	33	.598
Toronto Raptors	45	37	.549
Detroit Pistons	42	40	.512
Milwaukee Bucks	42	40	.512
Cleveland Cavaliers	32	50	.390
Atlanta Hawks	28	54	.341
Chicago Bulls	17	65	.207

WESTERN CONFERENCE

MIDWEST DIVISION	W	L	PCT
Utah Jazz	55	27	.671
San Antonio Spurs	53	29	.646
Minnesota Timberwolves	50	32	.610
Dallas Mavericks	40	42	.488
Denver Nuggets	35	47	.427
Houston Rockets	34	48	.415
Vancouver Grizzlies	22	60	.268

PACIFIC DIVISION	W	L	PCT
Los Angeles Lakers	67	15	.817
Portland Trail Blazers	59	23	.720
Phoenix Suns	53	29	.646
Seattle SuperSonics	45	37	.549
Sacramento Kings	44	38	.537
Golden State Warriors	19	63	.232
Los Angeles Clippers	15	67	.183

FINAL STANDINGS

2000–01 NBA Final Standings

EASTERN CONFERENCE

ATLANTIC DIVISION	W	L	PCT
Philadelphia 76ers	56	26	.683
Miami Heat	50	32	.610
New York Knicks	48	34	.585
Orlando Magic	43	39	.524
Boston Celtics	36	46	.439
New Jersey Nets	26	56	.317
Washington Wizards	19	63	.232

CENTRAL DIVISION	W	L	PCT
Milwaukee Bucks	52	30	.634
Toronto Raptors	47	35	.573
Charlotte Hornets	46	36	.561
Indiana Pacers	41	41	.500
Detroit Pistons	32	50	.390
Cleveland Cavaliers	30	52	.366
Atlanta Hawks	25	57	.305
Chicago Bulls	15	67	.183

WESTERN CONFERENCE

MIDWEST DIVISION	W	L	PCT
San Antonio Spurs	58	24	.707
Utah Jazz	53	29	.646
Dallas Mavericks	53	29	.646
Minnesota Timberwolves	47	35	.573
Houston Rockets	45	37	.549
Denver Nuggets	40	42	.488
Vancouver Grizzlies	23	59	.280

PACIFIC DIVISION	W	L	PCT
Los Angeles Lakers	56	26	.683
Sacramento Kings	55	27	.671
Phoenix Suns	51	31	.622
Portland Trail Blazers	50	32	.610
Seattle SuperSonics	44	38	.537
Los Angeles Clippers	31	51	.378
Golden State Warriors	17	65	.207

2001–02 NBA Final Standings

EASTERN CONFERENCE

ATLANTIC DIVISION	W	L	PCT
New Jersey Nets	52	30	.634
Boston Celtics	49	33	.598
Orlando Magic	44	38	.537
Philadelphia 76ers	43	39	.524
Washington Wizards	37	45	.451
Miami Heat	36	46	.439
New York Knicks	30	52	.366

CENTRAL DIVISION	W	L	PCT
Detroit Pistons	50	32	.610
Charlotte Hornets	44	38	.537
Toronto Raptors	42	40	.512
Indiana Pacers	42	40	.512
Milwaukee Bucks	41	41	.500
Atlanta Hawks	33	49	.402
Cleveland Cavaliers	29	53	.354
Chicago Bulls	21	61	.256

WESTERN CONFERENCE

MIDWEST DIVISION	W	L	PCT
San Antonio Spurs	58	24	.707
Dallas Mavericks	57	25	.695
Minnesota Timberwolves	50	32	.610
Utah Jazz	44	38	.537
Houston Rockets	28	54	.341
Denver Nuggets	27	55	.329
Memphis Grizzlies	23	59	.280

PACIFIC DIVISION	W	L	PCT
Sacramento Kings	61	21	.744
Los Angeles Lakers	58	24	.707
Portland Trail Blazers	49	33	.598
Seattle SuperSonics	45	37	.549
Los Angeles Clippers	39	43	.476
Phoenix Suns	36	46	.439
Golden State Warriors	21	61	.256

FINAL STANDINGS

2002–03 NBA Final Standings

EASTERN CONFERENCE

ATLANTIC DIVISION	W	L	PCT
New Jersey Nets	49	33	.598
Philadelphia 76ers	48	34	.585
Boston Celtics	44	38	.537
Orlando Magic	42	40	.512
Washington Wizards	37	45	.451
New York Knicks	37	45	.451
Miami Heat	25	57	.305

CENTRAL DIVISION	W	L	PCT
Detroit Pistons	50	32	.610
Indiana Pacers	48	34	.585
New Orleans Hornets	47	35	.573
Milwaukee Bucks	42	40	.512
Atlanta Hawks	35	47	.427
Chicago Bulls	30	52	.366
Toronto Raptors	24	58	.293
Cleveland Cavaliers	17	65	.207

WESTERN CONFERENCE

MIDWEST DIVISION	W	L	PCT
San Antonio Spurs	60	22	.732
Dallas Mavericks	60	22	.732
Minnesota Timberwolves	51	31	.622
Utah Jazz	47	35	.573
Houston Rockets	43	39	.524
Memphis Grizzlies	28	54	.341
Denver Nuggets	17	65	.207

PACIFIC DIVISION	W	L	PCT
Sacramento Kings	59	23	.720
Los Angeles Lakers	50	32	.610
Portland Trail Blazers	50	32	.610
Phoenix Suns	44	38	.537
Seattle SuperSonics	40	42	.488
Golden State Warriors	38	44	.463
Los Angeles Clippers	27	55	.329

THE STATS

NBA FINALS & ALL STAR GAME

NBA FINALS

YEAR	WINNER (DIV OR CONF)	LOSER (DIV OR CONF)	SERIES SCORE
1947	Philadelphia Warriors (Eastern)	Chicago Stags (Western)	4–1
1948	Baltimore Bullets (Western)	Philadelphia Warriors (Eastern)	4–2
1949	Minneapolis Lakers (Western)	Washington Capitols (Eastern)	4–2
1950	Minneapolis Lakers (Central)	Syracuse Nationals (Eastern)	4–2
1951	Rochester Royals (Western)	New York Knicks (Eastern)	4–3
1952	Minneapolis Lakers (Western)	New York Knicks (Eastern)	4–3
1953	Minneapolis Lakers (Western)	New York Knicks (Eastern)	4–1
1954	Minneapolis Lakers (Western)	Syracuse Nationals (Eastern)	4–3
1955	Syracuse Nationals (Eastern)	Fort Wayne Pistons (Western)	4–3
1956	Philadelphia Warriors (Eastern)	Fort Wayne Pistons (Western)	4–1
1957	Boston Celtics (Eastern)	St. Louis Hawks (Western)	4–3
1958	St. Louis Hawks (Western)	Boston Celtics (Eastern)	4–2
1959	Boston Celtics (Eastern)	Minneapolis Lakers (Western)	4–0
1960	Boston Celtics (Eastern)	St. Louis Hawks (Western)	4–3
1961	Boston Celtics (Eastern)	St. Louis Hawks (Western)	4–1
1962	Boston Celtics (Eastern)	Los Angeles Lakers (Western)	4–3
1963	Boston Celtics (Eastern)	Los Angeles Lakers (Western)	4–2
1964	Boston Celtics (Eastern)	San Francisco Warriors (Western)	4–1
1965	Boston Celtics (Eastern)	Los Angeles Lakers (Western)	4–1
1966	Boston Celtics (Eastern)	Los Angeles Lakers (Western)	4–3
1967	Philadelphia 76ers (Eastern)	San Francisco Warriors (Western)	4–2
1968	Boston Celtics (Eastern)	Los Angeles Lakers (Western)	4–2
1969	Boston Celtics (Eastern)	Los Angeles Lakers (Western)	4–3
1970	New York Knicks (Eastern)	Los Angeles Lakers (Western)	4–3
1971	Milwaukee Bucks (Western)	Baltimore Bullets (Eastern)	4–0
1972	Los Angeles Lakers (Western)	New York Knicks (Eastern)	4–1
1973	New York Knicks (Eastern)	Los Angeles Lakers (Western)	4–1
1974	Boston Celtics (Eastern)	Milwaukee Bucks (Western)	4–3
1975	Golden State Warriors (Western)	Washington Bullets (Eastern)	4–0
1976	Boston Celtics (Eastern)	Phoenix Suns (Western)	4–2
1977	Portland Trail Blazers (Western)	Philadelphia 76ers (Eastern)	4–2
1978	Washington Bullets (Eastern)	Seattle SuperSonics (Western)	4–3
1979	Seattle SuperSonics (Western)	Washington Bullets (Eastern)	4–1
1980	Los Angeles Lakers (Western)	Philadelphia 76ers (Eastern)	4–2
1981	Boston Celtics (Eastern)	Houston Rockets (Western)	4–2
1982	Los Angeles Lakers (Western)	Philadelphia 76ers (Eastern)	4–2
1983	Philadelphia 76ers (Eastern)	Los Angeles Lakers (Western)	4–0

Year			
1984	Boston Celtics (Eastern)	Los Angeles Lakers (Western)	4–3
1985	Los Angeles Lakers (Western)	Boston Celtics (Eastern)	4–2
1986	Boston Celtics (Eastern)	Houston Rockets (Western)	4–2
1987	Los Angeles Lakers (Western)	Boston Celtics (Eastern)	4–2
1988	Los Angeles Lakers (Western)	Detroit Pistons (Eastern)	4–3
1989	Detroit Pistons (Eastern)	Los Angeles Lakers (Western)	4–0
1990	Detroit Pistons (Eastern)	Portland Trail Blazers (Western)	4–1
1991	Chicago Bulls (Eastern)	Los Angeles Lakers (Western)	4–1
1992	Chicago Bulls (Eastern)	Portland Trail Blazers (Western)	4–2
1993	Chicago Bulls (Eastern)	Phoenix Suns (Western)	4–2
1994	Houston Rockets (Western)	New York Knicks (Eastern)	4–3
1995	Houston Rockets (Western)	Orlando Magic (Eastern)	4–0
1996	Chicago Bulls (Eastern)	Seattle SuperSonics (Western)	4–2
1997	Chicago Bulls (Eastern)	Utah Jazz (Western)	4–2
1998	Chicago Bulls (Eastern)	Utah Jazz (Western)	4–2
1999	San Antonio Spurs (Western)	New York Knicks (Eastern)	4–1
2000	Los Angeles Lakers (Western)	Indiana Pacers (Eastern)	4–2
2001	Los Angeles Lakers (Western)	Philadelphia 76ers (Eastern)	4–1
2002	Los Angeles Lakers (Western)	New Jersey Nets (Eastern)	4–0
2003	San Antonio Spurs (Western)	New Jersey Nets (Eastern)	4–2

YEAR	WINNERS	LOSERS	SCORE	VENUE
1951	East	West	111–94	Boston Garden
1952	East	West	108–91	Boston Garden
1953	West	East	79–75	Memorial Coliseum, Fort Wayne
1954	East	West	98–93	Madison Square Garden
1955	East	West	100–91	Madison Square Garden
1956	West	East	108–94	War Memorial Arena
1957	East	West	109–97	Boston Garden
1958	East	West	130–118	Kiel Auditorium
1959	West	East	124–108	Cobo Arena
1960	East	West	125–115	Convention Hall
1961	West	East	153–131	Onondaga War Memorial Hall
1962	West	East	150–130	Kiel Auditorium
1963	East	West	115–108	Los Angeles Sports Arena
1964	East	West	111–107	Boston Garden
1965	East	West	124–123	Kiel Auditorium
1966	East	West	137–94	Cincinnati Gardens
1967	West	East	135–120	Cow Palace
1968	East	West	144–124	Madison Square Garden
1969	East	West	123–112	Baltimore Civic Center
1970	East	West	142–135	The Spectrum
1971	West	East	108–107	San Diego International Sports Arena
1972	West	East	112–110	Los Angeles Forum
1973	East	West	104–84	Chicago Stadium
1974	West	East	134–123	Seattle Center Coliseum
1975	East	West	108–102	Veterans Memorial Coliseum
1976	East	West	123–109	The Spectrum
1977	West	East	125–124	Milwaukee Arena
1978	East	West	133–125	The Omni
1979	West	East	134–129	Silverdome
1980	East	West	144–136	Capital Centre
1981	East	West	123–120	Richfield Coliseum
1982	East	West	120–118	Brendan Byrne Arena
1983	East	West	132–123	Los Angeles Forum
1984	East	West	154–145	McNichols Arena
1985	West	East	140–129	Hoosier Dome
1986	East	West	139–132	Reunion Arena
1987	West	East	154–149	Kingdome

1988	East	West	138–133	Chicago Stadium
1989	West	East	143–134	Astrodome
1990	East	West	130–113	Miami Arena
1991	East	West	116–114	Charlotte Coliseum
1992	West	East	153–113	Orlando Arena
1993	West	East	135–132	Delta Center
1994	East	West	127–118	Target Center
1995	West	East	139–112	America West Arena
1996	East	West	129–118	Alamodome
1997	East	West	132–120	Gund Arena
1998	East	West	135–114	Madison Square Garden
1999	–	–	No Game Played	
2000	West	East	137–126	Arena in Oakland
2001	East	West	111–110	MCI Center
2002	West	East	135–120	First Union Center
2003	West	East	155–145	Philips Arena

THE STATS

HALL OF FAME

1959

The First Team Original Celtics
Forrest Clare Allen, Coach
Henry Clifford Carlson, Coach
Dr. Luther Gulick, Contributor
Edward J. Hickox, Contributor
Charles D. Hyatt, Player
Matthew P. Kennedy, Referee
Angelo Luisetti, Player
Walter E. Meanwell, M.D., Coach
George L. Mikan, Player
Ralph Morgan, Contributor
Dr. James Naismith, Contributor
Harold G. Olsen, Contributor
John J. Schommer, Player
Amos Alonzo Stagg, Contributor
Oswald Tower, Contributor

1960

Ernest A. Blood, Coach
Victor A. Hanson, Player
George T. Hepbron, Referee
Frank W. Keaney, Coach
Ward L. Lambert, Coach
Edward C. Macauley, Player
Branch McCracken, Player
Charles C. Murphy, Player
Henry V. Porter, Contributor
John R. Wooden, Player

1961

Buffalo Germans
Bernard Borgmann, Player
Forrest S. DeBernardi, Player
George H. Hoyt, Referee
George E. Keogan, Coach
Robert A. Kurland, Player
John J. O'Brien, Contributor
Andy Phillip, Player
Ernest C. Quigley, Referee
John S. Roosma, Player
Leonard D. Sachs, Coach
Arthur A. Schabinger, Contributor
Christian Steinmetz, Player
David Tobey, Referee
Arthur L. Trester, Contributor
Edward A. Wachter, Player
David H. Walsh, Referee

1962

Jack McCracken, Player
Frank Morgenweck, Contributor
Harlan O. Page, Player
Barney Sedran, Player
Lynn W. St. John, Contributor
John A. Thompson, Player

1963

New York Rens
Robert F. Gruenig, Player
William A. Reid, Contributor

HALL OF FAME

1964

John W. Bunn, Contributor
Harold E. Foster, Player
Nat Holman, Player
Edward S. Irish, Contributor
R. William Jones, Contributor
Kenneth D. Loeffler, Coach
John D. Russell, Player

1965

Walter A. Brown, Contributor
Paul D. Hinkle, Contributor
Howard A. Hobson, Coach
William G. Mokray, Contributor

1966

Everett S. Dean, Coach
Joe Lapchick, Player

1968

Clair F. Bee, Contributor
Howard G. Cann, Coach
Amory T. Gill, Coach
Alvin F. Julian, Coach

1969

Arnold J."Red" Auerbach, Coach
Henry G. Dehnert, Player
Henry P. Iba, Coach
Adolph F. Rupp, Coach
Charles H. Taylor, Contributor

1970

Bernard L. Carnevale, Coach
Robert E. Davies, Player

1971

Robert J. Cousy, Player
Robert L. Pettit, Player
Abraham Saperstein, Contributor

1972

Edgar A. Diddle, Coach
Robert L. Douglas, Contributor
Paul Endacott, Player
Max Friedman, Player
Edward Gottlieb, Contributor
W. R. Clifford Wells, Contributor

1973

John Beckman, Player
Bruce Drake, Coach
Arthur C. Lonborg, Coach
Elmer H. Ripley, Contributor
Adolph Schayes, Player
John R.Wooden, Coach

1974

Harry A. Fisher, Contributor
Maurice Podoloff, Contributor
Ernest J. Schmidt, Player

1975

Joseph R. Brennan, Player
Emil S. Liston, Contributor
William F. Russell, Player
Robert P. Vandivier, Player

HALL OF FAME

1976

Thomas J. Gola, Player
Edward W. Krause, Player
Harry Litwack, Coach
William W. Sharman, Player

1977

Elgin Baylor, Player
Charles T. Cooper, Player
Lauren Gale, Player
William C. Johnson, Player
Frank J. McGuire, Coach

1978

Paul J. Arizin, Player
Joseph F. Fulks, Player
Clifford O. Hagan, Player
John P. Nucatola, Referee
James C. Pollard, Player

1979

Justin M. "Sam" Barry, Coach
Wilton N. Chamberlain, Player
James E. Enright, Referee
Edgar S. Hickey, Coach
John B. McLendon, Jr., Coach
Raymond J. Meyer, Coach
Peter F. Newell, Coach

1980

Lester Harrison, Contributor
Jerry R. Lucas, Player
Oscar P. Robertson, Player
Everett F. Shelton, Coach
J. Dallas Shirley, Referee
Jerry A.West, Player

1981

Thomas B. Barlow, Player
Ferenc Hepp, Contributor
J. Walter Kennedy, Contributor
Arad A. McCutchan, Coach

1982

Everett N. Case, Coach
Alva O. Duer, Contributor
Clarence E. Gaines, Coach
Harold E. Greer, Player
Slater N. Martin, Player
Frank V. Ramsey, Jr., Player
Willis Reed, Jr., Player

1983

William W. Bradley, Player
David A. DeBusschere, Player
Lloyd R. Leith, Referee
Dean E. Smith, Coach
John "Jack" K. Twyman, Player
Louis G. Wilke, Contributor

HALL OF FAME

1984

Clifford B. Fagan, Contributor

James H. "Jack" Gardner, Coach

John Havlicek, Player

Samuel "Sam" Jones, Player

Edward S. Steitz, Contributor

1985

Senda Berenson Abbott, Contributor

W. Harold Anderson, Coach

Alfred N. Cervi, Player

Marv K. Harshman, Coach

Bertha F. Teague, Contributor

Nate Thurmond, Player

L. Margaret Wade, Coach

1986

William J. Cunningham, Player

Thomas W. Heinsohn, Player

William "Red" Holzman, Coach

Zigmund "Red" Mihalik, Referee

Fred R. Taylor, Coach

Stanley H. Watts, Coach

1987

Richard F. Barry, Player

Walter Frazier, Player

Robert J. Houbregs, Player

Peter P. Maravich, Player

Robert Wanzer, Player

1988

Clyde E. Lovellette, Player

Robert McDermott, Player

Ralph H. Miller, Coach

Westley S. Unseld, Player

1989

William "Pop" Gates, Player

K. C. Jones, Player

Leonard "Lenny" Wilkens, Player

1990

David Bing, Player

Elvin E. Hayes, Player

Donald Neil Johnston, Player

Vernon Earl Monroe, Player

1991

Nathaniel Archibald, Player

David W. Cowens, Player

Lawrence Fleisher, Contributor

Harry J. Gallatin, Player

Robert M. Knight, Coach

Lawrence F. O'Brien, Contributor

Borislav Stankovic, Contributor

HALL OF FAME

1992

Sergei Belov, Player
Louis P. Carnesecca, Coach
Cornelius L. Hawkins, Player
Robert J. Lanier, Player
Alfred J. McGuire, Coach
John "Jack" T. Ramsay, Coach
Lusia Harris-Stewart, Player
Nera D. White, Player
Phillip D. Woolpert, Coach

1993

Walter Bellamy, Player
Julius W. Erving, Player
Daniel P. Issel, Player
Ann E. Meyers, Player
Richard S. McGuire, Player
Calvin J. Murphy, Player
Uljana Semjonova, Player
William T. Walton, Player

1994

Carol Blazejowski, Player
Denzil "Denny" E. Crum, Coach
Charles J. Daly, Coach
Harry "Buddy" Jeannette, Player
Cesare Rubini, Coach

1995

Kareem Abdul-Jabbar, Player
Anne Donovan, Player
Aleksandr Gomelsky, Coach
John Kundla, Coach
Vern Mikkelsen, Player
Cheryl Miller, Player
Earl Strom, Referee

1996

Kresimir Cosic, Player
George Gervin, Player
Gail Goodrich, Player
Nancy Lieberman, Player
David Thompson, Player
George Yardley, Player

1997

Pete Carril, Coach
Joan Crawford, Player
Denise Curry, Player
Antonio Diaz-Miguel, Coach
Alex English, Player
Don Haskins, Coach
Bailey Howell, Player

1998

Larry Bird, Player
Jody Conradt, Coach
Alexander "Alex" Hannum, Coach
Marques Haynes, Player
Aleksandar Nikolic, Coach
Arnold "Arnie" Risen, Player
Leonard "Lenny" Wilkens, Coach

HALL OF FAME

1999

Wayne Embry, Contributor
Kevin McHale, Player
Billie Moore, Coach
John Thompson, Coach
Fred Zollner, Contributor

2000

Danny Biasone, Contributor
Robert McAdoo, Player
Charles Newton, Contributor
Pat Head Summit, Coach
Isiah Thomas, Player
Morgan Wootten, Coach

2001

John Chaney, Coach
Mike Krzyzewski, Coach
Moses Malone, Player

2002

Harlem Globetrotters, Team
Larry Brown, Coach
Earvin "Magic" Johnson, Player
Lute Olson, Coach
Drazen Petrovic, Player
Kay Yow, Coach

2003

Robert Parish, Player
James Worthy, Player
Dino Meneghin, Player
Leon Barmore, Coach
Earl Lloyd, Player
Chick Hearn, Contributor
Meadowlark Lemon, Player

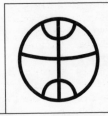

THE STATS

AWARDS

MOST VALUABLE PLAYERS

NBA MVP

YEAR	PLAYER
1955–56	Bob Pettit
1956–57	Bob Cousy
1957–58	Bill Russell
1958–59	Bob Pettit
1959–60	Wilt Chamberlain
1960–61	Bill Russell
1961–62	Bill Russell
1962–63	Bill Russell
1963–64	Oscar Robertson
1964–65	Bill Russell
1965–66	Wilt Chamberlain
1966–67	Wilt Chamberlain
1967–68	Wilt Chamberlain
1968–69	Wes Unseld
1969–70	Willis Reed
1970–71	Kareem Abdul-Jabbar
1971–72	Kareem Abdul-Jabbar
1972–73	Dave Cowens
1973–74	Kareem Abdul-Jabbar
1974–75	Bob McAdoo
1975–76	Kareem Abdul-Jabbar
1976–77	Kareem Abdul-Jabbar
1977–78	Bill Walton
1978–79	Moses Malone
1979–80	Kareem Abdul-Jabbar
1980–81	Julius Erving
1981–82	Moses Malone
1982–83	Moses Malone
1983–84	Larry Bird
1984–85	Larry Bird
1985–86	Larry Bird
1986–87	Magic Johnson
1987–88	Michael Jordan
1988–89	Magic Johnson
1989–90	Magic Johnson
1990–91	Michael Jordan
1991–92	Michael Jordan
1992–93	Charles Barkley
1993–94	Hakeem Olajuwon
1994–95	David Robinson
1995–96	Michael Jordan
1996–97	Karl Malone
1997–98	Michael Jordan
1998–99	Karl Malone
1999–00	Shaquille O'Neal
2000–01	Allen Iverson
2001–02	Tim Duncan
2002–03	Tim Duncan

Playoff MVP

YEAR	PLAYER
1968–69	Jerry West
1969–70	Willis Reed
1970–71	Kareem Abdul-Jabbar
1971–72	Wilt Chamberlain
1972–73	Willis Reed
1973–74	John Havlicek
1974–75	Rick Barry
1975–76	Jo Jo White
1976–77	Bill Walton
1977–78	Wes Unseld
1978–79	Dennis Johnson
1979–80	Magic Johnson
1980–81	Cedric Maxwell
1981–82	Magic Johnson
1982–83	Moses Malone
1983–84	Larry Bird
1984–85	Kareem Abdul-Jabbar
1985–86	Larry Bird
1986–87	Magic Johnson
1987–88	James Worthy
1988–89	Joe Dumars
1989–90	Isiah Thomas
1990–91	Michael Jordan
1991–92	Michael Jordan
1992–93	Michael Jordan
1993–94	Hakeem Olajuwon
1994–95	Hakeem Olajuwon
1995–96	Michael Jordan
1996–97	Michael Jordan
1997–98	Michael Jordan
1998–99	Tim Duncan
1999–00	Shaquille O'Neal
2000–01	Shaquille O'Neal
2001–02	Shaquille O'Neal
2002–03	Tim Duncan

ROOKIE OF THE YEAR

YEAR	PLAYER
1952–53	Monk Meineke
1953–54	Ray Felix
1954–55	Bob Pettit
1955–56	Maurice Stokes
1956–57	Tom Heinsohn
1957–58	Woody Sauldsberry
1958–59	Elgin Baylor
1959–60	Wilt Chamberlain
1960–61	Oscar Robertson
1961–62	Walt Bellamy
1962–63	Terry Dischinger
1963–64	Jerry Lucas
1964–65	Willis Reed
1965–66	Rick Barry
1966–67	Dave Bing
1967–68	Earl Monroe
1968–69	Wes Unseld
1969–70	Kareem Abdul-Jabbar
1970–71	Dave Cowens
1970–71	Geoff Petrie
1971–72	Sidney Wicks
1972–73	Bob McAdoo
1973–74	Ernie DiGregorio
1974–75	Jamaal Wilkes
1975–76	Alvan Adams
1976–77	Adrian Dantley
1977–78	Walter Davis
1978–79	Phil Ford
1979–80	Larry Bird
1980–81	Darrell Griffith
1981–82	Buck Williams
1982–83	Terry Cummings
1983–84	Ralph Sampson
1984–85	Michael Jordan
1985–86	Patrick Ewing
1986–87	Chuck Person
1987–88	Mark Jackson
1988–89	Mitch Richmond
1989–90	David Robinson
1990–91	Derrick Coleman
1991–92	Larry Johnson
1992–93	Shaquille O'Neal
1993–94	Chris Webber
1994–95	Grant Hill
1994–95	Jason Kidd
1995–96	Damon Stoudamire
1996–97	Allen Iverson
1997–98	Tim Duncan
1998–99	Vince Carter
1999–00	Elton Brand
1999–00	Steve Francis
2000–01	Mike Miller
2001–02	Pau Gasol
2002–03	Amare Stoudemire

DEFENSIVE MVP/COACH

Defensive MVP

YEAR	PLAYER
1982–83	Sidney Moncrief
1983–84	Sidney Moncrief
1984–85	Mark Eaton
1985–86	Alvin Robertson
1986–87	Michael Cooper
1987–88	Michael Jordan
1988–89	Mark Eaton
1989–90	Dennis Rodman
1990–91	Dennis Rodman
1991–92	David Robinson
1992–93	Hakeem Olajuwon
1993–94	Hakeem Olajuwon
1994–95	Dikembe Mutombo
1995–96	Gary Payton
1996–97	Dikembe Mutombo
1997–98	Dikembe Mutombo
1998–99	Alonzo Mourning
1999–00	Alonzo Mourning
2000–01	Dikembe Mutombo
2001–02	Ben Wallace
2002–03	Ben Wallace

Coach of the Year

YEAR	COACH
1962–63	Harry Gallatin
1963–64	Alex Hannum
1964–65	Red Auerbach
1965–66	Dolph Schayes
1966–67	Johnny Kerr
1967–68	Richie Guerin
1968–69	Gene Shue
1969–70	Red Holzman
1970–71	Dick Motta
1971–72	Bill Sharman
1972–73	Tom Heinsohn
1973–74	Ray Scott
1974–75	Phil Johnson
1975–76	Bill Fitch
1976–77	Tom Nissalke
1977–78	Hubie Brown
1978–79	Cotton Fitzsimmons
1979–80	Bill Fitch
1980–81	Jack McKinney
1981–82	Gene Shue
1982–83	Don Nelson
1983–84	Frank Layden
1984–85	Don Nelson
1985–86	Mike Fratello
1986–87	Mike Schuler
1987–88	Doug Moe
1988–89	Cotton Fitzsimmons
1989–90	Pat Riley
1990–91	Don Chaney
1991–92	Don Nelson
1992–93	Pat Riley
1993–94	Lenny Wilkens
1994–95	Del Harris
1995–96	Phil Jackson
1996–97	Pat Riley
1997–98	Larry Bird
1998–99	Mike Dunleavy
1999–00	Doc Rivers
2000–01	Larry Brown
2001–02	Rick Carlisle
2002–03	Gregg Popovich

NBA FIRST TEAM

YEAR	PLAYERS	YEAR	PLAYERS
1946–47	Joe Fulks Bob Feerick Bones McKinney Max Zaslofsky Stan Miasek	1955–56	Bob Pettit Bob Cousy Paul Arizin Neil Johnston Bill Sharman
1947–48	Joe Fulks Bob Feerick Max Zaslofsky Ed Sadowski Howie Dallmar	1956–57	Bob Pettit Dolph Schayes Bob Cousy Bill Sharman Paul Arizin
1948–49	Joe Fulks Max Zaslofsky George Mikan Bob Davies Jim Pollard	1957–58	Bob Pettit Dolph Schayes Bob Cousy Bill Sharman George Yardley
1949–50	Max Zaslofsky George Mikan Bob Davies Jim Pollard Alex Groza	1958–59	Bob Pettit Elgin Baylor Bob Cousy Bill Sharman Bill Russell
1950–51	George Mikan Bob Davies Alex Groza Ed Macauley Ralph Beard	1959–60	Bob Pettit Elgin Baylor Wilt Chamberlain Bob Cousy Gene Shue
1951–52	George Mikan Bob Davies Dolph Schayes Ed Macauley Paul Arizin Bob Cousy	1960–61	Bob Pettit Elgin Baylor Wilt Chamberlain Oscar Robertson Bob Cousy
1952–53	George Mikan Dolph Schayes Ed Macauley Bob Cousy Neil Johnston	1961–62	Bob Pettit Elgin Baylor Wilt Chamberlain Oscar Robertson Jerry West
1953–54	George Mikan Dolph Schayes Bob Cousy Neil Johnston Harry Gallatin	1962–63	Bob Pettit Elgin Baylor Oscar Robertson Jerry West Bill Russell
1954–55	Bob Pettit Dolph Schayes Bob Cousy Larry Foust Neil Johnston	1963–64	Bob Pettit Elgin Baylor Wilt Chamberlain Oscar Robertson Jerry West

NBA FIRST TEAM

YEAR	PLAYERS
1964–65	Elgin Baylor Oscar Robertson Jerry Lucas Jerry West Bill Russell
1965–66	Wilt Chamberlain Oscar Robertson Rick Barry Jerry Lucas Jerry West
1966–67	Elgin Baylor Wilt Chamberlain Oscar Robertson Rick Barry Jerry West
1967–68	Elgin Baylor Wilt Chamberlain Oscar Robertson Jerry Lucas Dave Bing
1968–69	Elgin Baylor Oscar Robertson Earl Monroe Wes Unseld Billy Cunningham
1969–70	Willis Reed Jerry West Billy Cunningham Connie Hawkins Walt Frazier
1970–71	Dave Bing Kareem Abdul-Jabbar Jerry West John Havlicek Billy Cunningham
1971–72	Kareem Abdul-Jabbar Jerry West John Havlicek Walt Frazier Spencer Haywood
1972–73	Kareem Abdul-Jabbar Jerry West John Havlicek Spencer Haywood Tiny Archibald

YEAR	PLAYERS
1973–74	Rick Barry Kareem Abdul-Jabbar John Havlicek Walt Frazier Gail Goodrich
1974–75	Rick Barry Bob McAdoo Walt Frazier Tiny Archibald Elvin Hayes
1975–76	Rick Barry Kareem Abdul-Jabbar Tiny Archibald Pete Maravich George McGinnis
1976–77	Kareem Abdul-Jabbar Elvin Hayes Pete Maravich David Thompson Paul Westphal
1977–78	Julius Erving Bill Walton David Thompson George Gervin Truck Robinson
1978–79	Moses Malone Elvin Hayes George Gervin Paul Westphal Marques Johnson
1979–80	Kareem Abdul-Jabbar Larry Bird Julius Erving George Gervin Paul Westphal
1980–81	Kareem Abdul-Jabbar Larry Bird Julius Erving Dennis Johnson George Gervin
1981–82	Larry Bird Julius Erving Moses Malone George Gervin Gus Williams

NBA FIRST TEAM

YEAR	PLAYERS	YEAR	PLAYERS
1982–83	Larry Bird Julius Erving Magic Johnson Sidney Moncrief Moses Malone	1991–92	Michael Jordan David Robinson Karl Malone Clyde Drexler Chris Mullin
1983–84	Kareem Abdul-Jabbar Larry Bird Isiah Thomas Magic Johnson Bernard King	1992–93	Michael Jordan Hakeem Olajuwon Charles Barkley Karl Malone Mark Price
1984–85	Larry Bird Isiah Thomas Magic Johnson Moses Malone Bernard King	1993–94	Hakeem Olajuwon Karl Malone John Stockton Scottie Pippen Latrell Sprewell
1985–86	Kareem Abdul-Jabbar Larry Bird Isiah Thomas Magic Johnson Dominique Wilkins	1994–95	David Robinson Karl Malone John Stockton Scottie Pippen Anfernee Hardaway
1986–87	Larry Bird Michael Jordan Magic Johnson Hakeem Olajuwon Kevin McHale	1995–96	Michael Jordan David Robinson Karl Malone Scottie Pippen Anfernee Hardaway
1987–88	Larry Bird Michael Jordan Magic Johnson Hakeem Olajuwon Charles Barkley	1996–97	Michael Jordan Grant Hill Karl Malone Tim Hardaway Hakeem Olajuwon
1988–89	Michael Jordan Magic Johnson Hakeem Olajuwon Charles Barkley Karl Malone	1997–98	Karl Malone Tim Duncan Shaquille O'Neal Michael Jordan Gary Payton
1989–90	Michael Jordan Patrick Ewing Magic Johnson Charles Barkley Karl Malone	1998–99	Karl Malone Tim Duncan Alonzo Mourning Allen Iverson Jason Kidd
1990–91	Michael Jordan David Robinson Magic Johnson Charles Barkley Karl Malone	1999–00	Kevin Garnett Tim Duncan Shaquille O'Neal Gary Payton Jason Kidd

NBA FIRST TEAM

YEAR	PLAYERS
2000–01	Tim Duncan
	Chris Webber
	Shaquille O'Neal
	Allen Iverson
	Jason Kidd
2001–02	Tim Duncan
	Tracy McGrady
	Shaquille O'Neal
	Jason Kidd
	Kobe Bryant
2002–03	Tim Duncan
	Tracy McGrady
	Shaquille O'Neal
	Kevin Garnett
	Kobe Bryant

NBA SECOND TEAM

YEAR	PLAYERS	YEAR	PLAYERS
1946–47	Ernie Calverley Frankie Baumholtz John Logan Chick Halbert Fred Scolari	1956–57	Neil Johnston Dugie Martin Maurice Stokes George Yardley Dick Garmaker
1947–48	Stan Miasek John Logan Fred Scolari Carl Braun Buddy Jeannette	1957–58	Dugie Martin Maurice Stokes Cliff Hagan Bill Russell Tom Gola
1948–49	Bob Feerick Bones McKinney John Logan Arnie Risen Kenny Sailors	1958–59	Dolph Schayes Dugie Martin Cliff Hagan Paul Arizin Richie Guerin
1949–50	Frankie Brian Fred Schaus Dolph Schayes Al Cervi Ralph Beard	1959–60	Dolph Schayes Bill Sharman Bill Russell Richie Guerin Jack Twyman
1950–51	Joe Fulks Frankie Brian Dolph Schayes Vern Mikkelsen Dick McGuire	1960–61	Tom Heinsohn Dolph Schayes Bill Russell Gene Shue Larry Costello
1951–52	Jim Pollard Vern Mikkelsen Larry Foust Bobby Wanzer Andy Phillip	1961–62	Tom Heinsohn Bob Cousy Bill Russell Richie Guerin Jack Twyman
1952–53	Bob Davies Vern Mikkelsen Bobby Wanzer Andy Phillip Bill Sharman	1962–63	Tom Heinsohn Wilt Chamberlain Bob Cousy Bailey Howell Hal Greer
1953–54	Jim Pollard Ed Macauley Bobby Wanzer Paul Seymour Carl Braun	1963–64	Tom Heinsohn Jerry Lucas John Havlicek Bill Russell Hal Greer
1954–55	Vern Mikkelsen Bill Sharman Harry Gallatin Paul Seymour Dugie Martin	1964–65	Bob Pettit Wilt Chamberlain Hal Greer Gus Johnson Sam Jones
1955–56	Dolph Schayes Dugie Martin Maurice Stokes Clyde Lovellette Jack George	1965–66	John Havlicek Bill Russell Hal Greer Gus Johnson Sam Jones

NBA SECOND TEAM

YEAR	PLAYERS		YEAR	PLAYERS
1966–67	Willis Reed Jerry Lucas Bill Russell Sam Jones Hal Greer		1976–77	Julius Erving Bill Walton Jo Jo White George McGinnis George Gervin
1967–68	Willis Reed Jerry West John Havlicek Bill Russell Hal Greer		1977–78	Kareem Abdul-Jabbar Pete Maravich Walter Davis Maurice Lucas Paul Westphal
1968–69	Willis Reed Jerry West John Havlicek Hal Greer Dave DeBusschere		1978–79	Kareem Abdul-Jabbar Walter Davis Bob Dandridge World B. Free Phil Ford
1969–70	Oscar Robertson Kareem Abdul-Jabbar John Havlicek Gus Johnson Lou Hudson		1979–80	Dennis Johnson Moses Malone Marques Johnson Dan Roundfield Gus Williams
1970–71	Oscar Robertson Willis Reed Walt Frazier Gus Johnson Bob Love		1980–81	Adrian Dantley Moses Malone Marques Johnson Otis Birdsong Tiny Archibald
1971–72	Wilt Chamberlain Billy Cunningham Bob Love Tiny Archibald Archie Clark		1981–82	Magic Johnson Sidney Moncrief Alex English Bernard King Robert Parish
1972–73	Rick Barry Dave Cowens Walt Frazier Elvin Hayes Pete Maravich		1982–83	Kareem Abdul-Jabbar Buck Williams Isiah Thomas George Gervin Alex English
1973–74	Dave Bing Bob McAdoo Spencer Haywood Elvin Hayes Norm Van Lier		1983–84	Adrian Dantley Julius Erving Sidney Moncrief Moses Malone Jim Paxson
1974–75	Dave Cowens John Havlicek Jo Jo White Spencer Haywood Phil Chenier		1984–85	Kareem Abdul-Jabbar Terry Cummings Ralph Sampson Michael Jordan Sidney Moncrief
1975–76	Dave Cowens John Havlicek Elvin Hayes Randy Smith Phil Smith		1985–86	Alvin Robertson Sidney Moncrief Hakeem Olajuwon Charles Barkley Alex English

NBA SECOND TEAM

YEAR	PLAYERS	YEAR	PLAYERS
1986–87	Isiah Thomas Charles Barkley Moses Malone Dominique Wilkins Fat Lever	1996–97	Scottie Pippen Glen Rice Patrick Ewing Gary Payton Mitch Richmond
1987–88	Patrick Ewing Dominique Wilkins Karl Malone Clyde Drexler John Stockton	1997–98	Grant Hill Vin Baker David Robinson Tim Hardaway Rod Strickland
1988–89	Patrick Ewing Kevin Johnson John Stockton Tom Chambers Chris Mullin	1998–99	Chris Webber Grant Hill Shaquille O'Neal Gary Payton Tim Hardaway
1989–90	Larry Bird Kevin Johnson Hakeem Olajuwon John Stockton Tom Chambers	1999–00	Karl Malone Grant Hill Alonzo Mourning Allen Iverson Kobe Bryant
1990–91	Patrick Ewing Kevin Johnson Dominique Wilkins Clyde Drexler Chris Mullin	2000–01	Kevin Garnett Vince Carter Dikembe Mutombo Kobe Bryant Tracy McGrady
1991–92	Patrick Ewing Charles Barkley John Stockton Scottie Pippen Tim Hardaway	2001–02	Kevin Garnett Chris Webber Dirk Nowitzki Gary Payton Allen Iverson
1992–93	Patrick Ewing Larry Johnson Joe Dumars Dominique Wilkins John Stockton	2002–03	Dirk Nowitzki Chris Webber Ben Wallace Jason Kidd Allen Iverson
1993–94	Mitch Richmond David Robinson Kevin Johnson Charles Barkley Shawn Kemp		
1994–95	Mitch Richmond Shaquille O'Neal Gary Payton Charles Barkley Shawn Kemp		
1995–96	Grant Hill Hakeem Olajuwon Gary Payton John Stockton Shawn Kemp		

OTHER AWARDS

Sixth Man

YEAR	PLAYER
1982–83	Bobby Jones
1983–84	Kevin McHale
1984–85	Kevin McHale
1985–86	Bill Walton
1986–87	Ricky Pierce
1987–88	Roy Tarpley
1988–89	Eddie Johnson
1989–90	Ricky Pierce
1990–91	Detlef Schrempf
1991–92	Detlef Schrempf
1992–93	Clifford Robinson
1993–94	Dell Curry
1994–95	Anthony Mason
1995–96	Toni Kukoc
1996–97	John Starks
1997–98	Danny Manning
1998–99	Darrell Armstrong
1999–00	Rodney Rogers
2000–01	Aaron McKie
2001–02	Corliss Williamson
2002–03	Bobby Jackson

Most Improved Player

YEAR	PLAYER
1985–86	Alvin Robertson
1986–87	Dale Ellis
1987–88	Kevin Duckworth
1988–89	Kevin Johnson
1989–90	Rony Seikaly
1990–91	Scott Skiles
1991–92	Pervis Ellison
1992–93	Mahmoud Abdul–Rauf
1993–94	Don MacLean
1994–95	Dana Barros
1995–96	Gheorghe Muresan
1996–97	Isaac Austin
1997–98	Alan Henderson
1998–99	Darrell Armstrong
1999–00	Jalen Rose
2000–01	Tracy McGrady
2001–02	Jermaine O'Neal
2002–03	Gilbert Arenas

OTHER AWARDS

J. Walter Kennedy Citizenship Award

YEAR	PLAYER
1974–75	Wes Unseld
1975–76	Slick Watts
1976–77	Dave Bing
1977–78	Bob Lanier
1978–79	Calvin Murphy
1979–80	Austin Carr
1980–81	Mike Glenn
1981–82	Kent Benson
1982–83	Julius Erving
1983–84	Frank Layden
1984–85	Dan Issel
1985–86	Michael Cooper
1985–86	Rory Sparrow
1986–87	Isiah Thomas
1987–88	Alex English
1988–89	Thurl Bailey
1989–90	Doc Rivers
1990–91	Kevin Johnson
1991–92	Magic Johnson
1992–93	Terry Porter
1993–94	Joe Dumars
1994–95	Joe O'Toole
1995–96	Chris Dudley
1996–97	P.J. Brown
1997–98	Steve Smith
1998–99	Brian Grant
1999–00	Vlade Divac
2000–01	Dikembe Mutombo
2001–02	Alonzo Mourning
2002–03	David Robinson

Sportsmanship Award

YEAR	PLAYER
1995–96	Joe Dumars
1996–97	Terrell Brandon
1997–98	Avery Johnson
1998–99	Hersey Hawkins
1999–00	Eric Snow
2000–01	David Robinson
2001–02	Steve Smith

ABOUT STATS INC.

In 1981, STATS, Inc. virtually created the high tech sports information industry by developing sophisticated data gathering networks to deliver the most in–depth, innovative sports information services in the world. Now with more than 20 years of experience in sophisticated sports data collection, processing and distribution—STATS, Inc. is the world's leading sports information and statistical analysis company.

Throughout its history, STATS has applied sports information and technology with an innovative flair that has changed the way sports are viewed, reported, and most importantly, enjoyed. STATS provides exclusive information and data from its proprietary databases to fans, professional teams, print and broadcast media, software developers and interactive service providers around the globe while serving as one of the industry's leading fantasy sports game management firms.

You can find STATS, Inc. on the world wide web at *www.stats.com*.

Or write to:

STATS, Inc.
8130 Lehigh Ave.
Morton Grove,
IL 60053

ABOUT THE AUTHOR

Marty Strasen is the sports producer for Tampa Bay Online (TBO.com), the two-time Edward R. Murrow Award-winning news site in Tampa, Florida, and writes regularly for *The Tampa Tribune*. He has co-authored the Michael Jordan Scrapbook and Basketball Almanac and is a former assistant editor of *Basketball Weekly* and *Football News*. He is a 1989 graduate of the University of Notre Dame.